# THE SOCIAL AND POLITICAL BODY

# Multidisciplinary Studies in Social Theory

A collectively edited Guilford Series devoted to transdisciplinary
understandings on key issues in contemporary social thought.

## Editors

**John Paul Jones III**　　　**Wolfgang Natter**　　　**Theodore R. Schatzki**
*Committee on Social Theory, University of Kentucky*


POSTMODERN CONTENTIONS: EPOCHS, POLITICS, SPACE
*John Paul Jones III, Wolfgang Natter, and Theodore R. Schatzki*, Editors
(originally published in the Mappings: Society/Theory/Space series)

OBJECTIVITY AND ITS OTHER
*Wolfgang Natter, Theodore R. Schatzki, and John Paul Jones III*, Editors

THE SOCIAL AND POLITICAL BODY
*Theodore R. Schatzki and Wolfgang Natter*, Editors

### Forthcoming

CONTEMPORARY DEMOCRATIC THEORY AND DEMOCRACY
*John Paul Jones III, Wolfgang Natter, and Theodore R. Schatzki*, Editors

DISCIPLINING BOUNDARIES
*Wolfgang Natter, Theodore R. Schatzki, and John Paul Jones III*, Editors

# The Social
# and
# Political Body

THEODORE R. SCHATZKI
WOLFGANG NATTER
EDITORS

THE GUILFORD PRESS
New York   London

**Library of Congress Cataloging-in-Publication Data**
The social and political body / [edited by] Theodore R. Schatzki,
  Wolfgang Natter.
    p.   cm.   —(Multidisciplinary series on social theory)
    ISBN 1-57230-139-2 (hard). — ISBN 1-57230-140-6 (pbk.)
    1. Social sciences—Philosophy.   2. Sociology—Political aspects.
  3. Political sociology.   I. Schatzki, Theodore R.   II. Natter,
  Wolfgang.   III. Series.
  H61.S5894   1996
    300—dc20                                              96-19771
                                                              CIP

# Preface

*The Social and Political Body* is the second installment in a series of collected volumes titled "Multidisciplinary Studies in Social Theory." Each volume contains essays from humanists and social scientists that focus on a key area of inquiry in contemporary social thought. The aim of the series is avowedly multidisciplinary. By collecting together essays in each book from a range of social disciplines, we aspire not only to remember the breadth of disciplinary perspectives that bear on central theoretical issues, but also to further the current surge of cross-disciplinary exchange. The greater the number of forums in which scholars from different social fields gather to examine common theoretical concerns, the quicker social theory will establish itself as a distinct, transdisciplinary field of inquiry. Our series seeks to help realize this goal.

The series of volumes arises out of the activities of the Committee on Social Theory at the University of Kentucky (UK). Each spring semester, the Committee sponsors a public lecture series/graduate seminar combination that is focused on a problem area of broad critical import in contemporary social thought. Each of the initial installments in the book series will contain the lectures delivered by the visiting scholars participating in a given spring's lecture series, together with essays written by the UK faculty coteaching that semester's graduate seminar. The visitors' contributions will generally be revisions of their public lectures that reflect discussions held with UK faculty and students during their stay in Lexington. The UK contributions, on the other hand, will grow out of the lengthy discussions conducted among these faculty and students in the weekly graduate seminar. The volumes in this series, consequently, will differ from standard anthologies, which generally publish commissioned works and/or compile conference proceedings.

The series' first volume, *Objectivity and Its Other*, was published in 1995. An earlier collection of essays with the same provenance, *Postmodern Contentions: Epochs, Politics, Space*, appeared in 1993 with The Guilford Press in a series called "Mappings: Society/ Theory/Space." *The Social and Political Body* is thus the third multi-disciplinary volume arising from the Committee's activities.

We would like to take this opportunity to thank the people and programs who have made the Committee's endeavors, and thus the series, possible. Initial financial support for the Committee came from the University of Kentucky's College of Arts and Sciences and its Graduate School. During the spring of 1992, when the current volume originated, support came from the College of Arts and Sciences, the offices of both the Vice President of Research and Graduate Studies and the Chancellor of UK's Lexington campus, and the Graduate School. We would like above all to thank Richard Edwards, Dean of the College of Arts and Sciences, for his steadfast support of the Committee's activities. We would further like to acknowledge the funding supplied by the offices of the Vice President and Chancellor. In addition, we wish to thank Ray Betts, Director of the Gaines Center for the Humanities, for the use of its marvelous facilities; assistants Hugh Bartling and Robert Shields; and our former MFAP adviser Dan Reedy, Dean of the Graduate School.

A general thanks is due the other members of the Committee and the students participating in the Committee's activities. Their enthusiasm and support make all this possible and worthwhile.

# Contributors

JUDITH BUTLER is Professor of Rhetoric, University of California, Berkeley, California.

KATHI L. KERN is Associate Professor of History and member of the Committee on Social Theory, University of Kentucky, Lexington, Kentucky.

THOMAS W. LAQUEUR is Professor of History and Director of the Townsend Humanities Center, University of California, Berkeley, California.

EMILY MARTIN is Professor of Anthropology, Princeton University, Princeton, New Jersey.

WOLFGANG NATTER is Associate Professor of Germanic Languages and Literatures and member of the Committee on Social Theory, University of Kentucky, Lexington, Kentucky.

JOHN O'NEILL is Distinguished Research Professor in Sociology, York University, Toronto, Canada.

KATHY PEISS is Professor of History, University of Massachusetts, Amherst, Massachusetts.

## Contributors

**HERBERT G. REID** is Professor of Political Science and member of the Committee on Social Theory, University of Kentucky, Lexington, Kentucky.

**THEODORE R. SCHATZKI** is Associate Professor of Philosophy and member of the Committee on Social Theory, University of Kentucky, Lexington, Kentucky.

**ERNEST J. YANARELLA** is Professor of Political Science and member of the Committee on Social Theory, University of Kentucky, Lexington, Kentucky.

# Contents

Contents

## III. Bodies Sociopolitical and Economic

# Sociocultural Bodies, Bodies Sociopolitical

### Theodore R. Schatzki
### Wolfgang Natter

Plato's analogy between human bodies and social bodies not only inaugurated a tradition of social theorizing but also seeped into popular usage, remaining to this day embodied in such turns of phrase as the "members" of organizations, the "heads" of councils and families, indomitable "corporations," and church, student, and ruling "bodies." Underlying the analogy and accompanying usage was the intuition that bodies and societies alike are systematically ordered assemblages whose elements, though dissimilar in form, function, and import, exist only in conjunction with one another.[1] Today, under the twin suspicions of theoretical insufficiency and political perniciousness, focused theoretical analogizing between human body and human society has largely lost appeal. The entwinement of the two domains, however, remains a pervasive theme.

Indeed, investigations of this entwinement have multiplied prodigiously in the twentieth century. For instance, Sigmund Freud (and Friedrich Nietzsche), associating the body with nature in opposition to culture, em-bodied a Hobbesian archetype in judging the taming of drives and desires to be a necessary task for the existence of (oppressive) societies.[2] Anthropological theorists, meanwhile, although generally accepting this thesis, also construed body and society less oppositionally in recording the traditional use made of bodily decorations and inscriptions to mark status, family, and group membership.[3] Mary Douglas, moreover, extended body–society semiotics in her investigations of the body as creation-medium of the classifications with which people explain disorder and reinstall order.[4] And Michel Foucault rewrote body–society metaphorics in conceiving of a "political anatomy" that "would be concerned with the 'body politic,' as a set of material elements and techniques that serve . . . and support . . . the power and knowledge relations that invest human bodies and subjugate them by turning them into objects of knowledge."[5] Over the last three decades, finally, feminists and other cultural theorists have examined how (mass) culture—above all, the representation of bodies—directly grips, shapes, and distorts bodies, especially female ones.[6]

The present volume explores diverse aspects of the body–society complex. This introductory chapter sets out that dimension of the interwovenness of socioculturated bodies (i.e., human bodies that incarnate and are transformed by sociocultural practices and phenomena) and bodies sociopolitical (i.e., social and political formations and institutions) that forms the overall subject matter for the individual contributions. This dimension is the dependency of the perpetuation of bodies sociopolitical on the production of socioculturated bodies cut to certain specifications. The particular aspects of this dependency scrutinized in subsequent chapters include the constitution of selves via the shaping of the body, the consolidation of bodies sociopolitical through the representation of human bodies, and the shaping of human bodies and representations thereof by political and economic forces.

## BODIES AND THE SOCIAL ORDER

The thesis that social phenomena shape and invest human bodies is a familiar one. By itself, however, it understates the scope and import of social "constitution." For it is not bodies alone, but more crucially individuals and their identities, that are constituted through the social shaping of bodies. There come to be individuals (subjects)—humans beings with particular identities, genders, characters, joys, understandings, and the like—largely through bodily transformations that result from the immersion of bodies in the field of social relations and power. In Foucault's words:

> Rather than seeing [the] soul as the reactivated remnants of an ideology, one would see it as the present correlative of a certain technology of power over the body. . . . [The soul] exists, it has a reality, it is produced permanently around, on, within the body by the functioning of a power that is exercised on those punished—and, in a more general way, on those one supervises, trains and corrects.[7]

Although individual subjects are socially "constituted," they are necessary components of social formations. A social formation exists only if it is incarnated in and/or organizes particular lives (which is not to claim that such formations consist only in individuals). Social formations, consequently, presuppose the sociocultural molding of bodies through which individuals come to be. The emergence, perpetuation, and transformation of bodies sociopolitic rests on the continuous production and recalibration of socioculturated bodies. This picture differs from Plato's suppositions that individual and society share a basic structure and their specific characters are causally interdependent, in contending that the very existence and perpetuation of society amounts largely to the existence and reproduction of socioculturated bodies.

A number of theorists have claimed that bodies are the medium through which social order and institutions are maintained. Bryan Turner, for instance, reformulates Thomas Hobbes' problem of order as an issue principally of the regulation of bodies.[8] He claims that any society must solve four tasks with regard to bodies: reproducing populations over time (e.g., through the system of patriarchal households), regulating populations over space (e.g., through the disciplines discussed by Foucault), restraining the interior of the body (e.g., with an ideology of asceticism), and representing the exterior body in space (e.g., via the face-work analyzed by Erving Goffman). The establishment of social order is at bottom a matter of solving these four tasks, failure at any of which engenders disorder.

A complementary conception of the centrality of bodies to the maintenance of the social order is displayed in Pierre Bourdieu's account of *habitus*. According to Bourdieu, a person's activities, thoughts, and perceptions are governed by a battery of practical senses (dispositions, *habitus*), which are acquired under certain objective conditions and perpetuate these conditions through the particular activities, thoughts, and perceptions they generate. These practical senses are not disembodied faculties of mind but schemes "inscribed" in the body:

> Practical belief is not a "state of mind," still less a kind of arbitrary adherence to a set of instituted dogmas and doctrines ("beliefs"), but rather a state of the body. . . . Practical sense, social necessity turned into nature, converted into motor schemes and bodily automatisms, is what causes practices. . . . Adopting a phrase of Proust's, one might say that arms and legs are full of numb imperatives.[9]

For Bourdieu, objective social structures are maintained by a molding within them of bodily dispositions that is such that how people act, think, and perceive, subsequent to acquiring these dispositions, perpetuates the structures involved.

John O'Neill articulates a highly similar template. "In everyday life," he writes, "we have—and must have—society in our bones." Social order is "never just a cognitive construct or an abstract system of rules and categories to which individuals conform,"[10] but something embodied. O'Neill suggests that the dimensions of the body that help perpetuate social institutions by carrying and engaging with their organization are threefold: the bio-body, home to well-being, health, and reproduction; the productive body, harborer of the labor and intellect expended in the reproduction of life; and the libidinal body, site of the desire that elevates the personality beyond family and economy.[11] People, *qua* multidimensional bodies, *eo ipso* are drawn into the reproduction of the cultures and societies they inhabit. Maintenance of social order thus demands care for these three bodies. Failure to provide for them, like failure to negotiate the tasks identified by Turner, occasions social anomie, conflict, and transformation.

In sum, the existence and perpetuation of social phenomena

and institutions is secured not just through the suppression of un-ruly impulses but also, as Foucault, Turner, Bourdieu, O'Neill, and others[12] have argued, through the production of bodily constitu-tions, senses, energies, activities, dispositions, and desires.

## THE CONTEXTUALIZED BODILY CONSTITUTION OF INDIVIDUALS

As suggested, the intuition that social orders rest upon the produc-tion of bodies is more fully rendered as the thesis that the constitu-tion of the individuals who people bodies sociopolitical transpires through the sociocultural shaping and informing of their bodies. To concretize this thesis, something must be said about human bodies, social shaping and informing, the contexts of shaping and inform-ing, and the resulting constitution of individual subjects.

Current discussions reveal four dimensions of the *human body* per se that are implicated in its socioculturation. The first is physi-cality, the neurophysiological, hormonal, skeletal, muscular, and prosthetic ensemble that composes any living human being. The operations of this ensemble support, execute, and make possible the remaining dimensions of the body. The second dimension is continuous bodily activity, which also "bodies forth" mental condi-tions. To say that activity "bodies forth" such conditions is to say that it is both the gateway to and presence (manifestation/signifi-er) of various dimensions of individuality in the public world (e.g., mind, gender, character).[13] The third aspect is the lived body, the body as experienced by the person it is. The lived body is the home of the distinction between self and body, thus of the theme of em-bodiment, with its Cartesian overtones and resulting dangers. The fourth dimension, finally, is the surface of the body, the slate upon which is "inscribed" the marks of culture, human coexistence, and social toil. This surface is the flesh that is symbolically and mean-ingfully punctured, incised, decorated, clothed, done up, disguised, and stylized. In the following, the term "corporeality"[14] will be em-ployed to emphasize that that body, through whose shaping bodies sociopolitical are maintained, is not simply physicality but activity, experience, and surface presentation as well: social bodies are maintained through the social molding of corporeality. Moreover, as many writers have insisted, instead of analyzing the body as if there were a single corporeality possessed by all, attention is due the possibly deep structural divergences in the above four dimensions along gender, racial, class, and ethnic fault lines.[15]

The *social molding* of the body is the social investment and shaping of corporeality. This overall process encompasses considerably varying components. Vis-à-vis physicality, for instance, social activities and their products are responsible for clogged arteries, cirrhosed livers, depressed immune systems, brain structures, and fetal misdevelopments. Description and diagnosis of as well as intervention into these matters fall to the activities and conceptualizations of particular social enterprises and traditions. Regarding bodily experience, moreover, it is within sociocultural contexts, e.g., family, therapy, school, TV talk shows, doctors' offices, and conversations among friends, that interpretations of experience are proffered, attention and care directed inward, feelings encouraged and scrutinized, and ways of dealing with bodily pain, incapacity, and felt or real failure and insufficiency developed. Only through a social imprinting along these lines can it transpire, for example, that "a generalized male witness comes to structure woman's consciousness of herself as a bodily being."[16] Vis-à-vis bodily activity and surface, finally, movements, gestures, acts, postures, and habits, on the one hand, and bodily shape, size, decoration, and ornamentation, on the other, are taught, enforced, proscribed, transmitted, exemplified, imitated, developed, discounted, and lauded. Caught up in this web of social conditioning and informing, bodies come to exhibit particular ranges and combinations of activities and surface presentations.

The *social phenomena* in which these modalities of social imprinting transpire are often construed in Foucaultian-impacted[17] contemporary analyses as discourses, practices, and institutions. Although very different conceptions exist of these phenomena, both within Foucaultian scholarship and elsewhere, discourses will be here understood as constellations of signification: interrelated ways of talking, thinking, and representing. Of importance in the current anthology is the dynamic of representation, both as process and outcome (e.g., visual images, mimetic contents). Practices, meanwhile, are organized activities of varying space–time extent. They range in scope from family eating practices, daily transportation practices, and those of personal grooming to practices of negotiation, banking, and religion. Since practices embrace both doings and acts of signification, discourses are components of them. Finally, institutions such as governments, schools, marriage, and economic systems are stabilized thickets of practice and discourse: regular, routinized, and interwoven ways of acting and "signifying" (writing, speaking, representing). Often lodged at particular locales in the built and natural environment, they are sites where individuals engage with and are subjected to nexuses of discourse and practice, thereby being constituted as the subjects they are. Foucault calls particular arrays of individual-constituting practices/ discourses "techniques" and treats the entire field of discourses, practices, and institutions as the site where power is opened and articulated.

Like the social investment in corporeality discussed two paragraphs above, the *constitution* of individual subjects within discourses, practices, and institutions is multiple. Four modalities are of particular importance in the present context. To begin with, there come to be people with particular corporealities through discipline in Foucault's sense, i.e., training, teaching, sanctioning, and punishment. Discipline takes place through the application of specific techniques (practices/discourses) to bodies. What, moreover, these activities, experiences, and surface presentations signify—including what genders, characters, and mental conditions they express—is established in discourses/practices. Examples of matters so established are a wave of the hand signifying greetings; crying, sadness; bad posture, moral depravity; and particular fashions, rebellion or staidness. Contemporary analyses of the cultural "inscription" of the body refer partly to this institution of bodily signifiers, together with what they signify, within discourse (and practice).[18] A second aspect of cultural inscription is the naming and classification of both bodily "parts," whose conditions are described via metaphors of war, and bodily diseases, which serve as metaphors for personality.[19] A further, more literal sense of "inscription" is the actual designing, engraving, and doing up of the body's surface as badge, symbol, or sign of family, gender, race, status, group affiliation, individuality, sense of style, and moral orientation, etc. Examples include tattoos, jewelry, and body painting as well as diagramming, hairstyles, and scarification. Finally, a fourth type of constitution—in addition to discipline, establishment, and inscription—is "normalization," here meaning conscious and nonconscious self-attending and -molding with an eye to sociocultural paradigms, idealizations, and norms. These four forms of constitution come together in Franz Kafka's story "The Penal Colony," which of late has received vigorous attention.

These and further types of constitution transpire through the integration of bodies into discourses, practices, and institutions. Through discipline, establishment, inscription, and normalization, bodies assume specific signifying ensembles of physicality, activity, experience, and surface. And it is through this assumption that there come to be individual subjects: people with particular mental conditions, genders, characters, senses of self, and the like. Being an individual, to utilize Judith Butler's apt phrase, is a style of the flesh.

## DETERMINISM AND NATURE

To some thinkers, constitution smacks of determinism. The question arises, how can subjects be socially constituted and at the same time be something more than sociocultural practice/discourse dopes (to update a phrase of Harold Garfinkel's)? Parallel questions regularly arise about resistance on Foucault's account: if power constitutes subjects, what is there to resist power and where might "it" be located? The key to answering such questions is to jettison the assimilation of constitution to determinism that underlies them and, coordinately, to abandon the search for sites of creativity, transformation, or resistance outside the sociocultural. Discourses, practices, and institutions do not determine, that is, causally necessitate, the existence of certain corporealities and hence individuals. Instead, to employ a figure of thought that Anthony Giddens above all has emphasized, these sociocultural phenomena "shape" and "invest" corporeality by constraining and, most importantly, *enabling* particular activities, experiences, and surface presentations.[20] Now, the "governing" effect of constraint and enablement is the opening of fields of possibility. It follows that the evolving corporeal ensembles of individuals depend partly on the specific discourses and practices in which they participate and partly on their previously constituted selves. People, consequently, are not mere putty in the hands of discourses and practices.

The notion of a field of possibility, moreover, eliminates the need to ascribe innovation, transformation, and resistance to something lying outside the sociocultural. The seeds of transformation and resistance are always present in discourses and practices in the form of possible corporealities that either are submerged by the current prescription and enforcement of other ones or are not yet articulated.[21] As a result, one source of innovation and transformation in corporealities and social life more generally is the marginalized and still unexplored nooks and fissures of individual discourses and practices. A second source is the multiplicity of discourses and practices—more specifically, the plural and diverging fields of actions, values, experiences, and surface presentations they open. A third source, emphasized by Judith Butler,[22] is the nonstandard and unfamiliar use of standard, normativized activities and surface presentations for the sake of destabilizing their standardized and normativized meanings (and therewith the standardized identities and individualities associated with them). A fourth potential fount of change and resistance is bodily possibilities unexplored or closed off in reigning sociocultural regimes. Examples are the alternative "economies of bodies and pleasures" called for by Foucault, the recalibration of reason and sensuousness under the aegis of the play-drive as envisioned by Schiller and Marcuse, and the anchoring of power in bodily meanings and capacities that do not pertain to control as advocated by Sheets-Johnstone.[23] A fifth wellspring, it should be added, is the power of self-consciousness, which Marxism and some strands of Freudianism highlighted as a path toward liberation.

We would further argue that the above account of subject constitution through the shaping of human bodies within social ones does not reinforce a culture–nature divide. The *corporeality* that is formed within discourses, practices, and institutions is anything but a purely natural thing. The body is indeed a *physical* thing. But even the physical body that is subjected to sociocultural molding is an always already *causally* socioculturally invested physical entity (even before birth),[24] not a piece of pristine nature—a purely biological organism—lying outside of and opposable to the sociocultural. The sociocultural shaping of the body does not presuppose (nor does it deny) a strong culture/nature contrast.

## REPRESENTED BODIES

It is important to stress, not only in the context of the present volume, the key role that representations of bodies play in the bodily constitution of individuals. In recent years, theorists of gender, race, and sexuality have pushed forward investigation of represented bodies.[25] Within the vicissitudes of stereotyping, caricature, and demonization, for instance, they have discussed how bodily parts of various types (e.g., nose, hair, and skin color) become markers of alterity seized upon and amplified into systems of social differentiation that "naturalize" domination.[26] With regard to normativization, furthermore, such representations as images of beauty and success in advertisements and films exert forcefully coercive and sometimes existentially and physically devastating effects on the bodily molding of self and other.[27] Susan Bordo, for example, analyzes these and other representations as crystallizing, encoding, and transmitting meanings that pertain, *inter alia*, to familial structures, the relative social positions of men and women, the moral and personal qualities of individuals and of men versus women, and class as well as racial distinctions. Among her many examples, she discusses how recent advertisements for contact lenses encode and enforce standards of feminine beauty that are held out even to those (i.e, non–European Caucasians) who are unable to realize them biologically.[28] By encoding and displaying dominant notions of masculinity, femininity, beauty, success, and the like, representations of bodies elicit, enforce, and enable activities that homogenize as well as normativize individuals and groups.

The current volume examines how bodies and representations of them impact the identity formation not only of individuals but also of groups. To appreciate this fact, one need only think of images of Christ, preserved bits of saints, fountains of blood (as in Tehran), portraits and statues of historical personages, the depiction of bodily parts on crests of arms, and the earlier mentioned bodily inscriptions *cum* badges of group membership.[29] Key elements in group formation and consolidation, bodies and their representations also form important sites of political struggle for both the politics of identity formation and that form of politics routinely analyzed in the Western philosophical tradition, i.e., politics as, in Oakeshott's words, the attending to general arrangements.[30] Since, on the one hand, subjects are constituted through the molding of bodies, corporeality is an important focus for feminists, gay activists, and others who politicize identity formation by locating it within and relating it to the public realm. At the same time, since the body politic is maintained through the sociocultural investment of bodies, the management of corporeality becomes an important focus for the decision-making and executive bodies that attend to general arrangements.[31]

These two genera of politics also commingle in a number of political projects centered on bodies. Insofar, for instance, as culture grips, shapes, and constrains the female body, women's liberation is at least partly an issue of freeing these bodies from certain sociocultural tentacles and opening up realms of greater self-determination and corporeal molding. To the extent, moreover, that the shaping and representation of corporealities solidify pernicious nationalistic, religious, ethnic, race, and class differences, opposing these differences encompasses the more specific projects of alternative shapings of bodies and alternative sets, or uses, of represented ones. In such cases as these, social and political transformation entails, among other things, the loosening, shedding, and transformation of embodied ideals of femininity, masculinity, nationality, race, and class. It thus calls for ensembles of activity, experience, presentation, discourse, and even physicality that confound, undermine, and present alternatives to enjoined and enforced combinations.

In the context of politics, it is worth remembering that the properties definitive of the atomistic self in the natural law tradition of political theory (e.g., reason and will) were conceived in this tradition as if they existed independently of the body; further, that feminists have argued that these properties are largely associated in Western culture with men as opposed to women.[32] Taken together, these two facts suggest that the individual countenanced in this line of political thought is, culturally viewed, a man.[33] If true, it might transpire that retheorizing these properties as being of bodies, or centering a conception of the political individual on properties associated with men and women equally, would underwrite key changes in this tradition's notions of rights, the social contract, the nature of freedom, and the limits of legitimate government power.[34] Another obvious possible gender political tactic in this context would be to undermine the cultural association of "disembodied" reason and will with men.

## BODIES AND SOCIOECONOMIC CONTEXT

That individual subjects are instituted through the social molding of corporeality implies that corporeality and individuality are bound to social context. Since the discourses, practices, and institutions that shape bodies and institute individuals evolve over time and diverge over space, corporeality and individuality vary across the social field. Perhaps this is obvious. Foucault's work highlights this state of affairs since both the disciplinary techniques discussed in *Discipline and Punish* and the practices of the self examined in *The History of Sexuality* are geohistorically specific phenomena primarily localized in the nineteenth- and twentieth-century West and in ancient Greece and Rome, respectively. "Political anatomy," like individuality and the sociocultural body, has both history and geography.

Susan Bordo illustrates this state of affairs in her discussions of normativizing idealized representations of male and female bodies. Muscular male bodies, for instance, have always symbolized masculine power as strength, but at one time they also connoted manual labor and hence proletarian existence (in addition to carrying racial meaning pertaining to the animality of black males). Today, by contrast, working out has become an activity for "anyone" (including a not insignificant proportion of women), whose sculpted product signifies glamour and sexuality and has lost suggestions of lower class status. Arguing, meanwhile, that hourglass figures in the 1950s and earlier were a "symbolic advertisement to men of women's reproductive, domestic sphere,"[35] Bordo observes that these figures, together with their encoding in film and advertising, are emphasized at historical junctures when women are encouraged to define their desire through service to home, husband, and family. As these examples suggest, the practices, discourses, and institutions that encode, enforce, and enable bodily forms and representations shift over social space–time.

If individuals and sociocultural bodies are tied to the shifting sands of bodies and phenomena sociopolitical, the question arises about what hand the economy has in their fortunes. From a neo-Marxist perspective, of course, economic phenomena are "ultimately" responsible in some sense for the bodies and individuals produced in specific regions of the social continuum. Although economic "determinism" has adopted considerably looser and less deterministic forms in this century, the idea that economic context explains developments in a vast range of noneconomic phenomena remains potent today. Even those generally hostile to this thesis are likely to admit that the economy makes significant contributions to countless social changes.

In recent years, the alleged emergence of a new form of capitalism, alternatively called, among other things, post-Fordism, fast capitalism, disorganized capitalism, and flexible accumulation, has served up a new economic phenomenon to which to refer a variety of developments in other domains. It has also fueled new articulations of the stronger, more deterministic thesis. One of the clearest diagnoses of noneconomic effects devolving from the new contours of the profit Leviathan is presented in David Harvey's *The Condition of Postmodernity*.[36] Harvey juxtaposes those economic transformations characteristic of a supposed shift from Fordist to post-Fordist economies (e.g., the switch from centralized production under one roof to decentered subcontracting of production tasks to firms in possibly far-flung geographic regions) with rapid technological innovation in telecommunications and transportation, and summarizes the resulting constellation as an economic-technological "compression of space and time." Analyzing how previous such space–time compressions in the mid-1800s and early 1900s occasioned fundamental cultural changes, Harvey hypothesizes that the economic-technological transition to post-Fordism is responsible for the advent of postmodern culture.

Harvey does not apply his hypothesis to the production of selves and bodies. Regardless, however, of the validity of his thesis with regard to postmodern culture, it appears that the transformations he takes as signaling the passage to a post-Fordist economy have instigated changes in corporeality and individuality through alterations in the discourses, practices, and institutions that produce selves by molding bodies.[37] This development mirrors similar changes that occurred in the wake of Taylorism and Fordism. Taylorizing the U.S. economy, for instance, entailed fitting the laboring body to appropriate clothing, housing, language, behavior, and institutions.[38] Furthermore, as Gramsci recognized, "Taylorism and rationalization in general demand a rigorous discipline of the sexual instincts and with it a strengthening of the family and of the regulation and stability of sexual relations"[39]—in short, monogamy. O'Neill's threefold model of the body also illustrates the supposition that economic changes issue in altered corporealities and selves, in the form of the productive body whose labor and skills anchor social order while varying with the economic systems that train and harness them. It seems safe to assume, however, that far more corporealities than those composing the productive body alone are tied to the state of economic affairs.[40]

\* \* \*

The chapters in this volume explore different facets of the sociocultural bodies—bodies sociopolitical complex. Part I, "Bodies and Selves," tackles the bodily constitution of selves. Judith Butler examines the performative construction of selves through a critique of Pierre Bourdieu that warns against theorizing this bodily construction with such dualities as subjective versus objective and linguistic versus social. Ted Schatzki then explores the different senses of constitution implicated in the bodily institution of individuals in social practices, tying together work of Foucault, Butler, and Wittgenstein. John O'Neill completes the opening trio with a subtle analysis of self-constitution *qua* response to death, as exemplified in the *Essays* and life of Montaigne. In emphasizing the role of representations in the "art of dying," his essay also serves as a transition to Part II.

This part, "Political Bodies, Discursively," examines the roles that representations of bodies play in the maintenance and internal dynamics of bodies politic. Kathi Kern begins by describing how representations of female and gay brains impacted political struggles in the United States. Tom Laqueur follows by considering a historical juncture in the early twentieth century when the representation of bodies served a key role in the consolidation of democratic subjectivities in Europe.

In Part III, "Bodies Sociopolitical and Economic," the effect of socioeconomic contexts on bodies and their representation comes into focus. Emily Martin explores recent parallel shifts in the structure of capitalism and representations of bodies. Kathy Peiss then examines the socioeconomic background against which the U.S. cosmetics industry developed in the late nineteenth and early twentieth century and interfaced with women's self-constitution through body ornamentation. In the final contribution to the volume, Ernest Yanarella and Herbert Reid analyze the development of the laboring body through different phases of capitalism and ponder what type of body is most suitable for opposing contemporary capitalist hegemony.

More detailed descriptions of the contributions follow.

## BODIES AND SELVES

In Chapter 2, Judith Butler kicks off the volume's discussion of bodies and selves by examining the constructive power of performatives, in particular their power vis-à-vis the constitution and reconfiguration of selves. Her general concern is how this power should be conceived once the body is established as the site where performativity is staged, inscribed, and resisted. Her overall thesis, developed through a reconstructive critique of Bourdieu's accounts of *habitus* and linguistic activity, is that performativity cannot be cast via such dualities as subjective versus objective and linguistic versus social. She begins by suggesting that Bourdieu's thesis, that action is the joint product of *habitus* and social fields, reinscribes the first of these dualities. She shows not only that each of these "orders of causality" is implicated in the other but that in Bourdieu's hands the social field is reified as an inalterable positivity. Butler then discusses Bourdieu's separation of linguistic and social dimensions of speech acts, a difference that mimes the opposition between subjective and objective while rehabilitating that between superstructure and base. Once again she demonstrates both the presence of each term in its alleged opposite and the reification of the objective term involved, in this case the social, in the form of institutional conditions or social positions. In the bodily performative constitution of the subject, consequently, both subjective and objective and discursive and social are inextricable. Butler's essay concludes with intimations of a nonreifying analysis of bodily performativity that stresses the constitutive powers of repeated processes of interpellation.

In Chapter 3, "Practiced Bodies: Subjects, Genders, and Minds," Ted Schatzki seeks to expose some of the complexity lurking under the moniker "the social constitution of the individual." He does so by working through a way of thinking that conceives this constitution as the establishment of individuals through the assimilation of bodies into social practices. The chapter proceeds by assembling the mutually complementary and corrective analyses of Foucault, Butler, and Wittgenstein around four axes: types of constitution, conceptions of the body, dimensions of individuality, and notions of practice. In their analyses, Schatzki argues, one encounters at least five different notions of constitution: incitement, production, conceptualization, delimitation/enforcement, and institution. From their texts there also emerges a conception of the human body as a naturally expressive, socially invested, and biophysically formed and operative entity whose activities manifest and signify the various components of individuality such as personhood and subjecthood, gender, and mind/action. Schatzki provisionally analyzes social practices, meanwhile, as collections of doings and sayings linked by rules/propositions and nonpropositional understandings. Collecting these strands yields a picture of the institution of individuals as a multidimensional investment of bodies within nexuses of activities. Through such a synthesis, Schatzki hopes to promote a diversified and thus more adequate understanding of the social constitution of the individual.

In Chapter 4, John O'Neill examines a form of self-constitution that can unfold in that most profound of bodily dimensions of human existence, one's own death. His reflections focus on a period of Western history, the late Renaissance, when the rise of individuality for the first time enabled portrayals of death to become forms of self-portraiture and observation. For O'Neill, Montaigne's *Essays* are a mode of self-fashioning through self-observation that epitomize an exemplary relation to death. Written after the death of Montaigne's friend La Boétie, and in the consciousness of his own mortality, the *Essays* are a practice of dying. The relation to death that they embody, however, has nothing of the morbidity that qualified then existent portrayals and ritual arts of dying as portrayals and arts of death. For Montaigne, the art of dying should instead be a matter of living. As O'Neill relates, Montaigne presages Martin Heidegger in conceiving the proper attitude toward dying as above all a steadiness in personal habits up to the moment of death, a disposition that in effect permits a continuous readiness for death. Such an attitude reveals at the moment of death the greatest "strength of the marriage [a man can] make between soul and body." The writing of the *Essays* exemplify this attitude by becoming Montaigne's habit, and also by articulating the human, all-too-human constancy between his conduct and his nature that is thereby revealed. These essays thus exemplify dying-by-living through self-inscriptional fashioning, what O'Neill calls an "embodied authenticity." What's more, in addressing and seeking readers as partners, the *Essays* exemplify a Socratic art of dying-by-living that conversationally constitutes the self for an indefinitely extendable literary community.

## POLITICAL BODIES, DISCURSIVELY

In Chapter 5, "Gray Matters: Brains, Identities, and Natural Rights," Kathi Kern considers two historical moments when medical theories of the brain that conceptualize it as the locus of identity, the self, and sexual preference impacted political struggles for

inclusion in the political process, for the provision of higher education, and for the protection of civil rights. The first episode centers
on the work of Helen Gardener, a nineteenth-century reformer
who attempted to disprove popular notions of women's mental inferiority. The second profiles contemporary brain specialist Simon
LeVay's theory of a "gay brain." Despite the passage of over a hundred years and the accompanying evolution of medical technologies, the two cases, Kern argues, are strikingly similar. This is partly
because in each episode the brain in question is analogously opposed to some "other" brain. The guiding notion of ninteenth-cen-
tury brain research was that male is to female as white is to black,
whereas contemporary research articulates a parallel opposition of
male is to female as heterosexual is to homosexual. Since the "gay
brain" is thus theoretically dependent on the female for its analytic
status vis-à-vis the straight male brain, this shows, Kern suggests,
that gender continues to structure brain research. In each episode,
furthermore, the materialization of sexually differentiated identities in brain size and structure was viewed by the groups involved
as promoting their struggles for inclusion in the political process
and for secure political-legal status. Kern, by contrast, points toward the troubled history of building a case for civil rights on the
naturalization of difference and urges caution in future employment of this strategy.

Thomas Laqueur's "Names, Bodies, and the Anxiety of Erasure" continues the volume's exploration of politically animated
and sustaining investments of bodies and their representations, focusing on the names and bodies of those killed in war. His interest
is to explain a specific constellation of names, bodies, and memory
in which the attachment of names to the bodies of soldiers preserves their individuality in memory. Laqueur points out that this
constellation appeared for the first time during the World War I
with the construction of monuments that either bore thousands of
names of dead soldiers or symbolized thousands of dead soldiers
with a nameless generic body. As explanations of this development, he first considers the expansion of democracy in the coun-
tries concerned, the political uses of such monuments, and the
need to come to terms with the sheer magnitude of the slaughter.
In each case he discovers that, although the cited factor was indeed

a context in which the commemoration practice developed, this development was more deeply rooted in certain underlying "political subjectivities" upon which democracy, politics, and the need in question were predicated. The subjectivities involved were two-fold: "an anxiety of erasure," which sought in the naming of bodies and the embodying of names a recovery and mastery of an inexorably lost past; and a new individualizing sensibility that each person has a life worthy of representation, which sought to preserve a sign-memory of each and every individual. The resulting democratic impulses to keep the past visible and to preserve every name were satisfied, consequently, by a preservation bureaucracy, a paradoxical result given the widespread contemporary sense of antithesis between sprawling bureaucracy and flourishing democracy.

## BODIES SOCIOPOLITICAL AND ECONOMIC

In Chapter 7, "The Body at Work: Boundaries and Collectivities in the Late Twentieth Century," Emily Martin explores the interplay between developments in the global political economy and changes in concepts and representations of the body. The economic background to her investigations is David Harvey's picture of a recent transformation of Fordist economies into post-Fordist regimes of flexible accumulation. This transformation can be summarily described as a shift from distinct, large-scale units to increasingly broken up, entwined, and blurred networks. Implicitly leaning on Harvey's contention that this economic shift underlies the emergence of postmodern culture, Martin documents the recent appearance of representations of the body that depict it as indistinct, blurred, and penetrable alongside existing representations of it as distinct, well defined, and guarded. This development is illustrated in three domains: images of the body vis-à-vis its ability to maintain health, the transmission of the human immunodeficiency virus (HIV), and corporate organization. The key notion and issue in each of these domains is boundaries, together with their distinctness/indistinctness and sealed-upness/penetrableness. Martin cautions that the univocity of these representational developments does not determine any particular future political-economic direction and that the positive departure from rigid bureaucratic demarcations might not turn into concrete democratic gains.

In Chapter 8, "Feminism and the History of the Face," Kathy Peiss scrutinizes the bodily self-constitution effected through bodily ornamentation. She seeks to destabilize several assumptions that underlie dominant contemporary feminist critiques of the beauty industry. Treating commerce in women's appearances as a site of oppression, these critiques construe the standards and paraphernalia of beauty as social control devices that are animated by a male sexual-aesthetic gaze and engineered by male-dominated capitalism. Through an examination of the rise of the cosmetics industry in late-nineteenth- and early-twentieth-century America, Peiss challenges this critique, in particular its presumed oppositions between powerful male institutions and passive female objects and between the repressed "natural" self and "artificial" selves. Although not denying that the cosmetics industry promoted the commodification and objectification of women, she argues that it also broke down cultural hierarchies among women, opened economic opportunities for them, and permitted the articulation of new claims for social legitimacy. Far from being the passive targets of commercialized inscriptions, women played major roles in the development and outreach of the cosmetics industry. Moreover, in a sociohistorical context where the constitution of the self through appearance was becoming increasingly visible as a performance, women utilized cosmetics in various ways as a means to remake identity: to achieve success in the workplace, participate in mainstream American society, assert and express individuality, and contest dominant norms. Although these modes of bodily self-constitution did not escape the wider patriarchal cultural context, they demonstrate that practices of appearance have multiple meanings, not all of them oppressive.

The touchstone for Chapter 9, the volume's concluding essay, is the model of internal transformation in Western industrial capitalism presented in Antonio Gramsci's celebrated essay, "Americanism and Fordism." Gramsci's critical but hopeful examination of the shift from craft to mass production effected by Taylorist scientific management and Fordist production techniques exposed the wider sociocultural fallout of these developments in the forms of new methods of work, a new type of worker, and new cultural practices and discourses. Ernest J. Yanarella and Herbert G. Reid show how Gramsci's study serves as a paradigm for grasping the discursive and practical changes in work, production, power, and gender that both accompany and influence the cultural landscape of post-Fordism. They pursue their analysis through investigation of the changing boundaries of those body–machine complexes, animal–human interfaces, and mind–body percepts that are involved either in the shift from craft to Fordist industry or in tendencies toward post-Fordism in contemporary Fordism. Foregrounding the notion of the American body—machine complex, they argue that despite important discontinuities, deep and camouflaging continuities exist between Fordism and post-Fordism in these dimensions. In order to clarify the stakes for democratic politics and cultural renewal in the resolution of the Fordist crisis, Yanarella and Reid conclude by juxtaposing and mediating two contending and contrasting renderings of the body–machine complex: humanware and cyborg. Drawing on such theorists as Carol Bigwood, Neil Everndon, and Mark Johnson, they seek to recuperate the role and foundation of the lived body, in opposition to cybernetic formulations offered by post-Fordist management theorists and even socialist feminists such as Donna Haraway.

\* \* \*

As emphasized earlier, increasing dimensions of the body–society complex have received intensifying scrutiny in the twentieth century. These dimensions include the body as the target of mass culture; as the site of embodiment; as a badge of identity; as a danger to civilization; as underpinning domination; as a source of symbolism and alternative intelligibilities and moralities; and as inscribed by culture, disciplined by techniques, and molded by prosthetic and industrial technology. Sporadic and insufficient attention, however, has been paid to the body as anchor of the social order, even though this theme intersects with those just mentioned. We hope that the current volume calls renewed attention to this facet of the body–society ensemble, thereby deepening appreciation of the depth of their embrace.

# NOTES

1. See Leonard Barkan, *Nature's Work of Art: The Human Body as Image of the World* (New Haven, CT: Yale University Press, 1975), pp. 77–79. Also Ernst Kantorowicz, *The King's Two Bodies* (Princeton, NJ: Princeton University Press, 1957); D.G. MacRae, "The Body and Social Metaphor," in *The Body as a Medium of Expression*, Jonathan Benthall and Ted Polhemus, eds. (New York: Dutton, 1975), pp. 59–73; and several essays in Michel Feher with Ramona Naddaff and Nadia Tazi, eds., *Fragments for a History of the Human Body*, Vol. 3 (New York: Urzone, 1989).
2. Sigmund Freud, *Civilization and Its Discontents*, James Strachey, trans. (New York: Norton, 1961), and Friedrich Nietzsche, *The Genealogy of Morals*, Walter Kaufmann, trans. (New York: Vintage, 1967); see also Norbert Elias, *The Civilizing Process*, Vol. 1: *The History of Manners* (New York: Urizen, 1978); Max Horkheimer and Theodor Adorno, *The Dialectic of Enlightenment*, John Cumming, trans. (New York: Continuum, 1972); and Herbert Marcuse, *Eros and Civilization* (Boston: Beacon Press, 1955). For commentary on what might be called the "*Trieb* factor" in this tradition, see Samuel Weber, *Return to Freud* (Cambridge, UK: Cambridge University Press, 1991). On the connection between Hobbes and Freud, see Dennis Wrong, *The Problem of Order* (New York: Free Press, 1994), especially Chaps. 4 and 5.
3. See, e.g., Terence Turner, "The Social Skin," in *Not Work Alone*, Jeremy Cherfas and Roger Lewin, eds. (London: Temple Smith, 1979), pp. 112–141, and Alphonso Lingis, *Excesses: Eros and Culture* (Albany: State University of New York Press, 1984).
4. Mary Douglas, *Purity and Danger: An Analysis of Concepts of Pollution and Taboo* (Harmondsworth, UK: Penguin, 1970), and *Natural Symbols: Explorations in Cosmology* (Harmondsworth, UK: Penguin, 1973).
5. Michel Foucault, *Discipline and Punish*, Alan Sheridan, trans. (New York: Random House, 1979), p. 28.
6. See, e.g., Susan Bordo, *Unbearable Weight: Feminism, Western Culture, and the Body* (Berkeley: University of California Press, 1993), and L. Grossberg, C. Nelson, and P. Treichler, *Cultural Studies* (London: Routledge, 1992).
7. Foucault, *Discipline and Punish*, p. 29.
8. Bryan S. Turner, *The Body and Society: Explorations in Social Theory* (Oxford, UK: Basil Blackwell, 1984), Chap. 4.
9. Pierre Bourdieu, *The Logic of Practice*, Richard Nice, trans. (Stanford, CA: Stanford University Press, 1990), pp. 68–9.

10. John O'Neill, *Five Bodies: The Human Shape of Modern Society* (Ithaca, NY: Cornell University Press, 1985), pp. 24, 49.

11. Ibid., p. 80.

12. On the production of sense, see Walter Benjamin, "The Work of Art in the Age of Mechanical Reproduction," in *Illuminations*, Hannah Arendt, ed. (New York: Schocken, 1969), pp. 217–252. See also Arthur Frank's scheme in which bodies, through immersion in discourses and institutions, achieve control, desire, self-relatedness, and relations to others, and in turn reproduce discourses and practices by carrying out the "bodily techniques" (in Mauss's sense) they thereby acquired. Arthur W. Frank, "For a Sociology of the Body: An Analytic Review," in *The Body: Social Process and Cultural Theory*, Mike Featherstone, Mike Hepworth, and Bryan S. Turner, eds. (London: Sage, 1991), pp. 36–102.

13. The expression "bodies forth" comes from Medard Boss, *Existential Foundations of Medicine and Psychology*, Stephen Conway and Anne Cleaves, trans. (New York: Jason Aronson, 1979), e.g., pp. 102–103. Characterizing bodily activity as the "gateway" to and "presence" of mind in the public world does not imply that mind is an interior sphere or space. For discussion, see Theodore R. Schatzki, "Wittgenstein: Mind, Body, and Society," *Journal for the Theory of Social Behavior 23*, No. 3 (September 1993): 285–313.

14. Frank, "For a Sociology of the Body," p. 49.

15. For a clear formulation, see Elizabeth Grosz, *Volatile Bodies: Toward a Corporeal Feminism* (Bloomington: Indiana University Press, 1994), p. 20.

16. Sandra Bartky, "Foucault, Femininity, and the Modernization of Patriarchal Power," in her *Femininity and Domination: Studies in the Phenomenology of Oppression* (New York: Routledge, 1990) p. 77.

17. See, e.g., Michel Foucault, "The Confession of the Flesh," in *Power/Knowledge*, Colin Gordon, ed. (New York: Pantheon, 1980), pp. 194–228, here especially pp. 194–198, and "Politics and the Study of Discourse," in *The Foucault Effect: Studies in Governmentality*, Graham Burchell, Colin Gordon, and Peter Miller, eds. (Chicago: University of Chicago Press, 1991), pp. 53–72.

18. For a general discussion of cultural inscription, see Grosz, *Volatile Bodies*, Chaps. 5 and 6.

19. See Emily Martin, "The End of the Body?," *American Ethnologist 19*, No. 1 (1992): 121–140; Donna Haraway, "The Biopolitics of Postmodern Bodies: Determinations of Self in Immune System Discourse," *Differences 1*, No. 1 (1989): 3–43, and Susan Sontag, *Illness as Metaphor* (New York: Farrar, Strauss, & Giroux, 1978).

20. See, e.g., Anthony Giddens, *The Constitution of Society* (Berkeley: University of California Press, 1984), pp. 169–179. What Giddens emphasizes is the substitution of constraint/enablement for determination, not the application of these notions to bodies.
21. A very similar picture operates in Michel Foucault's work; see his "The Subject and Power," an Afterword to Hubert Dreyfus and Paul Rabinow, *Michel Foucault: Beyond Structuralism and Hermeneutics* (Chicago: University of Chicago Press, 1983), pp. 208–228, especially pp. 219–222.
22. See, e.g., Judith Butler, *Gender Trouble: Feminism and the Subversion of Identity* (New York, Routledge, 1990), Chaps. 1 and 3.
23. See Michel Foucault, *The History of Sexuality*, Vol. 1, Robert Hurley, trans. (New York: Vintage, 1980), Pt. 5; Friedrich Schiller, "Letters on the Aesthetic Education of Man," in *Essays*, Walter Hinderer and Daniel Dahlstrom, eds. (New York: Continuum, 1993), pp. 86–178; Herbert Marcuse, *Eros and Civilization*, Chap. 9; and Maxine Sheets-Johnstone, *The Roots of Power: Animate Form and Gendered Bodies* (Chicago: Open Court, 1994), Epilogue. Incidentally, the picture sketched in the text need not deny that certain meanings of specific bodily behaviors are rooted in biological evolutionary heritage. See Sheets-Johnstone's conception of corporeal archetypes: meanings built through primate heritage into such behaviors as staring, averting the eyes, turning one's back, spreading one's legs, and increasing one's height; cf. ibid., Chaps. 2 and 3.
24. Sociocultural (i.e., environmental) investment of early fetal development is considered in Richard Lewontin, "Doubts about the Human Genome Project," *New York Review of Books* 39, No. 10 (May 28, 1992).
25. See, e.g., Emily Martin, *The Woman in the Body: A Cultural Analysis of Reproduction* (Boston: Beacon Press, 1987); Thomas Laqueur, *Making Sex: Body and Gender from the Greeks to Freud* (Cambridge, MA: Harvard University Press, 1990); Susan Suleiman, ed., *The Female Body in Western Culture* (Cambridge, MA: Harvard University Press, 1986); Sander Gilman, *Difference and Pathology* (Ithaca, NY: Cornell University Press, 1985); Mary Jacobus, Evelyn Fox Keller, and Sally Shuttleworth, eds., *Body/Politics: Women and the Discourses of Science* (New York: Routledge, 1990); Michelle Wallace, ed., *Black Popular Culture* (Seattle: Bay Press, 1992); and Henry Abelove, Michèle Aina Barale, and David M. Halperin, eds., *The Lesbian and Gay Studies Reader* (New York: Routledge, 1993).
26. See, e.g., "Elements of Anti-Semitism" in Horkheimer and Adorno, *Dialectic of Enlightenment*, pp. 168–208; Toni Morrison, *Playing in the*

*Dark* (Cambridge, MA: Harvard University Press, 1992); Sander Gilman, *Inscribing the Other* (Lincoln: University of Nebraska Press, 1991); and Wolfgang Natter and John Paul Jones III, "Identity, Space, and Other Uncertainties," in *Space and Social Theory,* Ulf Strohmayer and Georg Banko, eds. (Oxford, UK: Blackwell, forthcoming).

27. See, e.g., Bartky, *Femininity and Domination*; Wendy Chapkis, *Beauty Secrets* (Boston: South End Press, 1986); and Naomi Wolf, *The Beauty Myth* (New York: Morrow, 1991).

28. See Bordo, "Material Girl," in her *Unbearable Weight,* pp. 245–276.

29. See also Elaine Scarry's argument that at the end of wars injured bodies function to substantiate and materialize the cultural constructs—often closely related to the consolidation and preservation of groups—that "win" via the victory of one of the warring parties. Cf. Elaine Scarry, *The Body in Pain: The Making and Unmaking of the World* (Oxford, UK: Oxford University Press, 1985), Chap. 2, Sect. 4.

30. Michael Oakeshott, "Political Education," in *Rationalism in Politics and Other Essays,* expanded ed. (Indianapolis, IN: Liberty Press, 1991), pp. 43–69; especially p. 44.

31. See, e.g., O'Neill, *Five Bodies.*

32. See, e.g., Genevieve Lloyd, *The Man of Reason: "Male" and "Female" in Western Philosophy* (London: Methuen, 1984).

33. Good arguments to this effect are found in Carole Pateman, *The Sexual Contract* (Cambridge, MA: Polity Press, 1989), and Zillah Eisenstein, *The Female Body and the Law* (Berkeley: University of California Press, 1989).

34. For a critique pursued along the second line, see Chantal Mouffe, "Feminism, Citizenship, and Radical Democratic Politics," in *Feminists Theorize the Political,* Judith Butler and Joan Scott, eds. (London: Routledge, 1992), pp. 369–384.

35. Bordo, "Reading the Slender Body," in her *Unbearable Weight,* pp. 185–212; quoted p. 335, fn. 31.

36. David Harvey, *The Condition of Postmodernity* (Oxford, UK: Blackwell, 1989), Pt. 3.

37. See, e.g., Donald M. Lowe, *The Body in Late-Capitalist USA* (Durham, NC: Duke University Press, 1995).

38. See Martha Banta, *Taylored Lives* (Chicago: University of Chicago Press, 1993).

39. Antonio Gramsci, *Selections from the Prison Notebooks,* Quintin Hoare and Geoffry Nowell Smith, trans. and eds. (New York: International Publishers, 1971), p. 300.

40. This theme is scattered through the essays in Jonathan Crary and Sanford Kwinter, eds., *Incorporations, Zone 6* (New York: Urzone, 1992).

PART ONE

# BODIES AND SELVES

# Performativity's Social Magic

## Judith Butler

*Modalities of practices . . . are powerful and hard to resist precisely because they are silent and insidious, insistent and insinuating.*
—PIERRE BOURDIEU

The work of Pierre Bourdieu has become important to a number of intellectual inquiries across the social sciences and the humanities as much for its interdisciplinary range as for the theorization of social and linguistic practice that it offers. Clearly informed by a Marxian conception of class, although reformulated in less substantializing terms, Bourdieu's work offers a reading of social practice that reintroduces the market as the context of social power, arguing that social power is not fully reducible to the social practices they condition and inform.

Bourdieu insists that a certain intellectualism taking place recently under the rubric of "literary semiology" or "linguistic formalism" misconstrues its own theoretical construction as a valid description of social reality. Such an intellectual enterprise, according to Bourdieu, not only misunderstands the positions of social power that it occupies within the institutions of the legitimate academy but also fails to discern the critical difference between *linguistic* and *social* dimensions in the very textual practices that it attends.

He also argues, however, that a certain subjectivism[1] undermines the effects of an ethnographic practice that imagines itself to inhabit the very social practices that it reveals, and which does not consider the problem of translation that inevitably emerges between the taken-for-granted reality of the ethnographer and those of the subjects he or she attends. In relation to this latter problem, Bourdieu elaborates the conception of the *habitus*, those embodied rituals of everydayness by which a given culture produces and sustains belief in its own "obviousness."[2] In this way, Bourdieu underscores the place of the body, its gestures, its stylistics, its unconscious "knowingness" as the site for the reconstitution of a practical sense without which social reality would not be constituted as such. The practical sense is a sense of the body, where this body is not a mere positive datum but the repository or the site of incorporated history.[3]

The *habitus* maintains a constrained but noncausal relation to the practices that it informs. Composed of a set of dispositions that incline subjects to act in certain ways, the *habitus* does not determine that action causally. These dispositions may be said to motivate certain actions and, to the extent that these actions are regularized, to compel a set of practices. But practices are not unilaterally determined by the *habitus*; they emerge at the site of conjuncture between the *habitus* and what Bourdieu calls specific social "fields" where the ultimate or ultimately determining field is "the market."[4] Practices presuppose belief, where belief is generated by the *habitus* and, specifically, the dispositions out of which the *habitus* is composed. And yet, as a necessary counter to this apparently subjectivistic account of practices, Bourdieu argues that a set of fields and, indeed, the market as ultimate field will inform and limit practices from an objective direction.

For the moment, I propose first to consider the generative capacity of the *habitus* on practice and then to consider the "objective" determination of practice performed by fields. I also propose that the distinction between the subjective and objective dimensions of practice is itself difficult, if not impossible, to maintain, considered from the point of view of practice and its theoretical reconstruction. The distinction between subjective and objective will be shown to operate homologously to the distinction between the linguistic and the social, and to what is claimed for the "internal" dimension of performative language over and against what is "external" to language.

Bourdieu invokes the phenomenon of *social magic* to characterize the productive force of performative speech acts, and yet this same term might well apply to the *habitus*, his notion of "the bodily hexis," and the social effects that this embodied practice produces. The generative or productive domain of the *habitus* is not linked to the problem of performativity that Bourdieu elaborates in relation to the problem of intellectualism and linguistic formalism. In these latter contexts, Bourdieu rethinks the meaning of performative speech acts in a direction counter to J. L. Austin's in order to establish the dual and separate workings of social and linguistic elements in constituting what makes certain kinds of speech acts into "social magic," that is, what gives certain speech acts the efficacious force of authority. To what extent is the *habitus* structured by a kind of performativity, admittedly one that is less explicit and juridical than the examples drawn from the operation of state power, i.e., marriage, declarations, and pronouncements of various kinds? To what extent can performativity be thought as an embodied activity for which the distinction between the social and the linguistic would not be readily thinkable?

Bourdieu's work thus gives rise to two interrelated questions that will form the focus of this chapter: (1) can the "generative" dimension of the *habitus* be thought in relation to the efficaciousness of the illocutionary performative speech act, and (2) can the social and linguistic dimensions of the performative speech be strictly separated if the body becomes the site of their convergence and productivity? In other words, once the body is established as a site for the working through of performative force, i.e., as the site where performative commands are received, inscribed, carried out, or resisted, can the social and linguistic dimensions that Bourdieu insists on keeping theoretically separate be separated at all in practice?

## THE BODY AND ITS BELIEF

*The body believes in what it plays at: it weeps if it mimes grief. It does not represent what it performs, it does not memorize the past, it enacts the past, bringing it back to life.*
  —PIERRE BOURDIEU, "Belief and the Body"

Following Maurice Merleau-Ponty (1962), Bourdieu understands the body as a form of engagement with the world, where this engagement is understood as a kind of regularized activity that conforms to the "objective" demands of a given field. The body does not merely act in accordance with certain regularized or ritualized practices, but it *is* this sedimented ritual activity; its action, in this sense, is a kind of incorporated memory.[5] Here the apparent materiality of the body is recast as a kind of practical activity, undeliberate and yet to some degree improvisational. But this *habitus* that the body *is* is generated by the tacit normativity that governs the social game in which the embodied subject acts. In this sense, the body appropriates the rule-like character of the *habitus* through playing by those rules in the context of a given social field.[6] Its participation in the game is the precondition for a mimesis or, more precisely, a mimetic identification, that acquires the *habitus* precisely through a practical conformity to its conventions. "The process of acquisition," Bourdieu writes, is "a practical *mimesis* (or mimeticism) which implies an overall relation of identification and has nothing in common with an imitation that would presuppose a conscious effort to reproduce a gesture, an utterance or an object explicitly constituted as a model."[7] This acquisition is historical to the extent that the "rules of the game"[8] are, quite literally, *incorporated*, made into a second nature, constituted as a prevailing *doxa*. Neither the subject nor its body forms a "representation" of this conventional activity, for the body is itself formed in the *hexis*[9] of this mimetic and acquisitive activity. The body is thus not a purely subjective phenomenon that houses memories of its participation in the conventional games of the social field; its participatory competence is itself dependent on the incorporation of that memory and its knowingness. In this sense, one can hear strong echoes of Merleau-Ponty on the sedimented or habituated "knowingness" of the body, indeed, on the indissociability of thought and body: "Thought and expression . . . are simultaneously constituted, when our cultural store is put at the service of this unknown law, as our body suddenly lends itself to some new gesture in the formation of habit."[10]

To the extent that Bourdieu acknowledges that this *habitus* is formed over time and that its formation gives rise to a strengthened belief in the "reality" of the social field in which it operates, he understands social conventions as animating the bodies which, in turn, reproduce and ritualize those conventions as practices. In this sense, the *habitus* is formed, but it is also formative. The *habitus* is not only a site for the reproduction of the belief in the reality of a given social field—a belief by which that field is sustained—but it also generates *dispositions* that are credited with "inclining" the social subject to act in relative conformity with the ostensibly objective demands of the field.[11] Strictly speaking, the *habitus* produces or generates dispositions as well as their *transposability*. The problem of translating between competing or incongruent fields is potentially resolved through recourse to the *habitus*. Resolving the problem of translation is not simply a matter of conceptually or intellectually demarcating the conventions that govern a given social field other than one's own but, rather, of suspending the intellectualist conceit of a representational demarcation in favor of a mimetic and participatory "knowledge" decidedly more incorporative.

What precisely is the formative capacity of the *habitus*, and how does it work to "incline" action of a given kind without fully determining that action? First of all, the *habitus* does not act alone in the generation of dispositions, for the field exercises its demands as well. The distinction between the *habitus* and the field is a tenuous one, however, since the *habitus* does not merely encounter the *field*, as a subjective phenomenon encounters a countervailing objective one; rather, it is only on the condition that a "feeling for the game" is established, that is, a feeling for how to operate within the established norms of the social field, that the *habitus* is built up. Indeed, the *habitus* is the sedimented and incorporated knowingness that is the accumulated effect of playing that game, operating within those conventions. In this sense, the *habitus* presupposes the field as the condition of its own possibility.

And yet, Bourdieu invokes the trope of an epistemological encounter or event both to separate and to render dynamic the productive convergence of the subjective domain of the *habitus* and the objective domain of the field. The dispositions generated by the *habitus* are themselves "durably inculcated by the possibilities and impossibilities, freedoms and necessities, opportunities and prohibitions inscribed in the objective conditions"; further, the *habitus* will "generate dispositions objectively compatible with these conditions and in a sense pre-adapted to their demands."[12] The dispositions are thus generated by the *habitus*, but the *habitus* is itself formed through the mimetic and participatory acting in accord with the objective field. Indeed, the rules or norms, explicit or tacit, that form that field and its grammar of action are themselves *reproduced* at the level of the *habitus* and, hence, implicated in the *habitus* from the start.

This mutually formative relation between *habitus* and field, however, is occluded by the dramatic trope that figures their relation as an "encounter" or epistemological "event." This staging of the relation presumes that the *habitus* must be adjusted by the field and that an *external* relation between them will be traversed through the action by which a *habitus* submits to the rules of the field, thus becoming refashioned in order to become "congruent" or "compatible." Hence, the ideal of *adaptation* governs the relation between *habitus* and field, such that the field, often figured as preexisting or as a social given, does not alter by virtue of the *habitus*, but the *habitus* always and only alters by virtue of the demands put upon it by the "objectivity" of the field. Clearly an effort to avoid the pitfalls of subjectivism and idealism, the thesis of the objective field nevertheless runs the risk of enshrining the social field as an inalterable positivity.

Indeed, the question of whether or not the field itself might be altered by the *habitus* appears ruled out by virtue of the objective agency attributed to the field. Bourdieu continues the above remarks with the following: "The most improbable practices are therefore excluded, as unthinkable, by a kind of immediate submission to order that inclines agents to make a virtue of necessity, that is, to refuse what is anyway denied and to will the inevitable."[13] Bourdieu thus draws on the Althusserian formulation of "subjection" to ideology as the mastery of a certain practice in showing how submission to an order is, paradoxically, the effect of becoming savvy in its ways.[14] For Bourdieu, however, there is an "order" that "inclines" agents to "submission," but "inclination" is also conditioned by the *habitus* and so remains to a certain extent a site where the demands of the objective order and "regulated improvisations"[15] of the *habitus* are negotiated. If the order "inclines" and if the *habitus* is also that which produces dispositions that "incline," then whatever discrepant pressures exist between these separate sources that bear on inclination may well produce inclination itself as a site of necessary ambivalence. Indeed, the psychoanalytic argument would doubtless underscore that the mimetic acquisition of a norm is at once the condition by which a certain resistance to the norm is also produced; identification will not "work" to the extent that the norm is not fully incorporated or, indeed, incorporable. The resistance to the norm will be the effect of an incomplete acquisition of the norm, the resistance to mastering the practices by which that incorporation proceeds.[16] But because practical mimeticism works almost always to produce a conformity or congruence between the field and the *habitus*, the question of ambivalence at the core of practical mimeticism—and hence also in the very *formation* of the subject—is left unaddressed. Indeed, where there is discrepancy or "misrecognition" in Bourdieu, it is a function of an "encounter" between an already formed subject in an epistemological confrontation with an external and countervailing field.

For Bourdieu, practical mimeticism for the most part *works*, and this achieved congruence between field and *habitus* establishes the ideal of adaptation as the presiding norm of his theory of sociality. If the *habitus* is from the start implicated in the field, then the *habitus* only disingenuously confronts or "encounters" the field as an external and objective context. On the contrary, the "inclining" produced by the *habitus* and the "inclining" produced by the field may well be the *same* inclining. Discerning the discrepant pressures of either side of this conjectured encounter would be rendered impossible.

Indeed, one might well argue that if the incorporated and mimetic participatory engagement with the world that marks the *habitus* as such is constituted by the very field that it comes to encounter, then the figuring of the "encounter" as an epistemological face-to-face is itself a belated and imposed scenario, one which occludes the formative operations of the field in the formation of the embodied subject itself. Indeed, is there a subject that preexists its encounter with the field, or is the subject itself *formed* as an embodied being precisely through its participation in the social game within the confines of the social field? This question is important not only to underscore that the *habitus* does not primarily "encounter" the field as an external or objective field but to show that the field could not be reconstituted without the participatory and generative *doxa* of the *habitus*. Conversely, the *habitus* presupposes the field from the start and is itself composed of sedimented rituals framed and impelled by the structuring force of that field. Indeed, it seems that the subject, insofar as it is necessarily embodied and the body is itself the site of "incorporated history," is not set over and against an "objective" domain but has that "objectivity" incorporated as the formative condition of its very being.

## WHEN DOES A SPEECH ACT "ACT"?

*The essentially performative character of naming is the precondition of all hegemony and politics.*
—ERNESTO LACLAU, Preface to Zizek,
*The Sublime Object of Ideology*

The distinction between the subjective and objective domains of practice are offered by Bourdieu in order to illustrate both the necessary convergence of the two domains and their irreducibility to one another. This dualism, however, comes to haunt the very notion of practice that is supposed to render those disparate aims congruent or compatible. The presumption of an objective field or the "market" as a preexisting context, on the one hand, and a subject spatially positioned in that context, on the other hand, is sustained in the very notion of practice, constituting an intellectualist dualism at the core of a practical activity that may well enact the refutation of that very dualism.

The distinction between social and linguistic practice that emerges in the context of Bourdieu's various remarks on performative speech acts suggests not only that this distinction is a tenuous one but that it holds significantly restrictive consequences for his understanding of performativity as political discourse. Further, it seems that, apart from the "official" use of the speech act on the part of state authorities, a more tacit or covert operation of the performative produces prevailing *doxa* in much the same way that Bourdieu describes the *doxa*-generating capacity of the *habitus*.

In particular, there is the question of interpellations that might be said to "hail" a subject into being, that is, social performatives, ritualized and sedimented through time, that are central to the very process of subject formation as well as the embodied, participatory *habitus*. To be hailed or addressed by a social interpellation is to be constituted discursively and socially at once. Being called a "girl" from the inception of existence is a way in which the girl becomes transitively "girled" over time. This interpellation need not take on an explicit or official form in order to be socially efficacious and formative in the gendering of the subject. Considered in this way, the interpellation as performative establishes the discursive constitution of the subject as inextricable from the social constitution of the subject. Further, it offers an account of the social as formative of the subject where the dramatic scenario of the "encounter" between *habitus* and the social reduces that relation to that of a naive and disingenuous epistemological exteriority. Although Althusser's own account of interpellation does not suffice to account for the discursive constitution of the subject, it sets the scene for the misappropriation of interpellating performatives that is central to any project of the subversive territorialization and resignification of dominant social orders. Before elaborating this latter point, however, I would like to turn to Bourdieu's intervention in the debate on performative speech acts and consider the extent to which the dualism he maintains between the linguistic and social dimensions of performative acts produces a set of conceptual difficulties that undermine the political promise of his own analysis.

Linguistic utterances are forms of practice and are, as such, the result or consequence of a linguistic *habitus* and a linguistic market, where the market is understood as the ultimate field or, equivalently, the field in which a practice receives its final determination.[17] The linguistic *habitus* of the performative is, for Bourdieu, the *habitus* of official state speech or official discourse in general. Thus he argues that "politics is the arena *par excellence* of officialization strategies" and, further, that "the principle of the magical efficacy of this performative language which makes what it states, magically instituting what it says in constituent statements, does not lie, as some people think, in the language itself, but in the group that authorizes and recognizes it and, with it, authorizes and recognizes itself."[18]

Bourdieu's references here to the "some people [who] think" that the principle of the performative is to be found in language itself appears to be a reference to "literary semiology," the tradition of structuralism and poststructuralism:

> bracketing out the social, which allows language or any other symbolic object to be treated like an end in itself, contributed considerably to the success of structuralist linguistics, for it endowed the "pure" exercises that characterize a purely internal and formal analysis with the charm of a game devoid of circumstances.
>
> It was therefore necessary to draw out all the consequences of the fact, so powerfully repressed by linguists and their imitators, that the "social nature of language is one of its internal characteristics," as the *Course in General Linguistics* asserted, and that social heterogeneity is inherent in language.[19]

This last phrase is, I think, rich in ambiguity, for if this "social heterogeneity" is "inherent in language," then what is the status of its "heterogeneity"? Indeed, the two terms appear to war against one another, producing the question of whether the social that is internal to the linguistic is self-identically social or whether it does not, by virtue of its instrumentality, become a specific dimension of the linguistic itself. This problem reemerges for Bourdieu when he tries to account for the problem of performativity, itself a linguistic practice, in terms that recall his discussion above of *habitus* and field in their convergent and productive relation to practice more generally:

> Every speech act and, more generally, every action, is a conjuncture, an encounter between independent causal series. On the one hand, there are the socially constructed dispositions of the linguistic *habitus*, which imply a certain propensity to speak and to say determinate things (the expressive interest) and a certain capacity to speak, which involves both the linguistic

capacity to generate an infinite number of grammatically correct discourses, and the social capacity to use this competence
adequately in a determinate situation. On the other hand,
there are the structures of the linguistic market, which impose
themselves as a system of specific sanctions and censorships.[20]

It seems that the "action" which is the speech act is the conjuncture not merely between any causal series but between the
*habitus* and the field, as Bourdieu defined them. Further, there are
two "hands" here, which appear to be divided as the linguistic and
the social. Here the question is precisely how to read Ferdinand de
Saussure's claim that "the social nature of language is one of its internal characteristics"; what does it mean for the social to be "internal" to the linguistic? In the above, Bourdieu refers to "socially
constructed dispositions of the linguistic *habitus*," but is there a linguistic *habitus* that is distinguishable from a social *habitus*?[21] There
is a linguistic capacity, considered as an abstract and infinite potential, that is then subjected to a *social* capacity to use this competence adequately in a determinate situation. But to what extent
does the distinction between the social and the linguistic in this
instance presuppose the linguistic agent as a language *user*, that is,
one who uses or deploys language in an instrumental way? Can the
rich sense of the "practical" offered elsewhere by Bourdieu, related
as it is to the nondeliberate and ritualistic production of belief in
the social order's claim to ontological weight, be reckoned against
this notion of linguistic practice as the instrumentalized use of language? If the subject only comes "to be" within the *habitus* that ren-
ders that subject intelligible and possible, what does it mean to position that subject in an exterior and instrumental relation to the
language without which it could not be?

This becomes a problem for Bourdieu's account of performative speech acts because he tends to assume that the subject who
utters the performative is positioned on a map of social power in
a fairly fixed way, and that this performative will or will not work
depending on whether the subject who performs the utterance is
already authorized to make it work by the position of social power it occupies. In other words, a speaker who declares a war or
performs a wedding ceremony, and pronounces into being that
which he declares to be true, will be able to animate the "social

magic" of the performative *to the extent* that that subject is already authorized or, in Bourdieu's terms, *delegated* to perform such binding speech acts.[22] Although Bourdieu is clearly right that not all performatives "work" and that not all speakers can participate in the apparently divine authorization by which the performative works its social magic and compels collective recognition of its authority, he fails to take account of the way in which social positions are themselves constructed through a more tacit operation of performativity. Indeed, not only is the act of "delegation" a performative, that is, a naming which is at once the action of entitlement, but authorization more generally is to a strong degree a matter of being addressed or interpellated by prevailing forms of social power. Moreover, this tacit and performative operation of authorization and entitlement is not always initiated by a subject or by a representative of a state apparatus. For example, the racialization of the subject or its gendering or, indeed, its social abjection more generally is performatively induced from various and diffuse quarters that do not always operate as "official" discourse.

What happens in linguistic practices reflects or mirrors what happens in social orders conceived as external to discourse itself. Hence, in Bourdieu's effort to elaborate the paradox of a "social heterogeneity inherent in language," he construes a mimetic relation between the linguistic and the social, rehabilitating the base/superstructure model whereby the linguistic becomes epiphenomenal:

> The social uses of language owe their specifically social value to the fact that they tend to be organized in systems of difference ... which reproduce ... the system of social difference. ... To speak is to appropriate one or another of the expressive styles already constituted in and through usage and objectively marked by their position in a hierarchy of styles which expresses the hierarchy of corresponding social groups.[23]

Referring to the "generative capacities of language [to] produce statements that are *formally* impeccable but semantically empty," he proceeds to claim that "rituals are the limiting case of situations of *imposition* in which, through the exercise of a technical competence which may be very imperfect, a social competence is exercised—namely, that of the legitimate speaker, authorized to speak, and to speak with authority."[24] Of interest here is the equivalence posited between "being authorized to speak" and "speaking with authority," for it is clearly possible to speak with authority *without* being authorized to speak. Indeed, I would argue that it is precisely the *expropriability* of the dominant, "authorized" discourse that constitutes one potential site of its subversive resignification. For what happens when those who have been denied the social power to claim "freedom" or "democracy" appropriate those terms from the dominant discourse and rework or resignify those highly cathected terms to rally a political movement?[25] If the performative must compel collective recognition in order to work, must it compel only those kinds of recognition that are already institutionalized, or can it also compel a critical perspective on existing institutions? What is the performative power of claiming an entitlement to those terms—"justice," "democracy"—that have been articulated to exclude the ones who now claim that entitlement? What is the performative power of calling for freedom or the end to racism precisely when the one or the "we" who calls has been radically *dis*enfranchised from making such a call, when the "we" who makes the call reterritorializes the term from its operation within dominant discourse precisely in order to counter the workings of dominant discourse? Or, equally important, what is the performative power of appropriating the very terms by which one has been abused in order to deplete the term of its degradation or to derive an affirmation from that degradation, rallying under the sign of "queer" or revaluing affirmatively the categories of "blacks" or "women"?

The question here is whether the improper use of the performative can succeed in producing the effect of authority where there is no recourse to a prior authorization; indeed, whether the misappropriation or expropriation of the performative might not be the very occasion for the exposure of prevailing forms of authority and the exclusions by which they proceed?

Would such strategies work, though, if we were to accept Bourdieu's description of the constraints on who can wield the "social magic" of the performative?

Most of the conditions that have to be fulfilled in order for a performative to succeed come down to the question of the appropriateness of the speaker—or, better still, his social function—and of the discourse he utters. A performative utterance is destined to fail each time that it is not pronounced by a person who has the "power" to pronounce it, or more generally, each time that the "particular persons and circumstances in a given case" are not "appropriate for the invocation of the particular procedure invoked."[26]

Bourdieu's larger point is that the efficacy of performative speech acts (he refers to illocutionary acts in Austin's account) is based not in language but in the institutional conditions that produce and receive given linguistic practices. The "social magic" of the performative is thus extralinguistic, and this extralinguistic domain—marked as "institutional conditions"—is figured in a productive and mimetic relation to the linguistic practices that it authorizes. Here one would want to know whether this "productive and mimetic" relation is not itself one of signification, broadly construed, and whether the relationship of "reflection" figured as existing between language and its institutional conditions is not itself a theory of representation and hence a theory of language as well. For if "language" will signify "institutions," then surely an account of this notion of signification is in order given that it appears to condition—and hence to refute—the very claim of a set of institutions outside language.[27]

One might well return to the fields of "linguistic semiology" in order to ask a set of questions about how, in fact, institutions do come to enact their specific forms of social magic. If a performative brings about what it names, does it do this by itself or does it proceed through a kind of citation or appropriation of "authority" that effectively produces the *effect* of authority at deauthorized sites on the social map? What happens when this authority-producing effect takes place at "sites" that the social map fails to include as authorized "positions"?[28] If institutions "position" subjects, what are the means by which that positioning takes place? The domain of the social cannot be reduced to a spatialized context "in which" a temporalized *habitus* in general or the linguistic *habitus* in particular effects its rituals. For the question of how social positions are produced and reproduced will raise the question of the "temporality" of positions themselves. Although Bourdieu understands himself to reject the Marxian notion of class in its substantializing form through embracing a notion of "class position," is it not the case that the spatial metaphorics of "positions" can be just as reifying as the monolithic conception of class itself?[29] For "positions" are not mere spatial locations but temporally reproduced effects and hence, as subject to a logic of iteration, dependent on unstable forms of rearticulation.[30] Although Bourdieu underscores the temporal dimension of the *habitus* and of social practice as *ritual*, it seems that the focus on temporality disappears when he shifts to the "objective" domain of the social field, a field described almost exclusively in spatialized terms. Left unaccounted for within this topography are the critical questions of how "positions" achieve their spatial status within the current political imaginary and how this achievement might constitute precisely an erasure of the historical formation of "positions" as a theoretical foundation.

If a "social position" is produced in part through a repeated process of interpellation and such interpellations do not take place exclusively through "official" means, could this reiterated "being hailed into social existence" not become the very occasion for a reappropriation of discursive power, a further articulation of the *habitus*, a "regulated improvisation," to use Bourdieu's terms? Further, if this "unofficial" operation of the social performative does become repeated and ritualized as a *habitus*, how would such a notion of performativity recast Bourdieu's notion of a corporeal history, the embodied history of *having been called a name*? One need only consider how racial or gendered slurs live and thrive in and as the flesh of the addressee, and how these slurs accumulate over time, dissimulating their history, taking on the semblance of the natural, configuring and restricting the *doxa* that counts as "reality."

It is in this sense that the performative calls to be rethought not only as an act that an official language-user wields in order to implement already authorized effects, but precisely as social ritual, as one of the very "modalities of practices [that] are powerful and hard to resist precisely because they are silent and insidious, insistent and insinuating." The performative is not merely an act used by a pregiven subject; rather, it is one of the powerful and insidious ways in which subjects are called into social being, inaugurated into sociality by a variety of diffuse and powerful interpellations. In this sense the social performative is a crucial part not only of subject *formation* but of the ongoing political contestation and reformulation of the subject as well. In this sense, the performative is not only a ritual practice: it is one of the influential rituals by which subjects are formed and reformulated.

How would one distinguish—in practice—between the social and the linguistic on the occasion of that ritual of social inauguration and maintenance by which a subject is alerted to its "place" through the name it is called or a subject is formed through the name that it understands itself to be called without there having been an official call? If the *habitus* is both formed and forming, and if such interpellations are central to both that formation and its formative effects, then social interpellations will be performatives on the order of the *habitus*, and their effects will be neither linguistic nor social, but indistinguishably—and forcefully—both.

# NOTES

1. Bourdieu's work conducts a critique of intellectualism and subjectivism that draws on the kind of critical work of exposing false antinomies that Maurice Merleau-Ponty initiated in relation to the discipline of psychology in his *The Phenomenology of Perception* (1962).
2. Bourdieu's notion of the *habitus* might well be read as a reformulation of Louis Althusser's notion of ideology. Althusser writes that ideology constitutes the "obviousness" of the subject, but that this obviousness is the effect of a *dispositif*. That same term reemerges in Bourdieu to describe the way in which a *habitus* generates certain beliefs. Dispositions are generative and transposable. Note in Althusser's "Ideology and Ideological State Apparatuses" (1971) the inception of this latter reappropriation: "An individual believes in God, or Duty, or Justice, etc. This belief derives (for everyone, i.e. for all those who live in an ideological representation of ideology, which reduces ideology to ideas endowed by definition with a spiritual existence) from the ideas of the individual concerned, i.e. from him as a subject with a consciousness which contains the ideas of his belief. In this way, i.e.

by means of the absolutely ideological 'conceptual' device [*dispositif*] thus set up (a subject endowed with a consciousness in which he freely forms or freely recognizes ideas in which he believes), the (material) attitude of the subject concerned naturally follows" (p. 167).

3. See the editor's introduction to Bourdieu's *Language and Symbolic Power* (1991), p. 13.

4. Bourdieu argues that this conjuncture between *habitus* and field is for the most part congruent or compatible.

5. Bourdieu argues in a vein highly reminiscent of Henri Bergson's argument in *Matter and Memory* (1988) that the body acts as a repository for the entirety of its history. Bourdieu (1990) writes, "the *habitus*— embodied history, internalized as a second nature and so forgotten as history—is the active presence of the whole past of which it is the product" (p. 56). The metaphorics of the body as "depository" or "repository" recalls Bergson (and Plato's discussion of the *chora*, that famous receptacle in the *Timaeus*). But the presumption that the entirety of memory is preserved or "acted" in the present characterizes the temporal dimension of the body's materiality for Bergson: "memory itself, with the totality of our past, is continually pressing forward, so as to insert the largest possible part of itself into our present action" (1988, p. 168). Earlier in *Matter and Memory* he writes, "Habit rather than memory, it acts our past experience but does not call up its image" (p. 151).

6. To participate in a social game is not the same as acting according to a rule, for the rules that condition and frame actions are not fully explicit, and the "following of the rule" is not fully deliberate. For an interesting and helpful discussion of this Wittgensteinian problem as it emerges in Bourdieu's social theory, see Charles Taylor, "To Follow a Rule . . . ," in *Bourdieu: Critical Perspectives*(1993), pp. 45–60.

7. Bourdieu, *The Logic of Practice*, p. 73.

8. Ibid., p. 66.

9. Ibid., p. 69.

10. Merleau-Ponty, *The Phenomenology of Perception* (1962), p. 183.

11. For an interesting and thoughtful consideration of the paradoxes produced by Bourdieu's theory of "inclination" and "motivation," see Theodore R. Schatzki, "Overdue Analysis of Bourdieu's Theory of Practice," *Inquiry 30* (March 1987): 113–135.

12. Bourdieu, *The Logic of Practice*, p. 54.

13. Ibid.

14. Note the equivalence implied by the disjunctive "or" in the following passage from Althusser (1971): "The school teaches 'know how'

... in forms which ensure subjection to the ruling ideology or the mastery of its 'practice'" (p. 133).

15. Bourdieu, *The Logic of Practice*, p. 57.

16. See Jacquelyn Rose on the failure of identification in *Sexuality and the Field of Vision* (London: Verso, 1986), p. 91.

17. "It is in relation to the market that the complete signification of discourse occurs" (*Language and Symbolic Power*, p. 38). Bourdieu appears to presume the unitary or systematic workings of something called "the market" without questioning whether there are competing market forces that are not contained by a unitary notion of the market (i.e., the thesis that capitalism produces excess market phenomena that it cannot control and that undermine its own hypostatization as a unity). Nor does he consider that there might be a genealogy of "the market" that would undermine the thesis of its unitary and ultimately determining character. Further, he appears to codify the distinction between the economic and the cultural which Karl Polanyi has argued is the symptomatic conceptual effect of capitalism itself. See Karl Polanyi, *The Great Transformation* (Boston: Beacon Press, 1957).

18. Bourdieu, *The Logic of Practice*, pp. 109–110.

19. Bourdieu, Introduction, in *Language and Symbolic Power*, p. 34.

20. Ibid., p. 37.

21. For an excellent discussion of this problem, see William F. Hanks, "Notes on Semantics in Linguistic Practice," in *Bourdieu: Critical Perspectives*, pp. 139–155.

22. Bourdieu also argues that this magic is to be understood as the power to produce collective recognition of the authority of the performative and that the performative cannot succeed without this collective recognition: "One should never forget that language, by virtue of the infinite generative but also originative capacity—in the Kantian sense—which it derives from its power to produce existence by producing the collectively recognized, and thus realized, representation of existence, is no doubt the principal support of the dream of absolute power" (*Language and Symbolic Power*, p. 42).

23. Ibid., p. 54.

24. Ibid., p. 41.

25. For a relevant discussion of the phantasmatic promise of the performative, see Zizek, *The Sublime Object of Ideology* (1989), pp. 94–120.

26. From "Authorized Language," in *Language and Symbolic Power*, p. 111.

27. One might consider the usefulness of transposing Jean Baudrillard's critique of Marx to a critique of the social and linguistic distinction

in Bourdieu. Working within a very different tradition, one might consider the task that William F. Hanks holds out for rethinking the relation between linguistic formalism and semantics: "the challenge is to see the literal core of language as already permeated by context and subject to reconfiguration and novel production in activity" (Hanks, "Semantics in Linguistic Practice," in *Bourdieu: Critical Perspectives*, p. 155).

28. Derrida remarks that no performative can work without the force of iterability, that every appearance of a subject who works the performative is the effect of a "citation" that both offers the performative an accumulated force and belatedly positions "the subject" as the fictive and intentional originator of the speech act itself. See Jacques Derrida, "Signature, Event, Context," in *Limited Inc.*, Gerald Graff, ed. (Evanston, IL: Northwestern University Press, 1986), p. 18.

29. See "Concluding Remarks: For a Sociogenetic Understanding of Intellectual Works," in *Bourdieu: Critical Perspectives*, p. 264.

30. See the appropriation of the Gramscian notion of rearticulation in Ernesto Laclau and Chantal Mouffe, *Hegemony and Socialist Strategy* (London: Verso, 1986).

## References

Althusser, Louis. 1971. "Ideology and Ideological State Apparatuses." In *Lenin and Philosophy*, Ben Brewster, trans. New York: Monthly Review Press.

Bergson, Henri. 1988. *Matter and Memory*, N. M. Paul and W. S. Palmer, trans. New York: Zone.

Bourdieu, Pierre. 1990. *The Logic of Practice*, Rochard Nice, trans. Stanford CA: Stanford University Press.

Bourdieu, Pierre. 1991. *Language and Symbolic Power*, John B. Thompson, ed., Gino Raymond and Mathew Adamson, trans. Cambridge, MA: Harvard University Press.

*Bourdieu: Critical Perspectives*. 1993. Craig Calhoun, Edward LiPuma, and Moishe Postone, eds. Chicago: University of Chicago Press (originally a Polity Press publication).

Merleau-Ponty, Maurice. 1962. *The Phenomenology of Perception*, Colin Smith, trans. New York: Routledge.

Zizek, Slavoj. 1989. *The Sublime Object of Ideology*. London: Verso.

≈⟩

# Practiced Bodies:
# Subjects, Genders, and Minds

## Theodore R. Schatzki

Twentieth-century social theorists have challenged the reliance of their forebears on a disjoining of individual and society that has people psychologically integral independently of social phenomena. Conceiving the individual's psyche, identity, and personhood as at least partly the products of assimilation into such phenomena, social theory has undermined traditional strategies of legitimation, reconceptualized such central concepts as freedom, power, and rationality, and revised understandings of human life and society.

Toward the end of the current century, moreover, social theorists have increasingly viewed "practices" as the social phenomena that constitute individuals. In some ways this development, like the larger one, is a concretization of G. W. F. Hegel's *Sittlichkeit*. But the emergence of the dependency of intelligibility, signification, and understanding upon practices as a central topic of social and critical thought has secured profounder understandings both of practices and of constitution through participation therein. During the same period, theorists also began to consider more probingly exactly what is required for and entailed by the overcoming of Cartesian dualism. Those pondering what practices fasten upon in constituting individuals have arrived at the insight that it is in some sense the human body, and not a distinct mental sphere or mind, that comprises the required handle. The general notion of the social constitution of the individual has thus for some become the more specific idea that psyches, identities, and genders are constituted through the assimilation of human bodies into social practices.

This chapter aims to further this line of thinking. It examines how the analyses of Michel Foucault, Judith Butler, and Ludwig Wittgenstein complement, complete, and deepen one another, and thereby conjoin into a multidimensional and wide-ranging account of social constitution. My starting point will be the histories of Michel Foucault. In *Discipline and Punish* and *The History of Sexuality*, Vol. 1, Foucault describes key moments in the constitution of modern persons and subjects through the application of disciplinary techniques and "scientific" discourses to the human body. Butler and Wittgenstein supplement this analysis of persons and subjects with accounts of the constitution of gender and psyches. Their analyses, however, do not merely multiply the dimensions of individuality that can be theorized as constituted through social practical molding of the body. They also fill lacunae in Foucault's analysis of practices, advance more adequate conceptions of the body, and deepen understanding of the nature and modes of constitution.

## Persons and Subjects

Foucault's views are by now so widely disseminated that I will not outline his description of the development of bio-disciplinary power in the Western world during the past two centuries.[1] I will instead draw out those aspects that are central to my aims.

Being an individual is a multifaceted affair. An individual, *inter alia*, possesses a mind, enjoys an identity (or identities), has a gender, displays a character or personality, expresses a sexuality, and is a person of one or more types. Foucault's analyses do not provide a general theory of the constitution of individuality that clarifies all these dimensions. In fact, Foucault does not offer a theory of constitution at all. He simply tells a theoretically informed and politically charged story about the development of the bio-disciplinary matrix of techniques and discourses in which modern forms of individuality have been (partly) forged. Thereby illuminated are dimensions of individuality that were historically transformed within that matrix, e.g., personhood and subjecthood.

By "personhood" I mean the type of person one is. Examples are Type A individual, hyperactive child, nymphomaniac, homosexual, and delinquent. A person's type (or types) sums up important truths about what and who that person is. It can, as a result, form a central component of a person's identity and underlie others' expectations, hopes, fears, and attitudes vis-à-vis that person. By "subjecthood," moreover, I mean, in Foucault's words, "be[ing] tied to one's own identity by conscience or self-knowledge" (SP 212).[2] Being a person and being a subject are two dimensions of what Foucault means by the "soul" when he writes:

> The history of this "micro-physics" of the punitive power would then be a genealogy or an element in the genealogy of the modern "soul." . . . It would be wrong to say that the soul is an illusion, or an ideological effect. On the contrary, it exists, it has a reality, it is produced permanently around, on, within the body by the functioning of a power that is exercised on those punished. . . . The soul is the effect and instrument of a political anatomy; the soul is the prison of the body. (DP 29–30)

The modern forms of personhood and subjecthood examined by Foucault are correlates of modern techniques and discourses. In the case of person types, these techniques are those of punishment, surveillance, training, deployment, correction, and organization as implemented in schools, workplaces, families, militaries, and prisons; and the accompanying discourses are those of criminologists, psychiatrists, psychologists, educators, and the like. Vis-à-vis subjecthood, in particular sexual subjecthood, the techniques are a mix of confession, organization, observation, recording, correction, and punishment as implemented in homes, schools, doctors' offices, courts, and hospitals; while the accompanying discourses are similarly those of psychiatrists, moralists, planners, doctors, health specialists, naturalists, demographers, and criminologists. In both cases, particular types of persons and particular ways of being a subject were and are constituted by the application of these techniques and discourses to human bodies. What do "body" and "constitution" mean in this context, and what conception of social practices operates in Foucault's work? Let us begin with the body.

The body that is socially invested is a material thing with structure, organs, functions, sensations, pleasures, and physiological processes and systems (see HS 152, 154). At one point Foucault denies that there is anything constant about the body over time (NGH 153). What he writes there implies that sensations, pleasures, and physiological processes/systems are subject to social molding. This also presumably applies to structure and organs, although Foucault does not suggest this explicitly. Thus, although there just might for Foucault be something purely biophysical about the body, certainly the greater proportion of, and in any event the "most vital" (HS 152), bodily features are in his eyes also subject to social-historical transformation.

Many words have been spilled over whether Foucault recognizes anything lying outside the tentacles of power. Whether he does or does not is of little importance, for these words have concerned themselves with the nature of possible bases of resistance to power; and what possibly lies outside power—organs and anatomic structure—does not underwrite such opposition. What resists power in Foucault is something constituted by power: a person-ed and subject-ed body. This body is a purely biophysical thing only prior to the initial social investment (at birth or earlier), after which time it is a sociobiophysical entity. What transmits, is the target of, and is a potential site of resistance to power is a bio-social body in which biology and history are "bound together" (HS 152), hence something within power.

As for constitution, Foucault's histories highlight three types thereof. The first I will call "incitement." Incitement occurs when a technique or discourse fastens upon, singles out, or calls attention to some already existing feature of human bodily existence and, in so doing, intensifies, consolidates, transforms, or draws that feature out. The best examples of this process are found in Foucault's analyses of sexual subjects. Speaking of the techniques of confession and observation in relation to sexuality, he writes:

But so many pressing questions singularized the pleasures felt by the one who had to reply. They were fixed by a gaze, isolated and animated by the attention they received. Power operated as a mechanism of attraction; it drew out those peculiarities over which it kept watch. . . . We must not imagine that all these things that were formerly tolerated attracted notice and received a pejorative designation when the time came to give a regulative role to the one type of sexuality that was capable of reproducing labor power and the form of the family. These polymorphous conducts were actually extracted from people's bodies and from their pleasures; or rather, they were solidified in them; they were drawn out, revealed, isolated, intensified, incorporated, by multifarious power devices. The growth of perversions is not a moralizing theme that obsessed the scrupulous minds of the Victorians. It is the real product of the encroachment of a type of power on bodies and their pleasures. (HS 45, 47–48)

As these lines indicate, incitement can take a variety of forms, from a simple strengthening of pleasures, as occurred with the pleasures of masturbation following increased attention to them; to the relabeling of and discursive concentration on bodily functions and sensations, as transpired in the characterization of particular acts, sensations, and pleasures as perversions; to the transformation of sexual pleasures into an overpowering presence and object of concern in a person's life, as occurred in the sexualizing of the child's body. In all these cases, particular words, ways of speaking, and techniques such as confession and observation focus people's attention upon their bodies; and this increased attention, in the emotionally, ethically, spiritually, and scientifically charged atmosphere in which it occurs, induces a transformation in some physically based and socioculturally nurtured aspect of bodily existence. In constitution as incitement, consequently, "constitution" refers to the emergence of a transformed function, pleasure, sensation, act or combination of these.

A second type of constitution can be called "production." While incitement transforms already existing features, production brings them into being. "Newness," consequently, consists in the appearance of something that previously did not exist. Of course, since both production and incitement work with raw material, this difference between them is not absolute. Further differentiating them, however, is the fact that in incitement the body is set upon and transformed, whereas in production an individual is placed in particular material-disciplinary-discursive settings whereby he or she becomes something he or she was not before. An excellent example is offered in Foucault's discussion of the penal production of delinquents.

There came to be widespread delinquency in Western society in part because prisons took in criminals and transformed them into delinquents. A delinquent is a person whose upbringing, biography, or social position are such that he or she is inclined to commit crimes. Foucault argues that prisons helped create delinquency by producing individuals with such inclinations. What's more, they achieved this by subjecting prisoners to certain material, communal, and discursive conditions, e.g., isolation, filth, useless work, hierarchized criminal prison milieus, surveillance, and abusive staff. The production of delinquency, the bringing about of a type of person, was thus largely effected via the placement of bodies in particular material settings where they were exposed to certain conditions. In the case of production, therefore, unlike in that of incitement, there is no need to work on attention and thought. Merely subjecting a body to particular conditions suffices to produce persons of new types.

The third type of constitution, "conception," does not produce new objects. It instead consists in conceptualization, or conceptual innovation, that, in (re)organizing how reality is understood, becomes an axis around which people think about and interact with the world differently. The novelty it induces lies solely, at least initially, in new and changed ideas along with the accompanying (re)organized thoughts and behaviors. Such processes can lead to changes in individuality that are as dramatic as those induced by incitement and production. Consider Foucault's discussion of sex.

Sex, he writes, is not a real entity. Rather, it is a discursively cobbled together artificial unity, which is conceived as a reality and which in effect enables the grouping together of anatomic elements, biological functions, conducts, sensations, and pleasures (HS 152–154).[3] *Qua* entity, moreover, it is treated as a polymorphous causal principle lying behind rational consciousness that is responsible for pleasures, desires, behaviors, and physiological events. It is even considered the truth or essence of the human soul, the principle of the intelligibility of human existence. Sex, as an underlying causal and essential entity, is a conceptual innovation that transforms how people think about and act toward themselves and others (cf. also Foucault's discussion of instincts [HS 117]). It exemplifies the invention of, in this case, fictitious ideas about human bodily existence that effectively reorganize action and thought. Of course, it is only in retrospect that we can pronounce revisable judgments about whether particular conceptual novelties are fictitious constructions or discoveries of important truths.

Thus, Foucault's histories highlight three ways practices constitute individuals by molding person and subjecthood. Practices fashion person and subjecthood, first, by drawing out features of bodily existence through the shaping of attention to, perception of, and thought about oneself; they mold these, second, by placing bodies in particular material-disciplinary-discursive conditions; and they accomplish this, third, by establishing and altering thought about and behavior toward people (including oneself) through conceptual innovation. It should be noted that these forms of constitution can combine in manifold ways. Delinquents, for instance, were constituted not only through their production in particular material-disciplinary-discursive settings but also through their conceptualization within the discourses applied to prisoners in those settings.

> It is said that the prison fabricates delinquents; it is true that it brings back, almost inevitably, before the courts those who have been sent there. But it also fabricates them in the sense that it has introduced into the operation of the law and the offence, the judge and the offender, the condemned man and the executioner, the non-corporeal reality of . . . delinquency. (DP 255)

Indeed, the production of delinquents is not independent of their conceptualization in psychiatric and criminological discourses. Foucault relates how the idea that personal history underlies dispositions to criminality led to the recording of biographies, which in turn not only contributed to the prison atmosphere of surveillance and observation that bred delinquency but also formed prisoners' self-conceptions and consequent behavior.

Homosexuality, to take another example, was both incited by and conceived in the discourses that constituted it. Among other things, the conceptual innovation of treating homosexuality as an inner sensibility instead of a collection of particular acts led not only to the appearance of the homosexual as a type of person but also, once this conceptual innovation was assumed by the individuals so categorized, to both an intensification of sensations, pleasures, and functions and new ways of being and acting (see HS 43–47).

The second of the questions earlier broached about Foucault's analysis of the social constitution of the individual was, what are the practices that constitute persons and subjects? Foucault refers to these practices as "apparatuses" (*dispositifs*). Apparatuses consist of architectures, behaviors, and discourses and discursive elements (more precisely, of relations between these).[4] "Architectures" refers to built environments, not only buildings and other structures, but also the settings and spaces thereby set up. "Discourses and discursive elements," meanwhile, are statements made (*énoncés*)[5] and the propositional entities drawn on and presupposed in such statements. They thus include decisions, proffered reasons, rules, laws, programs, and scientific, philosophical, moral, and philanthropic propositions. By "behaviors," finally, I mean the learned and constrained, planned or taken for granted behaviors that Foucault labels "institutions" and characterizes as nondiscursive because they are not "utterances." Techniques of the sort discussed earlier, e.g., surveillance, confession, and punishment are combinations of all three elements: arrays of statements made and nonverbal behaviors performed (i.e., things said and done)[6] that draw on and presuppose specific propositional elements, transpire in particular settings organized in particular ways, and either record something about or effect some change in subjected persons' existence. Techniques are lines of power.

An apparatus is thus a matrix of knowledge, power, and individuality. Its knowledge is its discourses and discursive elements, an ensemble of made statements and propositions. Its power is its techniques, its setting upon and constituting of entities through discourse, procedures, and the organization of settings and behaviors. And its individualities are the types of persons and subjects thereby constituted.

Foucault's descriptions of the practice constitution of individuals have the not inconsiderable virtues of insight, suggestiveness, and concreteness. They are not, however, without lacunae. I will mention three. The first is that apparatuses are incompletely dissected. A discourse is not merely a collection of made statements and propositions but also whatever governs these and their possibilities. In earlier work, Foucault examined fields of possibility but settled for an overly discursive account in which it is more of the same, namely, rules (i.e., codifications, prescriptions, regularities, and relations) that govern the field of makable statements. Similarly, an "institution" is not merely a collection of performed nonverbal behaviors but also whatever governs these and their possibilities; and although I cannot discuss it here, this governance, too, cannot be understood primarily via rules and propositions.[7] So something is missing from Foucault's analysis. Moreover, Foucault's histories usually concentrate on scientific or pseudoscientific discourses. The vast range of everyday, "nonscientific" discourses, along with whatever role they play in the constitution of individuals, thereby recedes from view.

The second lacuna is that the three kinds of constitution highlighted by Foucault do not exhaust the range of possible types. Indeed, other types surface or are implicated here and there in *Discipline and Punish* and *The History of Sexuality* without being underscored as the three discussed types are.

Finally, the constitutive relation between the body, on the one hand, and persons and subjects, on the other, is poorly theorized in Foucault. He simply does not address the issue. He tends, furthermore, to accent how apparatuses seize bodies and mold them into persons and subjects, leaving uncommented the active, complicitory role the body plays in this constitution. This tendency reaches its apogee in talk of the "inscription" of significations on the "surfaces" (NGH 148) of bodies. Foucault does not deny that the body actively assumes and continuously constitutes individuality through its activities, but he also does not fully consider the relations between bodies and individuals.

## GENDERS

Judith Butler's analyses, whatever considerably else they might be, are Foucaultian in direction and outcome. She takes over from him the idea that individuals are constituted through the discursive molding of bodies in practices and applies that idea to a dimension of individuality underdiscussed in Foucault, viz., gender. In so doing, she builds the picture out in important ways.

As explicated in her *Gender Trouble*,[8] a central target of Butler's work is what she calls the "substance" conception of gender. This conception maintains that a person (or subject) is a substance, an inner core or ego, and that gender is an attribute of this substance. On this view, accordingly, it makes sense to say that the subject *is*, say, a man or a woman. Gender is a be-ing: an inherently nongendered person's being this or that gender. What's more, in treating sex as an inherent attribute of a person that underlies desire, acts, and thereby gender, this conception attributes a key role to sex in the determination of gender. Butler calls this the "expressive" model of gender, i.e., gender as an expression of a person's core attributes:

> [Monique] Wittig's view is corroborated by that popular discourse on gender identity that uncritically employs the inflectional attribution of "being" to genders and to "sexualities." The unproblematic claim to "be" a woman and "be" heterosexual would be symptomatic of that metaphysics of gender substances. In the case of both "men" and "women," this claim tends to subordinate the notion of gender under that of identity and to lead to the conclusion that a person is a gender and is one in virtue of his or her sex, psychic sense of self, and various expressions of that psychic self, the most salient being that of sexual desire. (GT 21–22)

Butler opposes the substance view of gender with a "performance" conception. Gender identity is not an attribute of a thing (the self) but a combining of four types of element: sex, gender, sexual practice, and desire.[9] "Sex" refers to significant anatomy, though not one that is necessarily fixed or binary in sexual possibilities. Bodies enter the world with certain anatomic parts that society treats as significant to sexuality and gender, and becoming a particular gender trades off the parts a body possesses (and acquires) and the significances they obtain. "Gender," meanwhile, can be understood for present purposes as an orienting of comportment (in-the-world). It embraces an array of identifications (transacted via phantasy) that orients how someone interacts with and carries herself amid people and other entities. "Sexual practices," furthermore, designates the sexual behaviors and acts a body performs, while "desire" means a positive wanting (or cathexis) to have or enjoy something. There comes to be a gendered individual through the performative combination of these factors: thus, through a body, with certain signifying anatomic parts, carrying on activities (including utterances) out of both orienting identifications and desires for particular objects and persons.

Of course, not every possible combination of these elements is permitted. Social regulatory practices prescribe certain combinations and punish individuals who adopt illicit ones. The space of gender possibilities opened in these practices contains a range of enjoined and favored combinations constituting different straight men or women, a range of sanctioned and to varying degrees prohibited combinations constituting a variety of homosexuals, and an *Abgrund* of unintelligible and bewildering combinations constituting unclassifiable individuals.[10] Gender, consequently, is a social construction.

A gender (combination), moreover, is a "corporeal style" established in a stylized repetition of acts (GT 140). It is a way of bodily being, a way of bodily comportment. All four elements of gender, in other words, and not anatomy and acts alone, pertain to the body. Desires and orientating identifications are not attributes of an inner substance that give rise to "outer" states such as behavior. They are instead something signified by the stylized repetition of acts, something exhibited not only in what a body with a specific significant anatomy says and does but also in how it says and does them (and suffers particular pleasures [GT 70–71]). Gender is thus a doing, a becoming through repeated doing, and not a being, a being such and such.

No doer, moreover, stands behind the stylized doings and sayings that constitute a gendered person. It is not that a preexisting person acquires a gender through the stylized repetition of acts. Rather, a person of such and such a gender comes to exist only through an anatomized body displaying such a style in its behavior. Only at this point is there a person at all. What, furthermore, underlies the illusion that there is a substance or person standing behind these bodily performances is precisely their stylization. The stylized repetition of acts signifies that one is such and such a gender and that one acts this way because one is that gender:

> In other words, acts, gestures, and desire produce the effect of an internal core or substance, but produce this *on the surface* of the body, through the play of signifying absences that suggest, but never reveal, the organizing principle of identity as a cause. Such acts, gestures, enactments, generally construed, are *performative* in the sense that the essence or identity that they otherwise purport to express are *fabrications* manufactured and sustained through corporeal signs and other discursive means. That the gendered body is performative suggests that it has no ontological status apart from the various acts which constitute its reality. (GT 136)

Finally, bodies come to combine enactively sex, gender, sexual practice, and desire and to signify illusorilly being a given gender through submission to social practices. As indicated, regulatory-disciplinary practices establish prescribed gender identities/enactive syntheses and police them. These gender norms, Butler explains in *Bodies That Matter* (e.g., p. 55), are the criteria of intelligibility for the enactment of gender, for the constitution of a gendered subject through bodily enactment.[11] Through the training and disciplining under the aegis of gender norms that they receive in these practices, acting bodies come to enact the normatized syntheses that constitute gendered persons. Practices, in other words, establish paradigmatic syntheses as regulative ideals emblematic of gender sense and prune individual enactments into reiterative variations of them. Gendered persons thus come to be through the "reiterative citation" of norms in a body's activities, which itself comes to pass through the subjection of that body to the norms concerned within the practices that carry them.

What, then, is the body that installs a gendered individual through enactive constitution? In treating the body as something active whose activity constitutes gendered individuals,[12] Butler highlights a bodily dimension neglected in Foucault. The body is not only a seized target that is formed and upon which are inscribed marks certifying personhood and subjecthood but also an active being that assumes and carries out the synthesis that is gender. Accordingly, the spotlight that Foucault's discussions of sexuality throw on such bodily properties as anatomy, sensations, pleasures, and physiological processes must be widened to encompass the features such as movement, gesture, and the uttering of words in which doings and sayings consist.

We saw earlier, furthermore, that Foucault acknowledges the historical investment of physiological systems, sensations, and pleasures, while conceding the biological contribution to bodily characteristics and even leaving open the possibility of purely biophysical anatomic organs and structure. I suspect Butler more or less shares the same position. In *Gender Trouble*, she criticizes Foucault for writing that "Nothing in man—not even his body—is sufficiently stable to serve as the basis for self-recognition or for understanding other men" (NGH 153), since his idea that social practices inscribe significations on the body implies—contradictorily—that there is a presocial, material body upon which they are written. In opposing the latter position,[13] Butler seems to imply that the body is socially invested in its entirety. As becomes clearer in *Bodies*, however, what Butler opposes is not the causal claims, that biophysics contributes to bodily functions/systems and that some bodily features might be primarily, if not entirely, so determined. Rather, she contests the idea of the body as a ready-made and purely "material," nonsignifying thing lying prior to discursivity, i.e., the idea of a transcendental signified, of something that is what it is prior to and independently of the possibilities of intelligibility articulated in discourse. Of course, Foucault, too, would have likely contested this idea and agreed that the intelligibility of a transcendental signified is articulated in discursive practices (as

Butler appears to suggest on pp. 33–35 of *Bodies*). Their positions, consequently, are substantially the same.

Note that discursivity lays down the intelligibility not only of the transcendental signified but also of the biophysical determination of the body (in Butler's words, the "demarcation" that "marks a boundary that includes and excludes, that decides, as it were, what will and will not be the stuff of" biophysical determination [*Bodies* 11]). Indeed, the intelligibility of any object or state of affairs, i.e., what is meant by and thus counts as "X" or "that Y," is beholden to discourse. And this means, as Butler writes, that discourse "constructs" that which it signifies, or more precisely, that it establishes the meaning and thus demarcation and possibility of something being X, things being Y, and the body being biophysically determined. This does not, however, gainsay the existence of biophysical determination in the way it problematizes the notion of a transcendental signified. Exactly what of significance for the topic of this paper follows from the articulation of intelligibility, boundaries, and possibilities within social practices is a matter to which I will return in the following section.

In any event, whatever of the body is biophysically determined underdetermines desire, sexuality, gender, and even sex. All these components of individuality are instead constituted in social practices. Since, moreover, the bodily synthesis of these four phenomena is in effect the materialization of gender norms and thus the matter of an intelligibly gendered body, the materiality of the gendered body is also fashioned in these practices. And because, in turn, only a so-mattered body establishes that there is a subject with this body, the body of the subject, too, is constituted there (*Bodies* 34).

Butler's analysis highlights two senses of constitution in addition to those presented in my discussion of Foucault. The first is constitution as delimitation and enforcement. (This sense of constitution lurks, though unhighlighted, in the Foucaultian texts discussed here [e.g., DP 28–29], having been explicitly wielded in a different conceptual framework in *The Order of Things* and *The Archaeology of Knowledge*; cf. also SP 220–221.) By "delimitation" I mean the laying down in practice of a realm of possibilities (in Butler's case, possible gender positions). Such realms are neither fixed nor delimitable. As practices evolve, so too do possibilities; and it is never possible to draw up a complete inventory of a field's contents. By "enforcement," meanwhile, I mean the realization of particular possibilities through normative sanction and coercion. That most bodies perform syntheses constituting heterosexual women and men results from the enforcement of regulatory ideals of gender synthesis. Gender, as a result, is socially "constituted" in the sense that the syntheses that bodies perform are made available by the same practices that, through normative sanction, direct and discipline them to enact and thereby reiterate particular possible syntheses.

The second additional type of constitution is institution. A body's performative synthesis of significant anatomy, orienting identifications, behaviors, and desire institutes an individual of such and such a gender. This type of constitution differs from incitement and production in neither adding to nor transforming the total stock of entities in reality. Constitution as institution instead establishes *that* something is the case, where something's being the case amounts to, or consists in, specific entities in the world being certain ways and doing certain things.

Constitution as institution yields an account of the relation of individuality to bodies that fills the third lacuna noted in Foucault. A person's gender is instituted, in Butler's language "signified," by bodily activity. Instead of being an attribute of a substantial self, gender is a bodily signification, a state of affairs instituted/signified by bodily activity. As we shall see, Wittgenstein extends this relation between gender and body to encompass the entire realm of the mental. He thereby provides a general model for the relation of individuality to bodies: all dimensions of individuality are instituted by bodily activities. Traces of this wider position can be found, moreover, in Butler. According to her post-Cartesian intuitions, there is no inner realm or soul. The illusion of a soul or interior space, like that of gendered substance, is signified by bodily performance:

> The figure of the interior soul understood as "within" the body
> is signified through its inscription *on* the body, even though its
> primary mode of signification is through its very absence, its

potent invisibility. . . . The soul is precisely what the body lacks . . . That lack which *is* the body signifies the soul as that which cannot show. In this sense, then, the soul is a surface signification that contests and displaces the inner/outer distinction itself, a figure of interior psychic space inscribed on the body as a social signification. (GT 135; cf. 67)

Finally, *Gender Trouble* is marked by an undertheorization of practices. Butler says almost nothing about practices and how they constitute individuals via bodies. Although this lacuna has now been addressed in *Bodies*, her focus there on discourse, "naming," and language confirms a suspicion about *Gender Trouble*, namely, that Butler works with an overly linguistic notion of practice. In *Bodies*, practices are signifying practices, more specifically, practices of signifying through language; and these in turn are chains of declaring and naming acts that reiteratively cite and rework norms and conventions (and do so only as part of these chains, thus as part of practices). Nowhere is the role of nonverbal doings thematized. Perhaps this neglect is simply the flip side of a spotlight on language. But a similarly overly linguistic concept of practice occasionally surfaces in *Gender Trouble* too. In one passage, for instance, Butler links the emergence, indeed the very intelligibility, of agency, identity, and selfhood to the occurrence of first person assertions:

> The rules that govern intelligible identity, i.e., that enable and restrict the intelligible assertion of an "I" . . . operate through *repetition*. Indeed, when the subject is said to be constituted, that means simply that the subject is a consequence of certain rule-governed discourses that govern the intelligible invocation of identity. (GT 145; cf. *Bodies* 95, 232)

Furthermore, although she speaks of "practices of identity," she conceptualizes these practices as structured around language:

> Indeed, to understand identity as a *practice*, and as a signifying practice, is to understand culturally intelligible subjects as the resulting effects of a rule-bound discourse that inserts itself in the pervasive and mundane signifying acts of linguistic life. Abstractly considered, language refers to an open system of signs

by which intelligibility is insistently created and contested. As historically specific organizations of language, discourses . . . (GT 145; cf. *Bodies* 107)

Language and rules (or "discourse" in Foucault's terminology) are important components of social practices. So, too, however, are nonlinguistic behaviors, behaviors that neither name nor declare something. A body already signifies personhood before it speaks, let alone makes assertions. Indeed, the capacity to make such assertions rests upon a body's being previously constituted as an "I/you" in both others' saying and its own and others' nonlinguistic behaviors. Moreover, both nondiscursive and discursive behaviors ride atop nonlinguistic dimensions of practices. All the acts and behaviors that constitute a child as an "I" transpire within force fields, undemarcated and undemarcatable in language, that govern intelligible sayings and doings. I do not claim that Butler denies the nonlinguistic dimension of practice (*a fortiori* nonlinguistic behavior), only that her focus on language allows them to recede from view. What more is there to the practices, through integration into which bodies come to enact gender, than naming and declaring activities and the norms and conventions governing/invoked by these? If we are fully to comprehend the constitution of individuality, we must bring the background more squarely into focus.

## MINDS

The story I am going to tell about Ludwig Wittgenstein is not a familiar one. Wittgenstein is best known for his thoughts on language, sensations, and knowledge, and for his opposition to the "Cartesian" picture of the mind as an inner, self-enclosed realm. Lying behind his remarks on mental concepts and phenomena, however, is an innovative and unique perspective on the nature of mind, one which construes mind as the expressed of the body. As noted, Butler's thesis—that enacted gender is a bodily signification—is kin to this wider Wittgensteinian perspective.[14]

Like Butler, Wittgenstein refuses the Cartesian (and contemporary cognitivist and functionalist) interpretation of mind as a substance, apparatus, or realm, real or abstract. Like gender, accordingly, "mental states" such as believing, desiring, hoping, thinking, and being in pain are neither properties of a substance, states of an apparatus, nor occupants of a realm. They lack the discreteness or subsistent reality (*Vorhandenheit*) required for them to be such entities.[15] Instead, in Wittgenstein "mind" is how things stand and are going for someone; and "mental states" are aspects of how, or ways in which, things stand and are going. I call such aspects or ways "conditions of life." Believing, desiring, hoping, and being in pain are all examples. Just as mind, how things stand and are going for someone, is neither a thing nor a subsistent realm, so too are mental states of affairs, understood as conditions of life, neither properties, states, nor occupants. They are more like modes of existence in a Heideggerian sense. On this view of mentality, the use of ordinary language "mental state" expressions such as "belief" and "pain" does not pick out discrete entities but instead articulates how things stand and are going for people. Incidentally, the term "condition" is used here in the sense of something's being, the "how-it-is" of something. It is not used in the sense of a prerequisite for something's occurrence or existence (as in Immanuel Kant's claim that the concept of an enduring object is a condition of empirical knowledge.)

Unlike René Descartes's *cogito*, furthermore, conditions of life do not stand in an unclear relation to a body independent of them. How things stand and are going for people is *expressed* (*ausdrücken*, *äussern*) by bodily activities, mostly behaviors (both doings and sayings) but also sensations and images. To say that conditions of life are expressed by bodily activities is to say that these activities make manifest in the world (experiential reality) how things stand or are going for people. Nervous fidgeting, for instance, can presence anxiety, expectation, fear, or any number of other conditions. Another way of putting this is that bodily activities and sensations are the spatiotemporal and temporal appearances of life conditions in the world. Conversely, conditions of life *consist in* (*bestehen in*) particular bodily activities in particular circumstances. To say that a condition consists in such activities is to say that these activities are what there is in the world to it in specific circumstances. Fear, for example, might on a particular occasion consist in grimacing, shaking, feelings of tension, and a gnawing in the stomach.

It must be emphasized that conditions of life do not reduce to the doings, sayings, sensations, and images expressing them. Wittgenstein is not a reductive behaviorist. Unlike bodily activities, for instance, conditions of life are not directly encountered, experiential entities. "The psychological verbs to see, to believe, to think, to wish do not signify [experiential] phenomena."[16] The activities that express a condition make it present in the world but do not exhaust its being. Indeed, the totality of expressions of a life condition can never exhaust what it is to be in that condition. But a condition of life is also not an inner psychic reality of which its expressions are emanations. For, just as in Butler, there is no such inner reality. A condition such as joy is a way things stand in life. It is neither a subsistent component of an inner psychic realm nor a thing in the experiential world in addition to its expressions. "'But "joy" surely designates an inward thing.' No. 'Joy' designates nothing at all. Neither something inner nor something outer" (Z 487).

A condition of life is not, in addition, an illusory signification. Butler interprets the soul as something signified by bodily activity; it is a "surface" social signification inscribed on the body. But it is also, as mentioned, an illusion. It is an illusory signification. Wittgenstein similarly construes desiring, believing, hoping, being in pain, and the like as states of affairs instituted in bodily activity. Conditions of life, however, are not illusions. They are states of affairs that actually hold of people. Wittgenstein denies only that these states of affairs are either "inner" psychic realities or "outer" experiential phenomena. As indicated in the previous section, moreover, Wittgenstein's views here offer a general answer to the question of the relation between individuality and bodies. Different components of individuality such as mind, gender, identity, personhood, and subjecthood can all be understood as dimensions of existence expressed by the active body.[17] They are all states of affairs instituted in bodily activities.

Importantly differentiating this Wittgensteinian view from most other contemporary and past conceptions of the mind is the noncausal nature of bodily expression. On most conceptions, mental states are causally or functionally responsible for bodily activities. In Wittgenstein, by contrast, conditions of life do not enter any causal relations, not even with the activities that express them. To say that doings, sayings, sensations, and images express life conditions is not to say that they are caused by these conditions. It is instead to say that these activities are that through which the conditions are made present (manifested) in the world. So an activity does not express a given condition by being its effect. Which conditions a bodily activity expresses depends instead on its place in the weave of behaviors and contexts of behavior.

Four types of context determine the expressive relation. The first is the past and future behavior of the person involved. Whether John's thought, "I'll get Albert," refers to Albert Gore or Albert Einstein depends partly on John's history of behavior. The second determinative context is the web of life conditions that already holds of someone. Which conditions of life are signified by a person's doings and sayings depends on the conditions the person is already in. The third context is the immediate and wider (social) situations in which people act. That nervous pacing at the airport expresses fear of missing the flight, not, say, anxiety over tomorrow's speech, might depend on an accompanying cospeaker's penchant for tardiness. The fourth determinative context is the practices in which people participate. I will explain later how practices help constitute mentality.

This Wittgensteinian picture of mind/action grants center stage to the body. Like Butler, Wittgenstein generally conceives of the body as active, though unlike her he views it as something animalistic. Underlying the complicated play of expressions performed by adult bodies is a repertoire of biologically determined natural expressions. An example is crying out as an expression of being in pain. Such reactions are prelinguistic (Z 541). Sociocultural education, in the form of initiation into and exposure to social practices, grafts upon this natural repertoire an extended and extendable realm of socially instituted expressions. Through this education, a person not only augments natural expressions with more elaborate bodily (including linguistic) expressions of the same conditions but also comes to express a wealth of conditions that have no natural expression.

The socially formed body expresses conditions of life in three ways. The expressive body is, first, a manifesting body that bodies forth into the world states of consciousness such as being in pain, imagining the Taj Mahal, and hearing Rush Limbaugh, as well as emotions and moods such as being joyful, being happy, and fearing. The body is the medium of manifestation for the instantaneous, moment-to-moment ebbs and flows of such conditions. The body is, second, a signifying body. Unlike emotions and states of consciousness, cognitive conditions such as believing, being certain, wanting, intending, and understanding are not continuously expressed while a person is in them. They are instead dispositions, in the sense that being in one means that certain sayings and doings can be expected in certain circumstances. The body is a signifying body, then, in signifying to others what a person's beliefs, doubts, understandings, etc. are, i.e., that a person can be expected to perform certain behaviors in specific circumstances. The body is, finally, an instrumental body. It is through the performance of bodily actions (e.g., raising an arm, uttering a few words) that the performance of other actions (e.g., signaling a turn, asking what time it is) is effected. I will not explain this further in the present context. Incidentally, actions are conditions of life because they, just as much as psychological conditions, are aspects of how things stand and are going in life. Like other conditions, they are expressed by bodily activities and consist in particular bodily activities in particular circumstances.

In sum, the expressive body, on this systemizing interpretation of Wittgenstein, is a socially molded and naturally expressive entity whose activities manifest, signify, and effect conditions of life.

Three notions of constitution figure prominently in this account. An expressive body, first of all, is *produced* out of a biological one by integration into social practices, whereby it comes to perform a complex and open-ended multiplicity of expressions. Mind/action, furthermore, is *produced*, *delimited*, and *instituted* in practices. Wittgenstein here identifies a particularly profound form of constitution. For the central component of individuality is the possession of mind and performance of action: all other components, such as subjecthood, gender, and character, presuppose it. Foucault's personhood and subjecthood, for instance, presuppose the performance of actions and the possession of attitudes, desires, conscience, and knowledge. Gender à la Butler, moreover, requires

69

desires and acts. In any event, mind is produced within practices because what it is to have a mind is to be in bodily expressed life conditions, and a person comes to perform doings and sayings and have sensations and images that express life conditions through initiation into such practices. Mind is, furthermore, delimited by practices since the range of nonnatural expressions and conditions of life open to people is delimited by the spectrum of extant practices. Mind, finally, is also instituted in practices because which condition(s) of life a given bodily activity expresses rests ultimately on practices.

Understanding this last point requires considering the notion of social practices that is pointed at by Wittgenstein's more natural historical (as opposed to pedagogical) uses of the term "language-game." This notion construes a practice as a temporally extended, open-ended set of sayings and doings that are linked by actors' shared understandings of both what they are saying/doing and how to go on. Initiation into a practice involves the acquisition of practical understandings that ensure that what people say and do is appropriate, intelligible to other participants, and continuous with past behaviors. These understandings do not dictate that people make particular statements and perform particular nonverbal actions in given situations; instead, they enable people to react flexibly, appropriately, and intelligibly in the face of constantly changing circumstances.[18] Understandings thus link sayings and doings into practices and are responsible for the latter's open character. So they also enmesh what people say and do, along with the rules and propositions pertaining to these sayings and doings, into practices (apparatuses). Practical understanding, consequently, is the component of practices missing from Foucault's account.

Foucault does not deny the existence of practical understanding. But his focus on the propositions and rules that govern what people say and do obscures its central and foundational role. Indeed, understanding underlies not only discourses and institutions (in Foucault's sense) but the different forms of constitution as well. For instance, the production of types of people transpires in part wordlessly through the behavioral assumption of understandings and unruled ways of proceeding that occurs when a person is placed in particular conditions. Similarly, the production of minds, i.e., there coming to be someone with a particular mind through the production of a body expressive of it, rests upon the acquisition of the understandings that underwrite the sayings and doings expressive of life conditions. Even the delimitation of fields of possibility, to take one last example, is crucially effected by the propagation and circumscription of understanding. The possibilities open to people rest centrally on the pool of practical understandings available to them since what understanding enables is the performance of an open-ended *range* of appropriate and intelligible actions.

An important feature of this notion of understanding, and hence of the sort of practice pointed at in Wittgenstein's work, is that the domain of intelligibility, *pace* Butler and others (e.g., *Bodies* 187), is not circumscribed by discourse, at least when discourse is understood as language. The realm of the intelligible carried and established in understanding cannot be exhaustively delimited in language. Language's impotence does not primarily show in the fact that understanding governs doings as well as sayings. Rather, it announces itself in the inability of language to express understanding fully. What is understood, for example, when someone is said to be happy, to believe something, to be a woman, and so on cannot be fully translated into explicit propositions: it cannot be exhaustively spelled out in words (this applies to all predicates, or signs, of natural language). The intelligibility operative in these statements, consequently, cannot be adequately marked in language. This is not the same as saying that the social relations/contexts in which someone characterized as happy (etc.) is suspended are so complex that the signifier involved cannot describe and summarize that which it names (e.g., *Bodies* 218). For, this latter claim does not imply that the totality of signifiers is incapable of accomplishing this; and the inexhaustibility of understanding is precisely the inability of this totality to spell out what happiness, belief, or being a woman are. I should add that Jacques Derrida's notion of the supplement (advocated by Butler) also suggests that the limits of intelligibility do not coincide with the limits of language. According to Derrida, what a signifier signifies always outruns what of it is fixed by the signifier. Signification, consequently, is never fully stabilized, even by a series of signifiers. This notion converges with Wittgenstein's thesis of the unformulability of understanding so long as signification is not reduced to linguistic signification, e.g., so long as doings as well as sayings count as signifiers. Unfortunately, the temptation to focus exclusively on language when considering discourse is powerful. Equally persistent and consequent recognition must be extended to the nonlinguistic practical as a constitutive feature of human practice.

I can now explain the thesis that mind is socially instituted in the sense that practices determine which condition(s) of life are expressed by given activities. One important way this works is for practices to establish expressive connections between particular conditions and activities. Some doings and sayings, for example, are extensions or augmentations of natural reactions—e.g., utterances of "Ow!" and "That hurts!", which augment a baby's crying. That these utterances express pain and not, say, joy lies in the way they were grafted upon the natural expression of pain. Many conditions, furthermore, especially emotions and moods, have characteristic expressions. These, too, are largely instituted, produced, and enforced by social practices.

More generally, practices—that is, the understandings they carry and outfit bodies with—establish the wider background of intelligibility against which given behaviors express particular conditions. I wrote above that three sorts of context in addition to practices determine the expressive relation: past and future behavior, webs of conditions, and immediate and wider situations. A particular behavior expresses a specific condition given the contexts of these three sorts in which it occurs, but also only on the background of the understanding of (the concept of) that condition. For this understanding establishes what it is, or means, to be in that condition. This understanding is a form of practical understanding expressed both in uses (and explanations) of the word that designates the condition and in reactions to the phenomena thereby characterized. Practices, consequently, institute mind/action because the understandings they carry establish (1) intelligible patterns of past, present, and future behavior, (2) intelligible combinations of life conditions, and (3) the relevance of immediate and wider circumstances to behavior. In acquiring these understandings by participating in practices, moreover, actors come to comprehend the ever-changing patterns, combinations of conditions, and lines of relevancy in participants' lives; they thus come to grasp doings and sayings as expressing particular conditions. By participating in and otherwise being exposed to practices, they also acquire the practical understandings through which they perform behaviors that manifest, signify, and effect particular conditions of life—behaviors, that is, that are informed by these patterns, combinations, and lines. The fact that people participate in the same practices is of course what establishes that their comprehension and execution of expressive behavior persistently harmonizes.

In sum, mind, the collection of life conditions characterizing a person's existence, is instituted in social practices on the background of the understandings operative there. Here Wittgenstein closes the further lacuna noted in Foucault's analysis concerning the role of everyday intelligibility and discourse in the constitution of individuality.

## Conclusion

Wittgenstein's conception of the practice institution of mind/action completes this chapter's attempt to concretize and diversify the widespread idea of the social constitution of the individual. The writers this attempt articulates share the central intuition that social life, in the form of practices, shapes individuals by molding human bodies. My synthesis has aimed at fashioning an account of individual constitution that comprises multifaceted, and thereby more comprehensive, grasps of practices, the complexity of the body, the multiple types of constitution, and the dimensions of individuality.

Social practices, we have seen, are open-ended collections of sayings and doings that (1) utilize rules and propositions while being governed by them and (2) are grounded in nonpropositional understandings that link these actions and elements into practices and are responsible for the open-ended nature of the latter. (There is, of course, much more to say about practices.) The body, furthermore, is a naturally expressive and biophysically formed and operative entity whose sensations, pleasures, and physiological systems are socially invested, and whose discursive and nondiscursive activities manifest and signify dimensions of individuality following training and learning within social practices. The dimensions thereby expressed include not only the central component of individuality, mind/action, but in addition other components such as gender, personhood, identity, and subjecthood that depend on it. In molding the body, finally, practices constitute these dimensions in a variety of ways. They, for example, institute minds and genders, incite pleasures, produce persons and expressive bodies, conceive of sex, delimit possible (and intelligible) genders and life conditions, and enforce the realization of certain behavioral syntheses.

This list does not exhaust the modalities at work. But it does show the complexity masked by the deceptively simple formula of the social constitution of the individual.

## NOTES

1. An excellent introductory overview can be found in Alan Sheridan, *Michel Foucault: The Will to Truth* (London: Tavistock, 1980).
2. Marked references to Foucault's texts are as follows:

   DP   *Discipline and Punish*, Alan Sheridan, trans. (New York: Vintage, 1980).
   HS   *The History of Sexuality*, Vol. 1, Robert Hurley, trans. (New York: Vintage, 1980).
   NGH   "Nietzsche, Genealogy, History," in *Language, Counter-memory, Practice*, Donald F. Bouchard, ed. (Ithaca, NY: Cornell University Press, 1977), pp. 139–164.
   SP   "The Subject and Power," in Hubert L. Dreyfus and Paul Rabinow, *Michel Foucault: Beyond Structuralism and Hermeneutics*, 2nd ed. (Chicago: University of Chicago Press, 1983), pp. 229–252.

3. See also Michel Foucault, "The History of Sexuality," in *Power/Knowledge*, Colin Gordon, ed. (New York: Pantheon, 1980), pp. 183–193, especially p. 185.

4. On the following, see Michel Foucault, "The Confession of the Flesh," in *Power/ Knowledge*, pp. 194–228, especially pp. 194–198.

5. In translating *énoncés* as "statements made" instead of "statements," I mean to emphasize that an *énoncé* is not merely a statement, *what* is said, but also an event, what *is said*. Statements are made primarily by people uttering and writing words. Unfortunately, this is not the place to engage the interpretive challenges posed by Foucault's use of the French word.

6. Cf. Michel Foucault, "Questions of Method," in *The Foucault Effect: Studies in Governmentality*, Graham Burchell, Colin Gordon, and Peter Miller, eds. (Chicago: University of Chicago Press, 1991), pp. 73–86, especially p. 75.

7. For discussion, see Pierre Bourdieu, *Outline of a Theory of Practice*, Richard Nice, trans. (Cambridge, UK: Cambridge University Press, 1976), Chap. 1, Sect. 1; also Hubert L. Dreyfus, *What Computers Can't Do: The Limits of Artificial Intelligence* (New York: Harper & Row, 1979).

8. Judith Butler, *Gender Trouble: Feminism and the Subversion of Identity* (London: Routledge, 1990). All references to this book (cited as GT) are contained in the text.

9. This formulation stems from ibid., p. 18, but is substantially compatible with the ideas articulated in Butler's more recent book, *Bodies That Matter: On the Discursive Limits of Sex* (New York: Routledge, 1993), hereafter called "Bodies." The main difference between the two texts with regard to the constitution of gendered individuals is that the earlier book highlights the "performative" establishment of such individuals in bodily activity, whereas the later work focuses on their "performative" institution through discourse and the repetition of gender signifiers therein. The two performativities are similar in that each is a type of "reiterative citation" of (the same set of) gender norms. Butler signals their compatibility in Chaps. 3 and 7 of *Bodies*, especially pages 107–108, 230–232, and 237–238. The discussion in these chapters also indicates that she still thinks that gender enmeshes the four phenomena mentioned on p. 18 of *Gender Trouble* (however little or much they have been reconceptualized in the meantime). In any event, the following discussion is organized around her earlier analysis of performative bodily activity and draws in later developments only to the extent necessary to fill out that analysis.

10. A good example of the latter is found in the film *Paris Is Burning* in the person Venus Xtravaganza.

11. This thesis seems to imply that homosexual genders are "unintelligible" and only heterosexual ones are "intelligible." In *Gender Trouble*,

by contrast, hetero- and homosexual genders are divided by a normative enjoining and sanctioning, i.e., a demarcation of right and wrong, that is not equivalent to the delineation of intelligible and unintelligible. In that work, accordingly, homosexual genders are intelligible but illicit. Interestingly, although Butler's discussions in *Bodies* of fields of intelligibility in general imply that homosexual genders are "unintelligible," when specifying the character devolving upon such genders in their demarcation from heterosexual ones she always uses other terms such as "unlivable," "unendurable," "not of value," "inviable," and "not mattering" (e.g., pp. 3, 16). I will not try to disentangle this thicket of intelligibility, normativity, livability, and mattering.

12. In *Bodies*, Butler describes "performativity" as the power of discourse to produce the effects it names. This type of performativity does not oppose that of bodily enactive activity. Discourse relates to such activity by constraining and molding it into a regular reiteration of norms, a forming and constraining without which that activity would have no shape. This does not, however, deny the performativity of the so-formed enactment. Indeed, Butler's discussions on pp. 107 and 231 (e.g., "the performing of gender norms") implicitly acknowledge the compatibility of the two performativities. Unfortunately, her repeated opposition of the performativity of discourse to the constitutive activity of a *subject* somewhat obscures the complementary and, moreover, necessary role of *bodily* enactive activity.

13. Foucault, too, as explained, opposes this position. There can be a purely presocial body only prior to the initial social inscription (assuming there is an initial one), after which time the body that is further written is an already socially molded biological thing. Butler does not give Foucault credit for rejecting biology and history as "consecutive" (HS 152) and instead construes them as entwined in a temporally extended and evolving melange.

14. For elaboration of the following interpretation of Wittgenstein, see my book *Social Practices. A Wittgensteinian Approach to Human Activity and the Social* (Cambridge, UK: Cambridge University Press, 1996), Chap. 2.

15. For parallel aspersions on the discreteness of mental states, see Donald Davidson, "Knowing One's Own Mind," *Proceedings and Addresses of the American Philosophical Association* 60 (1987): 441–458; also Daniel Dennett, *The Intentional Stance* (Cambridge, MA: MIT Press, 1987).

16. Ludwig Wittgenstein, *Zettel*, G.E.M. Anscombe and G. H. von Wright, eds., G.E.M. Anscombe, trans. (Berkeley: University of Cal-

ifornia Press, 1967), Sec. 471. (This book is cited in text references as Z.)

17. This interpretation of Wittgenstein shows the inpropitiousness of Butler's use of "expression" to characterize the view of gender she opposes (e.g., GT 141). Like other writers (e.g., Louis Althusser, *Reading Capital*, Ben Brewster, trans. [London: New Left Books, 1970], especially "Marx's Immense Theoretical Revolution," pp. 182–193), Butler attributes a metaphysical picture of inner and outer to "the expressive theory of X": the X which an outer phenomenon (e.g., bodily activity) expresses is an inner something. At least two types of expressive theories decline this metaphysical presupposition. One conceives of that which is expressed by spatiotemporal entities as ideal contents, in the sense of Gottlob Frege's thoughts, the other views what is expressed as ways of being, or modes of existence. Late Dilthey exemplifies the first view; Helmut Plessner (along with Wittgenstein), the second. See Wilhelm Dilthey, *Gesammelte Schriften*, Vol. 7 (Leipzig: Teubner, 1927); and Helmut Plessner, *Laughing and Crying: A Study of the Limits of Human Behavior*, James Spencer Churchill and Marjorie Grene, trans. (Evanston, IL: Northwestern University Press, 1970).

18. For an analysis of practical understanding, see Bourdieu's notion of *habitus* in his *Outline of a Theory of Practice*, Chaps. 2 and 3; also his *The Logic of Practice*, Richard Nice, trans. (Stanford, CA: Stanford University Press, 1990), Book I, Chaps. 3–5. For a different but related approach, see Hubert L. Dreyfus and Stuart E. Dreyfus, *Mind Over Machine* (New York: Free Press, 1986).

# Montaigne on the Arts of Aging and Dying

## John O'Neill

Like everything else in life, death has not always been what it is. Thus we can trace the "modernization" of death from the sixteenth century.[1] With the emergence of the individual, death is at once interiorized as a process of self-destruction and externalized in the discourse, emblems, hieroglyphs, and medical illustrations of the physiognomy and anatomy of musculature, skeletal structure, corpse, and cadaver. By the same token, the secularization of the discourses of death provoked a return of the repressed in the form of the macabre, perverse, and carnivalesque creature of Lady Death and her dance. Here knowledge and desire consume one another in the frenzy of the self-acknowledged limitations of birth, sexuality, and death. By the "postmodern" period, death is the absent player in a soap opera dominated by the power and eroticism of *General Hospital*. Here the theatricality of "near death" (like "near beer" or "safe sex") has consumed the early modern dramaturgy of death's torments in the psychodrama of hospital personnel relations enacted over a "dying process." The soap-patient's death is subordinated entirely to the heroic physician's struggle with the vicissitudes of the techno-medico morale of his subordinates. Eros and Thanatos become minor players in the soft pornography of hospitalized workouts in the service of sanitized "health."

The medicalization of the *memento mori*, however, had already begun in the Renaissance with the result that the eloquence of death was rendered beyond any denial in the medical illustrations of the *visible corpse*, flayed, sectioned, enumerated, and displayed as the ultimate object (Figure 4.1), the absolute certainty discovered in the inescapable vision of the eyeless skull, or the headless trunk of modern man.

Here the flesh of the world is given to itself in its loss, its disease, and its inevitable decay, at the same time that the living eye of science and medicine restores our mortality in an interiorized vision that is ethical rather than religious or mythological. We see

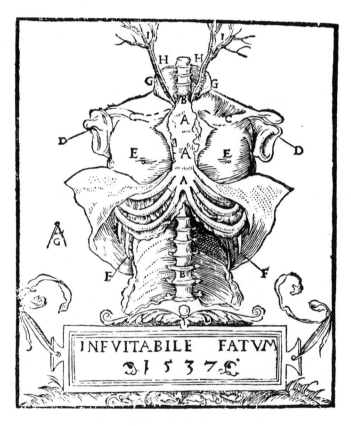

**Figure 4.1.** Dryander, *Anatomie* (1537).

ourselves: we live our death. By the same token, the portrait of death becomes a self-portrait, the highest achievement of Renaissance self-fashioning—as we may see from Michel de Montaigne's essaying of his own morbidity and mortality. Here the body's sad departure from the light of the living is no longer suffered with stoic regret. Rather, it is anticipated in the new light of self-observation. Montaigne's method, of course, is phenomenological and hermeneutical rather than an "autopsical" technique of the modern self that Michel Foucault has explored. Foucault's argument that only the autopsy permits true self-observation unnecessarily foreshortens the discursive history of modernity, even though his insistence upon the complementarity of the hand, the ear, and the eye is well taken.[2]

The discovery of the modern self required that the surgeon's hand open the body to the medical eye, thereby inaugurating the subject/object of the anatomy lesson that underwrites the incorporation of the modern self. Montaigne, by contrast, writes at that juncture in the history of the body's opening where the act of dissection is rhetorical, sacrificial, and theatrical, in search of a semiology of the self. The *Essays*[3] work in that zone between religion and medicine, between theology and science, where literature may claim to render the visible intelligible by making the visual textual. Montaigne's reflections on death start from his faithful record of the exemplary death of his friend La Boétie. The latter's injunction—that we live life as a preparation for death—weighed upon Montaigne, but as an example more honored in the breach. At first, however, the *Essays* are composed around the *double absence* created by La Boétie's exemplary life and death, on the one hand, and by Montaigne's near death, on the other hand, inasmuch as he had lost half of himself in his friend.

Here we introduce a series of constellations—or "grotesques," as Montaigne would think of them—in which we intend only to indicate the cross-cutting lines of attraction and repulsion, or of imitation and invention, which constitute the thematic elements in Montaigne's intricate treatment of life and death, of friendship and solitude, of separation and restoration (see Figure 4.2). At first, the exemplum of the great man in the hour of death challenged Montaigne's powers of portrayal. But then Montaigne also feared

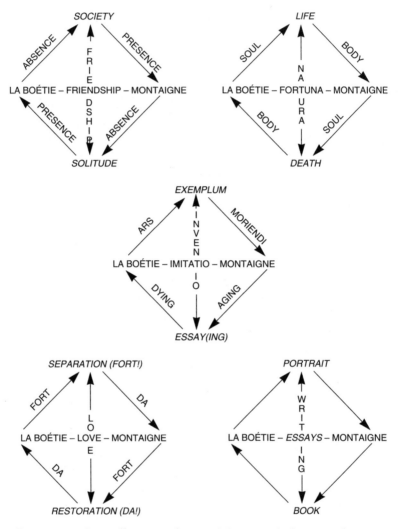

**Figure 4.2.** Constellations indicating Montaigne's thematic elements.

to fall into imitation and, even in his earliest writing, he was concerned to move away from the still life into the flux of the self-
essay. Of course, it would be foreign to the *Essays* to reduce the
phenomenological inquiry they exhibit to the minor geometric
structures shown in Figure 4.2 since they have no life apart from

the text from which they are drawn. In view of the practice of current literary criticism, however, it might be as well to point out
that these constellations are internal to the text's own deconstruc-
tive practice.[4] They "show" its relativization of contrastive concepts and its opposition and binding of contrary terms. But such
devices lose the rhetoric and stylistics of the *Essays* as a written inquiry motivated by the death of a friend and the reconstruction of
an abiding memorial to the lost image of a mutual love. To pursue
these matters, we are obliged to engage in our own "essay." Like
Roland Barthes, we abandon the abstract structure of the text for
the pursuit of its body.[5] We therefore forbid ourselves to look back
at these frozen constellations since they merely seduce us with
possession of the text. Like Orpheus, we have to learn that the
critic's gain lies ahead along a path carved out by his or her own art
and that he or she can work from no model behind him or her nor
return from any other depth.[6] The writer cannot look for inspiration in death. In order to write, the essayist must be able to write—
to write the body.[7] Thus, Montaigne conceived of death as the separation of oneself from oneself. The model of such splitting
(*Spaltung*) is to be found in the Aristotelian concept of friendship—and so we have to be cautious with the use of psychoanalytic
interpretation (as we shall show in our discussion of Anthony
Wilden's thesis). But Montaigne also discovered himself separated
from himself in language and in thought. Although he believed
himself to be mirrored in his friend, Montaigne discovered that he
could not hold this mirror to the *Essays*. Thus we shall explore how
Montaigne reconstructed the "absence/presence" of his friend La
Boétie in terms of the "*fort/da*" alternations between certainty and
doubt, between the solidity of the "example" (*exemplum*) and the
flux of the "essay."[8] As the *Essays* developed, Montaigne discovered that fidelity to his friend La Boétie required that he break the
mirror of example to work in the cracks and fragments of his self
opened up in the flow of writing, or of essaying himself. At the
same time, Montaigne put writing under the sign of speech inasmuch as it keeps trust with that unfinished conversation that
marked his love of La Boétie, his care of literature and of life itself,
until the moment death silences us, as it must. In this regard, the
*Essays* honor a Socratic art of dying, rising above the body's pains

to which the mind is nevertheless attached, and insisting to the very end upon the conversable company of humankind as our highest good. Yet despite the philosophical and religious tradition available to him, Montaigne resisted internalizing death as the soul's companion. Rather, he espoused an art of living, prepared at any moment to let go of life—as we must: "If I can, I shall keep my death from saying anything that my life has not already said" (I:7, 20).

For Montaigne death was as much a part of the landscape of his day as an event in time. He knew death quite early in his own family, and his home stood open to a countryside stalked by the deaths of civil war. Like Sigmund Freud, who in his middle age had most of his fame lying before him, Montaigne considered himself close to death when he retired to begin work on the *Essays*. One might pursue this circumstance, as Wilden[9] has done, by reading Montaigne as a man ridden by the anxiety of death, uncertain of his body, his sexuality, and his social position, and we shall consider this view later on. From such a perspective, the *Essays* are obsessed with "loss" and "absence" and are best read as an early essay on mourning and melancholy, repeating the great loss of La Boétie's friendship and enshrining his absence in the reflecting mirror of Montaigne's own self-portrait, itself copied from his lost image in the eyes of La Boétie, himself similarly doubled and lost. Thus we know that Montaigne intended to re-present La Boétie by placing his writings at the very center of the *Essays*, as a mirror from where he could explore himself as in life he was once beholden to his friend. But he did not do this. Rather, he published La Boétie's poems and discourses separately—in their own "write," so to speak, standing up for themselves and at a necessary distance from Montaigne inasmuch as he judged them to be too severe upon his countrymen. Did he, then, already betray his friend in death despite their protested fidelity in life? Or did Montaigne's judgment honor the differences rather than the similarities that he gradually discovered in the composition of his thoughts—against which the example of La Boétie acted as a necessary foil to exploit their difference and thus to honor the interplay that had constituted their friendship?

We know that Montaigne never ceased to meditate upon the

proportion of constancy and inconstancy in human affairs. Everything fed these meditations—and not the least the question of how
a man might conduct himself in the hour of death. Would he for-
swear himself, pleading with gods he had ignored during his life, or
by turning to hitherto unpracticed works of charity in recompense
for his sins? Did the high and mighty meet death any better than
the poor and humble folk? The Greeks had concluded that no man
is to be called happy until after he is dead. Did this mean that they
considered life a vale of tears, despite appearances? Or, rather, did
they have in mind the question of constancy, that is, how a man
might face death and not be altered in his essential character by
the pain of dying and the fear of annihilation? Now Montaigne
had before him, of course, a long philosophical and Christian tradition in which the exemplary deaths of Socrates and Christ, not to
mention the sages and saints, served to prepare one's meditations
on death and the practice of one's own conduct in the last hour
(Figure 4.3).[10] Nor does he ignore this tradition. But his use of it is
peculiar to him and cannot be appraised without treating the *Essays* as a whole as an exercise in the arts of aging and death upon
which they constitute a distinct innovation.[11]

Some seven years before beginning work on the *Essays*, Montaigne had relayed to his father an account of three days during
which La Boétie lay dying at the age of thirty-three or so.[12] He
presents a figure at times with Christ-like proportions but more
generally Socratic in his ability to converse with those around
him from whom in turn he took his leave. Setting aside public
life, acquitting his family duties, and settling his advice upon relatives and friends, La Boétie conducted himself in death before
his friend exactly as he had planned in life: "Il y a fort long temps
que j'y estois preparé, et que j'eu scavois ma leçon toute par
cueur."[13]

Montaigne's account of this exemplary death is both historical
and phenomenological—in part trapped in the stylistics of La
Boétie's *exemplum*, yet partially veering away to consider the mix-
ture of absolute conviction in La Boétie's last words and the slip-
page between mind and body that he saw not only in his friend but
also in himself, who was nevertheless called upon to witness forever La Boétie's quest for his "place":

**Figure 4.3.** From Alberto Tenenti, *La Vie et la mort à travers l'art du Xv^e siècle*, p. 117.

Then, among other things, he began to entreat me again and again with extreme affection to *give him a place*; so that I was afraid that his judgement was shaken. Even when I had remonstrated with him very gently that he was letting the illness carry him away and that these were not the words of a man in his sound mind, he did not give in at first and repeated even more strongly: "My brother, my brother, do you refuse me a place?" This until he forced me to convince him by reason and tell him that since he was breathing and speaking and *had a body*, consequently he had *his place*. "True, true," he answered me then, "I have one, but it is not the one I need; and then when all is said I have no being left." "God will give you a better one very soon," said I. "Would that I were there already," he replied. "For three days now I have been straining to leave."[14]

It may be said that Montaigne never found that "place" but also that he never abandoned the search for it that opened a path through himself, away from the world, into the *Essays* and back to the world from which only death could separate him by loosening his hand from the pages of his book. Not in death, but in the conversation sustained to the very end of the *Essays*, Montaigne remained loyal to La Boétie, returning the gift of two men caught in one another's talk, always putting off the closure of his own book.

The Preface to the *Essays* alerts us that they are to be used after Montaigne's death by his family, friends, and neighbors to remind them of him when alive. The *Essays*, have, therefore, to find Montaigne's "place" among his readers, just as La Boétie had begged his friend Montaigne to keep a place for him in his memory as dear as they had for each other when alive. The *Essays*, then, are not Montaigne's burial place any more than they are a monument to his place in literature, even to this day.

The essays are neither a history nor an autobiography, not a confession and not a discourse. They are an account of the most ordinary experiences of a man insofar as it is possible to record how one thinks and feels in the midst of everyone else without recourse to any undue perspective, ideology, or creed:

> Authors communicate with the people by some special extrinsic mark; I am the first to do so by my entire being, as Michel de Montaigne, not as a grammarian or a poet or a jurist. If the world complains that I speak too much of myself, I complain that it does not even think of itself. (III:2, 611)

How, then, can the *Essays* be true to La Boétie's example since they renounce his steadfast certainty and bend at every point under the weight of living into old age and the distance it puts between the rigidity of youth and its own slackness? How could such a book serve to keep Montaigne's memory in place when it renounces all attachments except detachment? Did La Boétie love only a ghost revealed in death to be less a thing than the wind it whistles? To be sure, at first Montaigne's body weighed heavily upon him separated from the joys of friendship and bound to the "obsequies" of remembering a lost goodness in which neither he nor La Boétie could be sure of a separate identity except as they savored moments apart that were flooded with each other's presence. Such repetition was all the more onerous inasmuch as Montaigne's capacity for intensity and focus had weakened with age, in one aspect, but was also undermined in another aspect by the experience brought with age, namely, that we can rarely sustain our intellectual and moral attachments.[15] Having lost his mirror image in La Boétie's youthful eyes, the old man stood staring at the blank page, summoning his weak nature to inscribe there the moving image of a mind whose body was drifting toward an ineludable death, catching at islands of goodness, sociability, limited well-being, and manageable pain. Never in the course of writing does Montaigne entertain a vision of himself outside of the season of his old age, yet without regret and never without compassion for youth—not once courting death. Seated in his library, where he kept La Boétie's books, given to him as part of his pledge to preserve their friendship, Montaigne devoted the last years of his life to the inscription of that Michel de Montaigne who had loved La Boétie and who was loved by him so unreservedly in a love that exceeded all reasoning, a love repeated only in the love with which Montaigne gave himself to the *Essays*, to find himself returned through them inasmuch as he could imagine readers similarly drawn into their company:

> In the friendship I speak of, our souls mingle and blend with each other so completely that they efface the seam that joined them, and cannot find it again. If you press me to tell why I loved him, I feel that this cannot be expressed, except by answering: Because it was I. (I:28, 139)

At this point, I think we must pause to confront Anthony Wilden's cleverly argued thesis to the effect that Montaigne's dependence upon La Boétie reduced him to a literary slave, half dead for fear of losing his place with La Boétie. For if we are to believe that Montaigne spent his last years enduring a living death, then we are surely wasting our time trying to develop an argument for Montaigne's remarkably sane approach to the hour of death. Wilden's thesis is argued from a combination of Marxian and psychoanalytic theory, together treating Montaigne as the victim of a double "loss"—the loss of his dead friend and the historical loss of his feudal sense of place, property, and self. As Wilden argues, this double loss nearly bled the life from Montaigne, resulting in the sickly modern self of the *Essays*, the first contribution to the dead culture of the bourgeoisie. Wilden treats La Boétie's friendship as the lost plenitude (*fort/da!*) of Montaigne's life, a loss that lured him into a perpetual search for a substantive self whose place had also been lost in the historical shift from feudalism to capitalism. On this view, Montaigne prefigures the dead souls of the new bourgeoisie, anxious and obsessed with property, clutching at a substantial self from which they are perpetually alienated. "Spoken by" the capitalist system, the Delphic injunction "know thyself" split Montaigne into a friend without a friend. Thus "La Boétie" is to be understood as a metaphor of social disintegration and the *Essays* as Montaigne's quest for authenticity in a broken world:

> With the death of La Boétie, Montaigne is reduced to a relationship, not with an ideal person, but with an ideal period. His quest is for the "ame de vieille marque" to whom the *Essays* are addressed—a situation out of which or through which there is no evolution whatsoever, since Montaigne never stopped writing the *Essays*: "Si mon ame pouvoit prendre pied, je ne m'essaierois pas, je me resoudrois" (II.2 782b). La Boétie becomes "La Boétie," a fiction in turn metaphorically replaced by all that it stands for in Montaigne's personal lexicon: stability, being, judgement, plenitude. At the same time the real absence of a referent for "La Boétie" creates in Montaigne's discourse all the things this absence stands for: flux, becoming, vanity, void. The goal of the *Essays* is both metonymically and metaphorically expressed in the words by which Montaigne characterizes La Boétie: "un'ame plein." And in all the passages where he describes the stability of his judgement, the stoicism of his attitude to life, the plenitude of his "regard dedans," it is "La Boétie" who speaks to Montaigne, rather than Montaigne to "La Boétie."[16]

The *Essays*, then, in their undue faithfulness to La Boétie, risked becoming a literary corpse, a "still life," so to speak, of La Boétie or else of Montaigne, himself mirrored in his dead friend. Or nearly so, as Wilden concedes, inasmuch as the quest for an embodied authenticity opened up in the *Essays* was to have a long residue in the struggle for bourgeois freedoms. Yet we may doubt that Wilden captures the subtle dialectic of self-possession and dispossession that Montaigne had experienced in friendship on the ancient model and which he set as a norm for evaluating freedom of speech in courtly and state affairs.[17] Nothing is sold more freely than the freedom of speech in bourgeois society; and no one speaks a dead language more than the politician and the businessman.[18] We must insist therefore that Montaigne did not try to preserve La Boétie's memory by enshrining his works within the *Essays*, any more than he portrayed himself in them as the lifeless relic of a friendship he did not know how to survive.[19] Rather, Montaigne's exploration of the last years of his life involved the persistent practice of an *anti-exemplary method* that far exceeded anything in the stoical formulations of La Boétie but which Montaigne nevertheless considered faithful to both sides of their friendship. Moreover, it was in this method of self-interpretation that Montaigne discovered the essayists' "balance" (*exagium*) of life and death—and with this exercise he filled his days to the end.

What Montaigne discovered is that life has no mirror that it can hold to itself even in the finest imagery of friendship and family life. The more he worked as an essayist, the more he realized that it is language itself that teaches us that it is only a broken mirror and that what we piece together are fragments whose lost unity challenges our judgment and interpretation. Only in this moment are we, so to speak, "ourselves," that is, when we "essay" things to the best of our ability and return our opinion, as we do in a conversation or in a game where we are challenged by a sufficiently equal partner. It is with the aim of finding such a *"suffisant lecteur"* that the *Essays* are so deftly composed. And it is because they so nearly realize their aim that the *Essays* find readers long after Montaigne's death, seeking, as we now do, to understand how it is that a loving mind can feed upon a dead past—yet not morbidly. What is broached here is an *ethical* conception of literature as a living community of the past, present, and future that transcends the life and death of its authority, much as the mind's witness to the body's limits is doubled in a friend's conception of the self. So far from offering us a dead legacy, as Wilden insists, the friendship between La Boétie and Montaigne opened a door to posterity through which the *Essays* were to be the vehicle of two moments of past understanding carried forward into the world's mind. Thus the gift of La Boétie's books entered Montaigne's library, from where there issued, in turn, the *Essays* to find that "place" in the world's library yearned for by La Boétie on his deathbed and won forever for them both by Montaigne.

If Montaigne feared old age and death, it was because he feared the pain of dying would loosen his tongue, separating his words from his thoughts and so excluding him from the company of men apart from whom he had no joy in living.[20] In other words, Montaigne only discovered himself in the flight of conversation; only in talk did he delight in himself. Thus he made it a rule to measure knowledge, his use of books, and all his associations—civic, conjugal, and filial—by the return of intimacy he experienced with himself as himself, neither too spiritual nor too physical but, rather, as a very natural metaphysician:

> I set forth notions that are human and my own, simply as human notions considered in themselves, not as determined and deemed by heavenly ordinance and permitting neither doubt nor dispute; matter of opinion, not matter of faith; what I reason out according to me, not what I believe according to God; as children set forth their essays to be instructed, not to instruct; in a lay manner, not clerical, but always very religious.
> (I:56, 234)

So, then, we may now set aside any argument that Montaigne labored half alive after the death of La Boétie or that the antique past lay upon him a deadly cultural burden from which he could not free himself and that consequently he could do nothing but stuff the *Essays* with dead thoughts into which he could breathe nothing of his own spirit.

After La Boétie's death, Montaigne installed himself in himself, pursued no other interest than himself, and thought of nothing else than how he thought or how he felt what he experienced. To do so, however, he needed to become a writer, not a copyist, not a historian, not a recluse, and not a confessor. To pursue the course of the *Essays*, he had in a certain sense to empty himself in order to be able to make the characteristic *clinamen*—swerve, deviation, or "schizz"—that so often turns the narrative of a given essay into a remarkable epiphany of "Montaigne on Montaigne." For example, in the essay "Of Presumption," in the course of taking stock of himself so as to set himself neither too highly nor too lowly, we catch Montaigne weighing himself, adding and taking away a given vice or virtue, as a painter might add or erase a given stroke of his brush, but always with a flash of insight into his bottom nature where he alone determines his worth:

> When things happen, I bear myself like a man; in conducting them like a child. The dread of falling gives me a greater fever than the fall. The game is not worth the candle. The miser is worse off for his passion than the poor man, and the jealous man than the cuckold. The lowest step is the firmest. There you need nothing but yourself. Constancy is founded there and leans only upon itself. (II:17, 489)

The *Essays* produce innumerable moments in which Montaigne discovers that happy constancy between his conduct and his nature that the ancients considered might only be revealed with any certainty in the hour of death. In this sense, the *Essays* are the daily practice of an art of dying (Figure 4.4). But, to say this requires that we resolutely set the *Essays* apart from any morbid philosophy as, in Montaigne's words, "not worth the candle." Although he may have begun by treating philosophy as an art of dying (along the lines portrayed above), Montaigne soon found he could not abide by such a view because it so plainly contradicts the *pleasure* (voluptuousness) that we seek in life and which requires that we give no thought to death. He who does so merely torments himself like a jealous husband living the event before it happens and lending it a reality it may never have—or that, as in death, we cannot know. In any case, Montaigne satisfies himself with the thought that he has already lived longer than many an excellent man whose virtues granted him no longer lease upon life. Thereafter, death will come

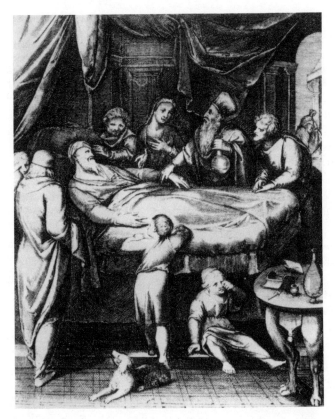

**Figure 4.4.** From Jules Brody, *Lectures de Montaigne*, p. 100.

in its own time and needs no avoidance: "It is uncertain where death awaits us: let us await it everywhere. Premeditation of death is premeditation of freedom" (I:20, 60). What Montaigne rejected in "premeditation" is that our own death cannot be an object for us in the same way that we can be aware of the death of others. To be a little more precise, Montaigne gradually distinguishes the death of *others* (*la mort*) from one's *own* death (*le mourir*).[21] What we may learn about death in the first case need have little bearing upon how we shall confront our own death and may even be an unnecessary impediment between us and our last act. Thus, while we may be conscious that "but for the grace of God" any present experience of ours might be otherwise than it is, if our fate were that of someone else, we cannot be elsewhere or other than who we are left to be:

> Let us never allow ourselves to be so carried away by pleasure that we do not sometimes remember in how many ways this happiness of ours is a prey to death, and how death's clutches threaten it. Thus did the Egyptians who, in the midst of their feasts and their greatest pleasure, had the skeleton of a dead man brought before them to serve as a reminder to the guests. (I:20, 60)

The bittersweet practice of the Egyptians, however, hardly amounts to a disciplinary practice of the kind that Montaigne sought to improvise. Above all, it lacks the introspective discipline that Montaigne had simultaneously to devise and to employ as the measure of his own attitude toward death so as to ensure that it would be consistent with his general outlook. Hence Montaigne wanted nothing to do with a debilitating morbidity, or with an otherworldly asceticism scrupulously in pursuit of the soul's release from its bodily prison—or from original sin. Yet he tells us that he has death constantly in his mouth and that if he were to make a book it would be to keep a register of famous deaths. The *Essays* proved not to be such a book. There he tells us he finds the loss of youth as great a loss as death even though he would be the last person to seek an unseasonable affectation of youth and its proper pleasures. But rather than one's age, it is the state of one's health that Montaigne considered the chief factor in his thoughts of death. Even though he tells how he had learned to live with his own most painful affliction—the kidney stone[22]—Montaigne conceded that ill health did tempt him to thoughts of death. Otherwise, he accepted without question the cycle of life and death. He recognized that we enjoy no good and no evil outside of it: "Life is neither good nor evil in itself: it is the scene of good and evil according as you give them room" (I:20, 65). We may no more rage at death than we do at birth. To do so is merely to abuse a life we already have and which we are hardly tempted to leave except as illness—and philosophizing may be such an illness—or old age weaken the pleasure we generally take in being alive and in the company of our fellow creatures. The measure of our lives is the use we make of life—not its length, any more than the measure of a man's humanity is his height. In this, our mother Nature treats us all the same.

It is rather our customs and rituals, says Montaigne, that create differences among us to the point where we believe it is possible to live and to die better than our fellow men and thus for us to fear that we may not have been born so well or that we may die less well than others do around us. But the fact is that in nothing else are we so equal as in death and, contrary to our practice and belief, there is nothing we can do to prepare for death, any more than for the hour of our birth. We may, of course, attend and comfort the death of others, as Montaigne stood by his dying friend. Each of us dies his own death, yet we need not die alone. This much we may hope of our friends and family, and we owe this practice to others as we may expect it upon our own behalf. Such is the *socio-logic of death* (*la mort*).

But with regard to the *hour of our dying* (*le mourir*), what Montaigne teaches us is that we are best known to ourselves through our habits. Habit is the core of friendship, family, and community.[23] Thus we might say that, more than anything else, Montaigne *is the physiognomist of habit*, if we understand by this something deeper than either the psychology of emotions and attitudes working in the service of modern predictability or the religious pedagogy of the schools. Our habits attach us to ourselves and to our friends. They cannot be masked and they make us thoroughly known to those who love us. By contrast, Montaigne considered that the ritual arts of dying practiced in his day merely continued the theater of masks.[24] Moreover, the rituals of dying are probably more frightening than dying itself. For these reasons, Montaigne hoped for a *sudden*—but not unprepared—death. He hoped, in fact, that when his time came he would go "quietly" and alone— and wherever he found himself while traveling, he was always ready to meet death. A sudden death might, of course, deprive him of the last rites. But Montaigne considered his daily habits, like those of a good gardener, sufficient preparation for death: "I want a man to act, and to prolong the functions of life as long as he can; I want death to find me planting my cabbages, but careless of death, and still more of my unfinished garden" (I:20, 62).

As it happened, Montaigne died three days after an attack of aphasia. He had communicated by jotting down his wish to take leave of his friends and neighbors who attended a bedside Mass during which he is said to have died at the moment of the elevation of the Host: HIC EST ENIM CORPUS MEUM. The postmortem accounts by his two friends Etienne Pasquier and Pierre de Brach are stylistically similar to Montaigne's own style in recording the death of La Boétie, and Hugo Friedrich[25] concludes that there is no reason to believe that Montaigne's death in any way belied the *Essays*.

Nonetheless, it may be thought that death properly concerns us as the most difficult exercise in philosophical reason. Here, surely, we might achieve more certainty in our belief and practice than is offered by the uncertain comforts of religion and ritual. But Montaigne did not think so. He certainly tried philosophy as a remedy for death. But, on balance, he considered that the philosopher's own practice is a kind of illness, rather like that of the jealous husband who pains himself with an (ir)reality he himself has created, suffering before his time an evil that he may never know beyond what he experiences in phantasy. The husband will only know how he will respond to his wife's infidelity once it occurs—it is then that he will play his true part in the comedy. The same is true of our philosophical selves, which are more likely to effect composure while discussing the arts of dying than in the final hour where the self is truly tested. Thus Montaigne judged that Solon's saying referred not to death as the harbinger of happiness but to the "hour of death" and to the question of our constancy when tested by it. It is then perhaps that a man may reveal the strength of the marriage he has made between soul and body—only then, in life's last embrace with death:

> In everything else there may be sham: the fine reasonings of philosophy may be a mere pose in us; or else our trials, by not testing us to the quick, give us a chance to keep our face always composed. But in the last scene, between death and ourselves, there is no more pretending; we must talk plain French, we must show what there is that is good and clean at the bottom of the pot:

At last true words surge up from deep
within our breast
The mask is snatched away, reality is left.
—LUCRETIUS (I:19, 55)

It is not that Death has the last word but, rather, that our last word is our death. Death is our witness—like a wife or a friend—the testimony of how well our soul was married to the body. Such, I believe, was the wedding of himself to himself that Montaigne solemnized in the daily habit of essaying the *Essays*. Apart from this, Montaigne practiced no other art of dying. Because of this, he is remembered. When Montaigne withdrew into his library tower, he did so to give birth to that study of himself which would reveal to the world every habit of his, for better or worse. Having kept this promise, he took leave of us in the Preface to the Reader:

> This book was written in good faith, reader. It warns you from the outset that in it I have set myself no goal but a domestic and private one. I have had no thought of serving either you or my own glory. I have dedicated it to the private convenience of my relatives and friends, so that when they have lost me (as soon they must), they may recover here some features of my habits and temperament, and by this means keep the knowledge they have had of me more complete and alive.

So Montaigne had long abandoned the earlier tradition of the arts of dying as a private act prepared for others who might vainly strive to see in the moment of death a moment of truth. Only the philosopher waits for the bride of truth. The essayist, more domesticated from the start, shuffles around himself, pushing and prodding at his thoughts and feelings, like a housewife choosing vegetables in the market. Each day the essayist repeats this work, as do ordinary folk whose living starts from no pride of knowledge or of wealth and who without privilege of place nevertheless build a home, raise a family, and never despair of themselves from day to day, despite their sorrows and their defeats.[26] Such people filled the countryside around Montaigne's chateau, and it was by their habits, rather than by those of the courtiers and the literati, that he measured himself. It was for their understanding that he wrote the

97

*Essays,* to reveal the man whose death they would soon receive— not in any grave but in the turning pages of the *Essays,* whose life remains open to this very day.

## NOTES

1. Gisèle Mathieu-Castellani, *Emblèmes de la mort: Le dialogue de l'image et du texte* (Paris: Libraire Nizet, 1988); Jean Roupet, *La Littérature de l'age baroque en France: Circe et Le Paon* (Paris: Libraire José Corti, 1954).
2. Michel Foucault, *The Birth of the Clinic: An Archaeology of Medical Perception* (New York: Vintage Books, 1975).
3. All quotations from the *Essays* are taken from *The Complete Essays of Montaigne,* Donald M. Frame, trans.(Stanford, CA: Stanford University Press, 1965).
4. John O'Neill, *Critical Conventions: Interpretation in the Literary Arts and Sciences* (Norman: University of Oklahoma Press, 1992).
5. John O'Neill, "Breaking the Signs: Roland Barthes and the Literary Body," in *The Structural Allegory: Reconstructive Encounters with the New French Thought,* John Fekete, ed. (Minneapolis: University of Minnesota Press, 1984), pp. 183-200.
6. Maurice Blanchot, *The Gaze of Orpheus, and Other Literary Essays* (Barrytown, NY: Station Hill Press, 1981).
7. John O'Neill, *The Communicative Body: Studies in Communicative Philosophy, Politics, and Sociology* (Evanston, IL: Northwestern University Press, 1989).
8. John O'Neill, "The Essay as a Moral Exercise: Montaigne," *Renaissance and Reformation 21,* No. 3 (1985): 210-218.
9. Anthony Wilden, "Pars divers moyens on arrive à pareille fin: A Reading of Montaigne," *Modern Language Notes 83* (1968): 577–597; and "Montaigne on the Paradoxes of Individualism: A Communication About Communication," in his *System and Structure: Essays in Communication and Exchange* (London: Tavistock, 1972), pp. 88– 109. I have discussed Wilden's thesis at length in my *Essaying Montaigne: A Study of the Renaissance Institution of Writing and Reading* (London: Routledge & Kegan Paul, 1982), Chap. 4, "The Paradox of Communication: Reading the "Essays' Otherwise."
10. Alberto Tenenti, *La Vie et la mort à travers l'art du XV^e^ Siècle* (Paris: Libraire Armand Colin, 1952); Sister Mary Catherine O'Connor, *The Art of Dying Well: The Development of the* Ars Moriendi (New

York: AMS Press, 1966); Nancy Lee Beatty, *The Craft of Dying: The Literary Tradition of the* Ars Moriendi *in England* (New Haven, CT: Yale University Press, 1970).

11. O'Neill, *Essaying Montaigne*, Chap. 7, "On Living and Dying as We Do."

12. Claude Blum, "De la 'Lettre sur la mort de La Boétie' aux 'Essais'; allongeail ou répétition?" *Revue d'histoire littéraire de la France* 88, No. 5 (September–October 1988): 809–943.

13. Montaigne, *Oeuvres Completes*, Textes établis par Albert Thibaudet et Maurice Rat (Paris: Bibliothèque de la Pléiade, 1962), p. 1353. See also Gabriel A. Perouse, "La Lettre sur la mort de La Boétie et la première conception des Essais," in *Montaigne et les Essais, 1580-1980*, Actes du Congrès de Bordeaux (Juin 1980), presentés par Pierre Michel (Paris and Geneva: Champion-Slatkine, 1983), pp. 65–76.

14. Jean Starobinski, *Montaigne in Motion*, Arthur Goldhammer, trans. (Chicago: University of Chicago Press, 1985), pp. 46–47. Emphases are in the original.

15. François Rigolot, "Montaigne's Purloined Letters," *Yale French Studies* No. 64 (1983), Montaigne: Essays in Reading, pp. 145–166. It has also been argued that Montaigne was "feminized" by the loss of his mirror in La Boétie; see Marc E. Blanchard, *Trois portraits de Montaigne: Essai sur la représentation à la Renaissance* (Paris: Libraire A.G. Nizet, 1990).

16. Wilden, "Par divers moyen . . . , loc. cit., p. 588.

17. John O'Neill, "Power and the Splitting (Spaltung) of Language," *New Literary History* 14 (1982/83): 695–710.

18. John O'Neill, *Plato's Cave: Desire, Power and the Specular Functions of the Media* (Norwood, NJ: Ablex, 1991).

19. Michel Butor, *Essais sur les Essais* (Paris: Gallimard, 1968). I have shown at some length how Butor's fantasy of the absent center of the *Essays* structures them by the means of a set of arbitrary images of the tower, the labyrinth, and the observatory. See O'Neill, *Essaying Montaigne*, pp. 168–182.

20. M. Dreano, "Montaigne et la préparation à la mort," *Bibliothèque d'Humanisme et Renaissance* 22 (1960): 151–171.

21. See the excellent study by Claude Blum, *La Représentation de la mort dans la littérature Française de la Renaissance* (Paris: Libraire Honoré Champion, 1989), Vol. 2. In Chap. 4, "La Représentation du mourir: Le 'moi' et sa mort," Blum says,

> Pour représenter le "mourir" Montaigne ne garde de la représentation de "l'heure de la mort" que la structure ex-

terne (conscience, subconscience, unconscience) et l'in-
vestit d'une figuration empruntée à la représentation chréti-
enne de la mort et de l'au-delà immédiat: les "derniers in-
stants," le trepas, "l'Etat intermédiare." Le mélange d'une
structure reprise de la tradition de "l'heure de la mort" et de
représentations qui fondent, depuis toujours, la vision chré-
tienne de la mort et de l'au-delà amène Montaigne à envis-
ager ce qui n'avait jamais été possible avant lui, le "passage"
et "l'état intermédiare" dans une perspective uniquement
terrestre. (p. 789)

See also Blum, op. cit., note 12, above.

22. John O'Neill, "Essaying Illness," in *The Humanity of the Ill: Phenome-
    nological Perspectives*, Victor Kestenbaum, ed. (Knoxville: University
    of Tennessee Press, 1982), pp. 125–141.
23. Pierre Bourdieu, "Structures and the Habitus," in his *Outline of a
    Theory of Practice* (Cambridge, UK: Cambridge University Press,
    1979), Chap 2.
24. Jules Brody, in his *Lectures de Montaigne* (Lexington, KY: French Fo-
    rum, 1982), Chap. 4. "Montaigne et la mort: Deux Études sur Que
    philosopher c'est apprendre à mourir," pp. 1, 20.
25. Hugo Friedrich, *Montaigne* (Paris: Gallimard, 1985), pp. 313–315.
26. O'Neill, "An Introduction to Communicative Sociology," in his *The
    Communicative Body*, pp. 181–233.

PART TWO

# POLITICAL BODIES, DISCURSIVELY

# Gray Matters: Brains, Identities, and Natural Rights

## Kathi L. Kern

Scientific theorizing about the human brain, its physiological structure and operation, has often amounted to much more. Like "the body" whose nature is socially constructed and historically conditioned, the brain has for generations served as a screen for the competing views of scientists and social commentators. Perhaps more than any other region of the body, the brain has been privileged as a key site for the locating and fixing of identity. As early as 1615, through the work of anatomist Helkiah Crooke, the brain ascended to the position of "the most noble part of the body."[1] Since then, the brain has been conceptualized variously as the locus of reason, the self, sexual difference, racial difference, and, most recently, sexual preference. This essay will explore two historical moments in which medical findings about the brain took on social and political dimensions. The first episode focuses on the work of Helen Gardener, a nineteenth-century reformer who attempted to disprove popular notions of women's mental inferiority. The second discussion profiles the work of contemporary brain specialist Simon LeVay and his theory of a "gay brain." In each case, new medical discoveries about the brain raised issues of profound social consequence.

## Nineteenth-Century Brain Debates

In the pages of the *Popular Science Monthly* of 1887, Helen Gardener took on New York neurologist and former U.S. Surgeon General Dr. William Hammond and his views on women's brains and mental capacity.[2] Hammond was only the most recent of medical authorities to report scientific evidence of women's cranial inferiority. Western scientists had begun in earnest to collect, measure, and study skulls and brains in the early nineteenth century. In 1873, Alexander Bain, also a leading physician of the day, had reported a difference in brain weights between European men and women. The average male brain outweighed the average female by a total of 5 grams. These findings, coupled with those of many other brain specialists, weighed in against the higher education of women.[3]

Rebuking the medical community, Gardener compared nineteenth-century doctors to medieval priests, arguing that physicians were only the most recent in a long line of woman's detractors. But the climate of debate was changing, according to Gardener, as "hell went out of fashion. . . . Conservatism, Ignorance, and Egotism, in dismay and terror, took counsel together and called in medical science, still in its infancy, to aid in staying the march of progress. . . . It was no longer her soul, but her body, that needed saving from herself."[4]

Or most recently, her brain. Hammond had asserted in print the measurable inferiority of women's brains. He testified to "numerous and striking" sex-based differences in the size and structure of male and female brains. "The male brain is larger," Hammond argued, "its vertical and transverse diameters are greater proportionately, the shape is quite different, the convolutions are more intricate, the sulci deeper, the secondary fissures more numerous, and the gray matter of the corresponding parts of the brain decidedly thicker." All of these differences revealed woman's lack of mental capacity, which rendered her incapable of "accuracy," "sustained or abstract thought," "unbiased judgment . . . judicial fairness," and "the accomplishment of any really first-class or original work in the fields of science, art, politics, invention or even literature."[5]

Furthermore, a lack of capacity mandated different educational needs for girls. In an article on "brain-forcing" (or cramming) in children, Hammond warned against the particular dangers in overeducating girls:

> The effort to cram mathematics, for instance, into the female mind almost always results in failure. . . . I have seen many cases of girls whose nervous systems have been woefully disturbed in the endeavor to master algebra, geometry, spherical trigonometry, and other mathematical branches of knowledge that could not by any possibility be of use to them. . . . Their minds revolt at the idea. Nevertheless, not only are the higher branches of mathematics kept in the curricula of many of our schools for girls, but even civil-engineering and other applied mathematical studies are pursued. I do not think that absurdity can go much further than this.[6]

Gardener's chief concern was that Hammond's ideas—"aided by the circulation and prestige of the leading journals of the country which publish them as authoritative"—would inevitably influence "school directors, voters and legislators." Consequently, Gardener set out to ascertain how far science had proceeded in demonstrating actual sex-based differences in the brain and "how far the usual theories advanced are gratuitous assumptions, founded upon legend and fed by mental habit and personal egotism."[7]

Gardener was herself a student of biology, but she decided that her best shot at Hammond would be to enlist the support of brain specialists. She claimed to have personally visited twenty physicians and to have submitted written questions to others. All paths of inquiry led to one man, Dr. E. C. Spitzka, who was reputed to be the leading brain specialist in the United States. None of her medical contacts, however, would introduce Gardener to him. Not to be thwarted, Gardener told audiences of women that "I took my life in my hands, put on my best gown—I had previously discovered that even brain anatomists are subject to the spell of good clothes—and went." Despite Gardener's fears, Spitzka responded in a friendly manner and Gardener made many subsequent pilgrimages to see him. The connection with Spitzka proved very useful to Gardener because, although he did not share her belief in woman's equality, Spitzka was willing to admit "when knowledge stopped and guessing began" on the issue of the human brain.[8]

Gardener waged two main challenges to Hammond's assertions. The first, and the one directly aided by her connection with Spitzka, was to demonstrate that Hammond's findings were contradicted by other scientists or simply insupportable by the existing information. On the issue of brain size, Hammond had conceded that the relative size and weight of the brain in the sexes was about the same, or slightly in women's favor. This concession proved to be irrelevant, however, because according to the doctor, absolute—not relative—size determined intellectual power. Gardener enjoyed pointing out that within this model, "an elephant would out think any of us, and the whale, whose intellectual achievements have never been looked upon as absolutely incendiary (if we except Jonah's friend), would rank the greatest man on record, and have brain enough left to furnish material for a fair-sized female seminary."[9] Similarly, in challenging Hammond's claim that "the specific gravity of both the white and gray matter of the brain is greater in man than in woman," Gardener responded that many scientists had demonstrated that the specific gravity of woman's brain *actually increased* with old age and insanity.[10]

On questions of brain structure, Gardener countered with the increasingly popular "environmental" argument. Hammond had asserted that '"the female brain . . . is not only smaller than that of man, but it is different in structure, and this fact involves much more as regards the character of the mental faculties than does the element of size.'" The frontal lobes, believed to contain the highest intellectual faculties, were reputed to be more highly developed in men than in women, in both sheer size and "convolutions" of gray matter. Consequently, Hammond argued, "'the part of the brain which is especially concerned in the evolution of mind is the gray matter, and this is increased or diminished in accordance with the number and complexity of the convolutions. The frontal lobes contain a greater amount of gray cortical matter than any other part of the brain, and they are, as we have seen, larger in man than in woman.'"[11] Rather than disputing these alleged sex-based differences, Gardener pursued a different strategy.

Gardener proposed to test the brains of infants to determine if the supposed differences between adult male and female brains were "fundamental and pre-natal, or . . . the result of outside artificial influences." If one tested fifty male and fifty female brains of infants of the same age and weight, and held constant for Gardener's other concerns—health and "parentage"— would the brains be distinguishable by any of Hammond's criteria, "weight, shape, size, quality or convolutions?" While Hammond rebuffed Gardener's challenge, Spitzka and others insisted that if such differences existed in the brains of infants, it was not "known to those who make a specialty of brain study."[12]

In fact, Gardener pointed out, the available scientific knowledge on this subject revealed significant differences among members of the same sex. Take the brains of two renowned poets, for example: Byron reputedly weighed in at 1807 grams, whereas a light-headed Dante totaled only 1320 grams, a difference of 487. Or, consider two historically prominent statesmen: Oliver Cromwell, who allegedly could claim the largest healthy brain on record at 2210 grams, put a poor Léon-Michel Gambetta to shame at just 1241 grams, a difference of 969 grams. "Surely," Gardener argued, "it would not be held because of this, that Gambetta and Dante should have been denied the educational and other advantages which were the natural right of Byron and Cromwell. Yet it is upon this very ground, by this very system of reasoning, that it is proposed to deny women equal advantages and opportunities, although the difference in brain weight between man and woman is claimed to be only 100 grams."[13]

Natural differences between the sexes could only be proven by studying the brains of infants, Gardener concluded, and not the disadvantaged brains of adult women. "After a woman's waist and brain are put into tight laces and shaped to fit the fashion, it is rather a poor time to judge of her natural figure, either physical or mental." Gardener's experts concurred. While no such test had been conducted, Spitzka and others maintained that it would be impossible to distinguish between the brains of infants of different sexes. While Hammond claimed in the pages of the *Popular Science Monthly* that his assertions were well known to the medical profession, Gardener insisted that "the truth is that the positive knowledge on the subject is not sufficient at this moment to form even an intelligent guess upon," despite "all the talk, the pathetic warnings, and the absolute statements to the contrary."[14]

In her analysis to this point, Gardener essentially used the methods of scientific inquiry to debunk what she termed Hammond's "pseudo-science." Gathering expert testimony, she undermined Hammond's central assertion that women's mental capacity could necessarily be inferred from differentials in size, specific gravity, or structure of the brain. In response to Hammond's claims regarding measurable differences in the brains of women and men, Gardener challenged the reliability and authenticity of those supposed differences. And she suggested that where differences did exist, they could be explained more persuasively by a contrast in environment and opportunity, rather than a contrast in innate structure. In sum, Gardener exposed the "hereditary bias" of male-dominated medical science and its efforts to reinforce a vision of women's inferiority.

But she did not stop there. Gardener offered a second and rather peculiar challenge to Hammond and to women generally. Her careful analysis of Hammond's research led Gardener to a crucial discovery:

> The brain of no remarkable woman has ever been examined! Woman is ticketed to fit the hospital subjects and tramps, the unfortunates whose brains fall into the hands of the profession, as it were, by mere accident; while man is represented by the brains of the Cromwells, Cuviers, Byrons and Spurzheims. By this method the average of men's brains is carried to its highest level in the matter of weight and texture; while that of women is kept at its lowest, and even then there is only claimed 100 grammes difference! It is with such statistics as these, it is with such dissimilar material, that they and we are judged.[15]

This discovery formed the cornerstone of Gardener's mission among womens' rights advocates. Women's claims to equality were marred not only by the distortions of a false science but by the lack of representative specimens for potential investigation. And here was where women could act. Women must assume an active role in offsetting the prejudices of science by taking "a hand in the future investigations and statements themselves." In her speeches and published essays, even in the *Popular Science Monthly* go-around with Hammond, Gardener virtually obsessed about the need to measure the brains of "eminent" women:

> I sincerely hope that the brains of some of our able women may be preserved and examined by honest brain students, so that we may hereafter have our Cuviers and Websters and Cromwells. And I think I know where some of them can be found without a search-warrant—when Miss Anthony, Mrs. Stanton, and some others I have the honor to know, are done with theirs.[16]

Of all the available brains of "eminent" women, that of suffragist Elizabeth Cady Stanton was always Gardener's leading candidate to "make as fair a show as those of these gentlemen [Baron Georges Cuvier, Daniel Webster, Lord Byron]."[17] Eminent large-brained women like Stanton, Gardener asserted, were needed to counter the misrepresentation of womanhood by the brains of lower class women whom Gardener variously categorized as tramps, prostitutes, hospital subjects, imbeciles, and unfortunates. But was it privilege and environment that had so engorged Stanton's brain, or nature? Gardener failed to say.

Gardener's denunciation, then, centered on her observation that Hammond had not so much mismeasured heads as he had selected the wrong heads to measure. She ultimately accepted Hammond's assertions about a sex-based discrepancy in brain weights but implied that the connection between brain size and intellectual capacity could not be inferred from the *available* specimens. While Gardener began by challenging "male" science, she was ultimately co-opted by its central assumption that an individual's capacity could be deduced from nature, specifically brain size. The attention to difference, however, should be shifted away from a male–female dichotomy to uncover the real and measurable difference among members of the same sex. We begin to see the class-specific tone of Gardener's challenge. Clearly, she disputed Hammond not on behalf of gender equality per se but, rather, to entitle one particular racial and social group of women to the privileges of their male peers.

In drawing distinctions between themselves and their "cerebral inferiors," Gardener and her followers did not classify the "tramps, prostitutes and other unfortunates" by racial or ethnic heritage. That is not to imply that race as a category was absent from her conclusions. While she seldom mentioned race explicitly, when she did it was to make a rather extreme point. To invalidate the relationship between absolute brain size and intelligence, for example, Gardener parenthetically mentioned that the largest brain on record belonged to a "Negro criminal idiot."[18]

In analyzing the Gardener–Hammond controversy, we get a clearer view of the class- and race-based notions of gender underlying the political rhetoric of the woman's movement. This attack on women's equality prompted feminists to redraw the boundaries of gender to exclude women who were perceived to be confusing the scientific results—women paupers, "imbeciles," and criminals. Gardener and her followers suggested, in essence, that as educated white women they were more like men than like the subjects of the scientific research, poor and institutionalized women.

It is perhaps not surprising, given the primacy of polarized sexual difference in Victorian ideology, that women suffragists attempting to erode political boundaries would locate their struggle on the body itself. In defending "woman" against this false science, however, it becomes clear that the woman to be salvaged is white, educated, middle class—the very woman whom suffragists began to argue should have the right to vote on the basis of educational qualifications. Indeed, the politics of the brain-size debate were reflected in the policies and future direction of the suffrage movement into the 1890s and beyond. Identifying themselves as "native born Americans," suffrage leaders at the turn of the century increasingly resisted throwing in their lot with "women" as a group. In both scientific and political debates, they argued for narrowing the margins of womanhood to exclude women whose lack of privilege was perceived to be retarding the emancipation of white, middle class, "eminent" women.

Adopting new methods of classifying and stratifying social groups, both biological determinists and feminists of the twentieth century abandoned the physiology of the brain as their primary strategy. By 1905 research indicated that the size and structure of the brain were not reliable indicators of intelligence. Historian

Cynthia Russett has argued that it was the work of a British woman anatomist in particular that began to erode earlier theories of gender difference based on brain size. Publishing in 1902, Alice Lee demonstrated that in fact the cranial capacities of her sample of women college students put to shame that of some of the male anatomists. Similarly, future research demonstrated that claims of sexual and racial difference— previously thought to be evident in the weight, size, and complexity of the frontal lobe of the brain— were refuted by physical evidence.[19] In the wake of what Russett termed the "Great Brain Theory," scientists turned their attention to intelligence testing as a means of ranking social groups. For feminists, including Helen Gardener, classist assumptions about women's brain size would give way to a "feminist eugenics," riddled with its own class-based fears of "race suicide."[20] Yet, despite new scientific strategies to justify social stratification, echoes of the earlier brain debates persisted as well.

As promised, Gardener ultimately willed her brain to Cornell Medical School.[21] She would have been pleased to learn that her brain did not sit idly by soaking up formaldehyde, but on the contrary, as the *New York Times* reported, "The Study of Helen Gardener's Brain Revives the Controversy Over Mental Equality of the Sexes." Gardener had passed away in 1925, and in 1927 the study of her brain by a Dr. James W. Papez was published in *The American Journal of Physical Anthropology* and extensively reported in the *Times* as well.[22] Dr. Papez concluded :

> The brain of Helen H. Gardener has been compared in each of its details with the brains of twenty other men and women. Among them were the brains of a number of eminent men and several cultured women. In the structure of her own brain Mrs. Gardener has presented abundant evidence that the brain of a woman need not be inferior to that of a man of equal rank. In its entire organization it reveals a wealth of cortical substance, or gray matter, that is only equaled, but not exceeded by the best brains in the Cornell collection, which includes those of doctors, professors, lawyers and naturalists.
>
> Her peculiarities appear to be well reflected in the wealth of development of certain areas of the brain which are regarded as being devoted to the scholarly pursuits. The fact that she was

a keen student of human affairs, a writer and publicist, must be kept in mind.

... There is nothing to indicate that hers was a one-sided or single track mind, or that she possessed any mental peculiarities out of the ordinary.[23]

The *Times* concluded their coverage of Gardener's brain by remembering her "Sex in Brain" writings of 1888 in which she took on Hammond and the conservative branch of the medical community, "On that speech she rested her case. Her own brain has now added its testimony."[24]

## TWENTIETH-CENTURY BRAIN DEBATES

Gardener would have considered the published report on her brain a triumph for the cause of "eminent" women of her day. But how much has the nineteenth-century rhetoric of the sexualized brain seeped into our contemporary notions of gender difference? According to the popular press, cutting-edge neuroscience of the 1990s has focused on delineating sex-based differences in the brain. Many of the conclusions sound hauntingly familiar: differences in male and female brains are hormonally based; language formation takes different paths in the brains of men and women; these different patterns of thinking result in men's superiority in computational and spatial skills and women's dexterity in verbal skills.[25]

In fact, actual measurable differences in the brains of men and women have proven speculative and elusive. Sexual dimorphism, the commonly used medical term for sexual difference, had been documented in the preoptic region in the brains of laboratory rats in the early 1970s. In 1991, UCLA researchers Roger Gorski and Laura Allen, building upon earlier studies on rats, documented a sex-based difference in the size of the corpus callosum in human cadavers. The corpus callosum, the section of the brain that bridges and communicates between its left and right hemispheres, was found to be 23 percent larger in women than in men.[26] This finding added weight to the already considerable evidence suggesting different patterns of brain usage by women and men. Or, as one popular magazine translated the importance of the finding for its readers, "in male brains, the right and left side barely know what the other is doing, while in women there's practically nonstop chitchat."[27]

Indeed, the gendered brain, recently revived and tenuously documented, is nevertheless so universally accepted that we find reference to it saturating contemporary popular culture. *Reader's Digest*, for example, offered readers the chance to discover "What Sex Is Your Brain?" in a multiple-choice test abstracted from the British publication *Brain Sex: The Real Difference Between Men and Women*. Cartoonist Cathy Guisewite introduced greeting card consumers to the "male brain" in which the cranial lobes are divided into two large competing regions, sports and sex, with a smaller region remaining for food.[28]

The latest incarnation of the sexualized brain is the gay brain. But exactly how new is it? Even Simon LeVay, the researcher whose findings have garnered the most discussion, admits that gay and straight brains are differentiated "in curiously analogous fashion" to female and male brains. Specifically, LeVay argues, a section of the hypothalamus isolated in the brains of gay men, straight men, and women (sexual preference unknown) show that a particular nucleus (INAH3) is significantly smaller in the gay male brains than in the straight male brains. This nucleus, LeVay contends, is the presumed correlate of sexual orientation.[29]

A newer study by Allen and Gorski discovered yet another structural difference in the brains of straight and gay men. The anterior commissure—a collection of nerve cells responsible, like the corpus callosum, for connecting the two hemispheres of the brain—was larger in the brains of gay men than in the brains of straight men. LeVay applauds this study because it strengthens his conviction that the brains of gays and straights are in fact structurally different. And perhaps even more at issue, the differential in size of the anterior commissure is proof of a higher caliber, as the anterior commissure is not involved in sexual activity. Its enhanced size in the brains of gay men, then, cannot result from a lifetime of homosexual activity, a criticism frequently charged against LeVay's findings on the nuclei of the hypothalamus.[30]

The medical community has greeted LeVay's documentation of a gay brain with ambivalence. While most medical researchers agree with LeVay's basic assumption that "sexual orientation in humans is amenable to study at the biological level," many commentators raise troubling questions about the science behind the findings.[31] William Byne, a research associate at the Albert Einstein College of Medicine of Yeshiva University, summarized concerns raised by researchers since the first publication of LeVay's study.[32] First and foremost, LeVay's findings have not been replicated. More importantly, Byne echoes the concern of other researchers that LeVay's brains all came from AIDS patients. "His inclusion of a few brains from heterosexual men with AIDS did not adequately address the fact that the time of death virtually all men with AIDS have decreased testosterone levels as the result of the disease itself or the side effects of particular treatments," Byne charges. The measurable difference in the size of the nucleus in question (INAH3) attributed to sexual orientation might actually be the result of hormonal changes associated with AIDS, a finding that has been documented by other researchers. Finally, LeVay's assumption that the hypothalamus nucleus (INAH3) is the key correlate of sexual orientation in the brain is also under fire. Byne points out that LeVay's guiding assumption about the importance of the INAH3 relies too heavily on the analogous research performed on laboratory animals and, at best, incorporates that research imprecisely. At the same time, other scholars have focused their attention on regions of the brain other than the specific nucleus of the hypothalamus so critical to LeVay's findings. Allen and Gorski's conclusions on the size differential of the anterior commissure as they relate to sexual preference might add force to Byne's critique, except that he finds similar problems with their data.[33] Allen and Gorski's findings have been refuted by other scientists. But even if the size differentials are granted, how can they best be explained? Some critics caution that the differences in the size of the nuclei is evidence of the effect of homosexuality, not the cause.[34]

Finally, commentators have taken LeVay to task for his categorical definitions of sexual preference. In his research design LeVay considered a male patient to be "homosexual" if he engaged in any same-sex sexual activity "irrespective of the number of sexual encounters with women."[35] Self-reporting bisexuals, in other words, became "homosexual" for the purposes of the study. The faulty design of the study, "with subjects drawn from a small, highly selected, nonrepresentative sample," caused Joseph Carrier and George Gellert of the Orange County Health Care Agency (in California) to protest its publication. Should a study as flawed as LeVay's "receive the kind of international attention and credibility that publication in a journal with the stature of *Science* lends?" they asked.[36]

Like Helen Gardener, whose career as a public intellectual escalated with her "Sex in Brain" work, Simon LeVay became a media celebrity seemingly overnight and, by his own admission, on the basis of one three-page article.[37] Both his popularity—and, for some, his notoriety—stem from different sides of the same coin: the use of his findings to "naturalize" homosexuality. As *Newsweek* alerted readers: "Theoretically, it could gain them the civil-rights protections accorded any 'natural' minority, in which the legal linchpin is the question of an 'immutable' characteristic."[38] Curiously, other researchers publishing similar kinds of data did not provoke the same high-pitched reaction. To what extent were readers responding to the messenger as well as the message?

Part and parcel of the popularization of LeVay's research is the accompanying narrative of his personal struggle with sexuality, a veritable coming-of-age story. Plot twists include his knowledge at an early age of his homosexuality; his aversion to "rough sports"; his strained relationship with his father; his ultimate rejection of Freudian theories of homosexuality ("as I got to know large numbers of gay men and lesbian women, it became harder and harder to see them, or myself, as the products of defective parenting; we just seemed too normal"); his earlier work on environmental influences on development; the death of his lover from AIDS; an ensuing depression; and finally, his decision to search for the biological basis of homosexuality. "I felt if I didn't find anything," LeVay told *Newsweek*, "I would give up a scientific career altogether."[39] Instead, LeVay made a career move to Hollywood, where he runs the West Hollywood Institute for Gay and Lesbian Education and appears regularly on talk shows as an expert witness for the biological basis of homosexuality.[40]

## Conclusion

In comparing nineteenth- and twentieth-century debates about the brain, one is struck, at first glance, by how much has changed. Contemporary researchers' focus on the hypothalamus would seem alien to their nineteenth-century predecessors who saw variations in cranial size as the chief indicator of difference. Or more dramatically, the new technologies—functional magnetic resonance imaging and position emission tomography—that permit live brains to be scanned and analyzed *in use* have revolutionized brain studies previously dependent upon brain specimens rescued from corpses. But even the context by which those specimens become available marks an important difference in these two inquiries. The harsh realities of the AIDS epidemic have replaced the anonymous brain that Gardener railed against with brains richer in medical and social history.

Then, too, the dominating paradigms in brain research have shifted in telling ways. The guiding analogy of nineteenth-century brain research—male is to female as upper class is to lower class or as white is to black, which posed gender as a surrogate for social class or race—has given way to a new paradigm: male is to female as heterosexual is to homosexual.[41] While the brains of women patients rarely figure prominently in the research, gender nevertheless pulls more than its own conceptual weight. In the latest research, the gay brain is rhetorically dependent upon the female brain for its analytical status vis-à-vis the straight, male brain.[42] These hierarchies of power and their juxtaposition inform the very questions researchers pose about the brains they study. In an earlier historical and political context, Gardener disrupted the dominant analogy of power—male–female—by studying the differences in the brains of members of the same sex. Her argument persuaded white, upper-class women of the existence and importance of class- and race-based differences in the bodies of women, a difference they could further document with the donation of their own brains.

A brain is rarely simply a brain. Rather, it always points beyond itself to an essentialized identity whose power and capacity is understood in relation to that of other similarly situated brains.

Such reasoning allows for the possibility of the existence of a "gay brain," where the privileged analogy is heterosexual–homosexual but where other hierarchies are both masked and presumed. (The "gay brain" is assumed to be a male brain and a white brain.)

The development and popularization of the gay brain theory begs feminist analysis. The differences between the brains of straight and gay men are understood as significant because those differences were first located (by Laura Allen) in the brains of men and women. The size of the hypothalamus nuclei INAH3 was initially polarized along a male–female axis when LeVay first began to question if the same differences could be found between straight and gay men. When LeVay reported success in finding those same differentials in size—incidentally, a difference so slight, indeed invisible to the human eye, that its variation among men would only be considered significant because it had been established as a sex-based difference— all attention shifted to the new axis, straight–gay. For all practical purposes, the brains of women fell out of the equation. Because gay women have been underrepresented among AIDS victims, researchers have been unable to test the gay brain theory on the brains of women (although LeVay has theorized that, according to his model, gay women should have an INAH3 size comparable to that of straight men). We are left with significant questions. Only a small number of women's brains have been studied, all AIDS victims and all presumed heterosexual, and yet from this sample the theory of the gay brain draws its analytical power. Not unlike the nineteenth-century debates, the contemporary brain discussions reify "woman's brain" to privilege a different analogy: the relationship of straight to gay men. Ultimately, the gay brain theory contributes little or nothing to our understanding of the bodies of women, gay and straight. Certainly there is little room within the gay brain conceptual schema for lesbians whose unstudied brains seem to hold the key to many of the questions raised by LeVay's study. And for feminists generally, who have devoted careers to disproving the adage "biology is destiny," the gay brain theory leaves much to be desired as a political strategy.

Despite these obvious changes in the focus, strategies, and context of brain research, similarities persist. In addition to creating a surplus of available brains, the AIDS epidemic has underscored the urgency of the research mission to establish a biological basis for homosexuality. Not unlike Helen Gardener, who searched the brain itself for evidence of women's equality at a time when women were denied entrance into male institutions, Simon LeVay and others work to establish a gay brain in a historical moment when homophobia has reached new heights. Countering the popular belief that gays choose their sexual preference and willingly risk disease, LeVay and colleague Dean Hamer hope to "dispel some of the myths about homosexuality that in the past have clouded the image of lesbians and gay men."[43] The biology versus choice explanations for homosexuality are considered by many scientists to be a "false dichotomy." In the current cultural climate, however, "choice" falls well short of ensuring social acceptance or civil rights protection. As one researcher suggests: "Could Christians . . . continue to define homosexual behaviour as sinful if it were known to stem from some hardwired neural structure?"[44] Nothing is more legitimizing, apparently, than biological evidence. "Perhaps . . . we should also be asking ourselves why we as a society are so emotionally invested in this research," William Byne has suggested. "Perhaps the answers to the most salient questions in this debate lie not within the biology of human brains but rather in the cultures those brains have created."[45]

For Helen Gardener, the assumptions of women's mental inferiority were so insurmountable that no counterargument based on women's cultural experience could deflate them. They were medical claims that called for medical rebuttal. Garderner negotiated the arguments for bodily difference first by focusing on the brains of infants, indistinguishible by sex. However, her ultimate faith in the body as the key site of difference led her back to mining the brain as a natural repository for class and race distinctions. Gardener's campaign and related ones that attempted to demonstrate the cranial inferiority of people of color strike us today as obvious examples of scientific racism, bad science polluted with imperialist motives. That nineteenth-century science failed in the strugggle to locate social, racial, and sexual difference in the *size* of the brain may shed light upon our contemporary fixation on the microscopic differences found in the brains of men and women, heterosexuals and homosexuals. Just as the brain threatens to transcend bodily difference, the proof of difference moves to a microscopic level. From Gardener's quest over a hundred years ago, however, we now understand some of the risks involved in basing a claim to political entitlement on the slippery ground of "biological equality." Women are still fighting that battle as newer studies recycle familiar results regarding women's allegedly inferior computational and spatial skills. Moreover, in laying claim to their own biological equality with men, white women like Gardener self-consciously separated themselves from the biological destinies of other women. Does LeVay risk comparable problems with the development of the gay brain? LeVay acknowledges that "increasing knowledge of biology may eventually bring with it the power to infringe on the natural rights of individuals and to impoverish the world of its human diversity."[46] Rushing into the speculative void aroused by such vague disclaimers, the popular press spelled out the obvious fear: the abortion of "gay fetuses."[47] In the wake of brain studies of the nineteenth century that "proved" the biological superiority of men over women, whites over blacks, contemporary gays may take little comfort in the new evidence of their "natural" status. Choice may not prove a viable political alternative, but resting the case for civil rights on the natural status of the body brings with it a long and troubled history.

# NOTES

The author whishes to thank the following for comments on portions of this work: Karla Goldman, JoEllen Kaiser, Joanne Meyerowitz, Ellen Rosenman, Leila Rupp, Ted Schatzki, Monica Uvardy, and Nan Woodruff.

1. Londa Schiebinger, *The Mind Has No Sex?: Women in the Origins of Modern Science* (Cambridge, MA: Harvard University Press, 1989), p. 170.
2. See *Popular Science Monthly* 31 (June 1887): 266–268; 31 (August 1887): 554–558; 31 (September 1887): 698–701; 31 (October 1887): 846.
3. Cynthia Eagle Russett, *Sexual Science: The Victorian Construction of Womanhood* (Cambridge, MA: Harvard University Press, 1989), pp. 35–39.

4. As quoted in Helen Hamilton Gardener, "Sex in Brain," in her *Facts and Fictions of Life* (Chicago: Kerr, 1893), p. 96.
5. As quoted in ibid., pp. 110, 121.
6. William Hammond, "Brain-Forcing in Childhood," *Popular Science Monthly 30* (June 1887): 732.
7. Gardener, "Sex in Brain," p. 100.
8. Ibid., pp. 104, 100.
9. Ibid., p. 111.
10. Ibid., p. 119.
11. As quoted in ibid., p. 112.
12. Ibid., p. 113.
13. Ibid., pp. 116–117.
14. Ibid., pp. 120–121.
15. Ibid., pp. 122–123.
16. Ibid., p. 124.
17. Gardener to Editor, *Popular Science Monthly 31* (September 1887): 699.
18. Gardener, "Sex in Brain," p. 117.
19. Russett, *Sexual Science*, pp. 164–165. See also, Stephen Jay Gould, *The Mismeasure of Man* (New York: Norton, 1981), pp. 73–108.
20. For a discussion of "feminist eugenics," see Linda Gordon, *Woman's Body, Woman's Right: A Social History of Birth Control in America* (New York: Viking Penguin, 1974, 1990), 130.
21. Last Will and Testament of Helen H. Gardener, p. 15. Helen Hamilton Gardener Papers, Arthur and Elizabeth Schlesinger Library on the History of Women, Radcliffe College, Cambridge, MA.
22. "The Human Brain Still Puzzles Scientists," *New York Times* (October 9, 1927): 3; James W. Papez, "The Brain of Helen H. Gardener," *American Journal of Physical Anthropology* (October–December, 1927).
23. "The Human Brain Still Puzzles Scientists," loc. cit.
24. Ibid.
25. Kathryn Phillips, "Why Can't a Man Be More Like a Woman . . . and Vice Versa?," *Omni* (October 1990): 42–48.
26. Roger Gorski, "Interview," *Omni* (October 1990): 71–76.
27. Sharon Begley, "Gray Matters," *Newsweek* (March 27, 1995): 51.
28. Anne Moir and David Jessel, "What Sex Is Your Brain?," *Reader's Digest* (October 1991): 115–117.
29. Simon LeVay, "A Difference in Hypothalamic Structure Between Heterosexual and Homosexual Men," *Science* (August 30, 1991): 1034–1037.
30. Laura S. Allen and Roger A. Gorski, "Sexual Orientation and the

Size of the Anterior Commissure in the Human Brain," *Proceedings of the National Academy of Science, U.S.A.* 89 (1992): 7199–7202. See also Simon LeVay, *The Sexual Brain* (Cambridge, MA: MIT Press 1994), p. 124.

31. LeVay, "A Difference in Hypothalamic Structure Between Heterosexual and Homosexual Men," p. 1036.

32. William Byne, "The Biological Evidence Challenged," *Scientific American* 270, No. 5 (May 1994): 53.

33. Ibid.

34. John Maddox, "Is Homosexuality Hard-wired?," *Nature* 353 (September 5, 1991): 13.

35. Joseph M. Carrier and George Gellert to Editor, "Letters," *Science* 254, No. 5032 (November 1, 1991): 630.

36. Ibid.

37. See, for example, "American News," *Women's Penny Paper* (London) (November 17, 1888): 2; "Sex in Brain" speech reprinted in *Report of the International Council of Women* (Washington DC: 1888); also in Gardener, *Facts and Fictions of Life*, p. 96; see also LeVay, *The Sexual Brain*, p. xii.

38. David Gelman et al., "Born or Bred?," *Newsweek* (February 24, 1992): 48.

39. LeVay, *The Sexual Brain*, p. xiii; Gelman et al., "Born or Bred?," p. 49.

40. Gelman et al., loc. cit.

41. Stephen Jay Gould, "Morton's Ranking of Races by Cranial Capacity: Unconscious Manipulation of Data May Be a Scientific Norm," *Science* 200 ( May 5, 1978): 503–506.

42. "Men Who Want to Be Women Might Have Brain Structure That's Already Female," *Lexington Herald Leader* (November 2, 1995): A7. My thanks to Linda Minch for this citation.

43. Simon LeVay and Dean H. Hamer, "Evidence for a Biological Influence in Male Homosexuality," *Scientific American* 270, No. 5 (May 1994): 44–49.

44. Maddox, "Is Homosexuality Hard-wired?," p. 13.

45. Byne, "The Biological Evidence Challenged," p. 55.

46. LeVay and Hamer, "Evidence for a Biological Influence in Male Homosexuality," p. 49.

47. Gelman, "Born or Bred?," p. 48.

# Names, Bodies, and the Anxiety of Erasure

## Thomas W. Laqueur

This chapter is about the relationship between names, bodies, and memory—both personal and political. Specifically, I want to explore what I think is a distinctly twentieth-century constellation of sensibilities and practices: acts of devotion and infusion of meaning through the display of names on surfaces and spaces of diverse sorts, through their conspicuous attachment to bodies, or through bodies whose meaning arises from their being forever, and impenetrably, nameless.

Let me be more specific still. When the British Expeditionary Force went off to Belgium in August 1914 there were no plans to deal with the dead in any way different from how they had been dealt with in previous wars: "shoveled into the ground and so forgotten," as Tennyson put it. But sometime during the late fall things changed. "It became our job," writes a member of a new British Red Cross unit in his war diary, "to search for graves, identify soldiers, mark them with a cross, register their position."[1] But it speaks of a new sensibility that Catherine Stevens, sister of the poet Wallace Stevens, would record in her journal that upon seeing still another cross during her almost phantasmagoric ride over Flanders' field she "just had to go and see if I could read the name."[2] The journal was returned with her dead body from the western front.

POLITICAL BODIES, DISCURSIVELY

By 1930, a total of 557,520 soldiers of the British Empire (454,574 from the United Kingdom) had been buried, or reburied, in identified graves. Another 180,861 bodies were put each in a separate unidentified grave. The names of these men and of a further 336,912 whose bodies had simply disappeared, blown into the air or ground into the mud, were inscribed in stone on a monument, near the place where they were thought to have died. These are the imposing major monuments of the western front, bearers of the names that stand in for the dead.

Ypres: Despite cramming, 1200 panels up all of the major columns, along stairs, and on the walls of terraces that abut the ramparts of Sir Arthur Blomfield's arch/tunnel would hold only 54,896. (This was quite literally the first monument in history to display names on anything approaching this scale, and Blomfield asked for, and got, from a notoriously parsimonious patron an extra £500 to build a mockup of one panel just to see whether the calculations about letter size, spacing, "leading," etc. would give the required density. Miscalculations of one-eighth inch, he pointed out, would result in over 2000 too many or too few names.)[3] The names that remained from the Ypres Salient, men who died after the night of August 15–16, 1917, the night of the Battle of Langemark in the Passchendaele, are inscribed on the seemingly endless walls of Tyne Cot. Producing the lists themselves, and more sensitively, deciding whose name went where, was another novel and enormously difficult task. "Was there," the bureaucrat in charge asked his superior, "any reasonable interpretation of the term that would give us as low a figure as 50,000 'missing' [for Menin Gate] and if so what interpretation?"[4] In any case, the leftovers from Ypres, 34,888 names, surround 11,908 individual gravestones at Tyne Cot.

And the disembodied names continue down the front. Those of 11,447 men—the dead of battles from Armentières and Aubers Ridge in 1914 to Hazebrouck and Scherpenberg in 1918—line the colonnades of the Ploegstreet Memorial. I skip some. About 30 kilometers south is the Duds Corner Memorial, where one enters a courtyard formed by panels with 20,589 names from the battles around Loos. Then, 10 kilometers on, over 11,000 names of Canadians with no known graves stretch out from two of Walter Allard's monumental figures on Vimy Ridge. I pass by Cambrai, some 30 kilometers to the south-southwest, with 7048 names on the cemetary walls. Due south 30 kilometers stands Lutyens' massive reworking of the architectural vocabulary of nearby Albert Cathedral. There the sixteen weight-bearing columns that hold up the towers of the great monument at Thiepval are faced on three or four sides with panels holding the names of 73,367 men with no known resting place who died in the Battle of the Somme. Like a great altar screen through which some graves are visible, this is the monument that Maya Lin invoked when she designed the Vietnam Memorial in Washington, DC.

There are other British repositories of names, not to speak of hundreds of cemeteries with between a score or so to over 10,000 grave markers, some with names, others with the notation that here lies a soldier whose name is known but to God. The pyramids pale by comparison with the sheer scale of British, let alone German, French, Belgian, Portuguese, and American commemorative imposition on the landscape. One enters the German cemetery at Langemark, for example, through a gatehouse flanked by two chapels. In one there is a register of the over 40,000 men buried there; the walls of the other are carved with the names of students who died in the October 1914 offensive. Immediately ahead is a wreath surrounding a fragment of verse from Isaiah (43:1): "But now thus says the Lord, he who created you, O Jacob, he who formed you O Israel: 'Fear not for I have redeemed you; *I have called you by name* and you are mine'" (my emphasis). And past the wreath a mass grave containing 24,834 men is surrounded on three sides by name-bearing bronze pillars. ("Name" in epitaphs is not, I should point out, traditional. The phrase chosen by Rudyard Kipling for the Stone of Remembrance that sits in every British war cemetery—"Their names Liveth Evermore"—is from Ecclesiasticus in the Apocrypha, had not been used before, and was thought extremely odd by those to whom it was first proposed.)

At the opposite end of the same discursive strategy that is evident in this enumeration, this veneration, of names on the battlefront are the great national memorials at home at whose core lies a soldier whose defining characteristic is eternally not having a name. In the British case, his is the *only* repatriated body and served literally as *the* generic body. It makes the attribute of being forever unnamed—not lost or disappeared or simply forgotten, but so anonymous as to become universal—sacred. These are the bones that stand for all bones, the body that could be any body, the cor-poreal "distributive singular term," as the logicians would have it: "*The* Unknown Warrior."

Each of these practices—naming and the sanctifying of anonymity—have had powerful resonances in our century. In 1943, in the Warsaw Ghetto, "not naming" was already enough part of the Western cultural inheritance for Chaim Kaplan to use the term in quotation marks, to hope that "the day will come when the Jewish people will erect a memorial here, where the common grave holds all these brothers forever. [He says nothing of sisters.] . . . Here lie our 'unknown soldiers,' whom all of us should honor and remember."[5]

The passion in our century for naming, and more particularly for embracing the name as the specific placeholder for all that a person means, is fairly evident: the furor about the MIAs (missing in action), which were commonplace in wars before this century, the NAMES project that coordinated the AIDS quilt, and of course the Vietnam Memorial, to pick three. The actor Jimmy Stewart goes to Maya Lin's great black, reflecting marble wall of names every time he is in Washington. "There are 57,000 names there." His voice becomes soft as he speaks of his son Ronald, a marine lieutenant killed at Danang. "But I can pick out my son's name almost with my eyes closed."[6] An aged veteran of the most horrible day of the most horrible battle of the twentieth century— the first day of the First Battle of the Somme, July 1, 1916, told a BBC 4 interviewer that he had felt badly about a comrade whose wounded body had been left in a German trench, subsequently abandoned. It was never found. The old man's spirit came to rest on this matter, he says, when he found his comrade's name among the almost 74,000 others on Lutyens' monument. Only in 1986, more than a half century later, could he say in the presence of the name that "I felt I had not abandoned him."

These—naming in relation to bodies and sanctifying the namelessness of an eternally anonymous body—are the memorial practices that I want to account for as modern phenomena that came to full and sudden flower during and after the Great War. By this I do not mean that names and lists of names did not exist before then: one can point to the monastic *Liber memorialis* or to the quite different *Memor Bücher* of the high medieval Jewish communities of central and western Europe, or to Memorial Chapel at Harvard, or to the Civil War monuments and lists of veterans in hundreds of towns. Still, the explosion of naming in memorialization at the beginning of this century is so quantitatively striking as to constitute a qualitatively new phenomenon. Until our time "none else of name," as the herald after the battle of Agincourt intoned in Shakespeare's Henry V, was an acceptable response to mass death.

More importantly, in making a claim for the novelty of the connection between names, bodies, and memory during the Great War, I definitely do not want to suggest that the emotions or sensibilities that make it possible are new. Quite to the contrary. Names—serious names—demand that we read a great deal into them: as Marcel Proust puts it at the beginning of *The Guermantes Way*, they offer us "an image of the unknowable which we have poured into their mould"; they are, as he says about Guermantes' house, "transformed to suit the life of our imagination."[7]

As for the connection of names, bodies, and the memory, William Wordsworth, for example (in *Essays on Epitaphs* 1), claims that there is nothing more natural in the history of reason than that a name and an epitaph should that mark the dead—of war or not of war. "Almost all nations," he says, "have wished that certain external signs should point out the places where their dead are interred." This is because of the consciousness of immortality that is implanted, he thinks, "in all men naturally." Without it "man could never have awakened in him the desire to live in remembrance of his fellows."[8] The existential poignancy of name and epitaph, as Paul de Man observes, allows Wordsworth to claim a restoration, in the face of death, one that seems to both constitute and be made possible by the immortality of the soul.[9]

And, finally, the creation of a memorial landscape that is constituted by the nexus of name, body, and place—at least its constitution in the imagination—has deep cultural roots. Simonedes, the poet whom both Quintilian and Cicero single out as "the first person to discover an art of memory," was able to identify bodies of guests at a banquet ("to restore to each man his own dead")—despite the fact that the relatives of the deceased "were unable to distinguish not merely the faces but even the limbs of the dead"—because he remembered where each guest had been sitting.[10] The almost obsessive concern for identifying bodies that led the British authorities to record on ordinance survey maps the location within 10 meters of over 300,000 disinterred bodies on the western front is a large-scale reenactment of this originary moment. But why now, in the early twentieth century, do hoary if not eternal human murmurings find such abundant new resonance?

One obvious answer is democracy. Simply leaving bodies to rot and disappear, as was done in the past, turned out to be out of the question, at least in the case of the western European powers. A delegation of Labour M.P.s, for example, visited the battlefields just after the war "on behalf of the thousands whom we represent . . . who have not yet been able to visit the graves of those dear to them, [to be sure] that these graves are being fittingly cared for." They left satisfied that "our brothers of every class" were lovingly cared for, that "equality of treatment" meant that they saw "every rank of soldier from General to Private, lying side by side, under the same simple headstones, silent witnesses to future generations of the world's greatest tragedy."[11] Clearly the fate of dead bodies and of names representing bodies in our century does tend to be part of a new, democratic, more broadly public and demanding history of persons. But why this should be the case is not clear. Of some 3000 soldiers who died in the most democratic of armies at Valley Forge in the winter of 1777/78, only one is buried in a marked grave. The American Civil War was the first in which some efforts were made, at least by the Union side, to identify and mark the graves of individual soldiers: to name them. But the army issued no identification disks (these are a product of the Boer War), and in general the process was haphazard. Each soldier was responsible for buying or making, and for carrying, something with his name on it—an identification tag, buckle, broach, or simply a shred of paper—so that his dead body might be identified after battle. The care exercised at the first national cemetery at Gettysburg, rather more a memorial field to military units than to individual men, was an exception even for Union soldiers, and of course the remains of Confederates who died at that famous battle were scrupulously excluded. Moreover, the Great War began without anyone having any intention of doing anything different from what had been done with bodies at Malplaquet or Waterloo. Nothing is visible there of the carnage that bloodied these fields, and nothing more was planned at Mons. New political arrangements thus do not self-evidently demand a new aesthetics of memory. Or, put differently, the fact that every body now demands a name somewhere in proximity to it, or that every name can become, in Proust's sense, "transformed to suit the life of our imagination," is, indeed, a feature of the political subjectivity upon which democracy is predicated. But the question of the nature of that subjectivity itself remains.

A second and related answer is politics more generally. The uses of commemorative practices have particular national histories. German memorials and cemeteries are much more rapidly and overtly politicized than British ones, for example; considerable efforts in the British case go into making each monument bearing names representative of the empire as a whole. And there were supposedly immediate instrumental gains to be had, some argued, from this or that public remembrance. Allowing the general public an opportunity for seats in Westminster Abbey at the burial ceremonial for the Unknown Warrior would, an adviser of Lloyd George hoped, "be a bold and dramatic stroke, because you might find the Duchess next to the Charwoman; it might even have its effect, however small and imperceptible, upon the industrial situation."[12] In a war fought, at least publicly, for freedom and democracy it was terribly important that Princess Beatrice visiting the grave of her only son, Prince Maurice of Battenberg, should have met, and be known to have met, "an aged fellow" from New Zealand who was on a pilgrimage to the identically marked and cared for grave of his only son. The *News of the World* published the account of their commiseration in a cemetery near Ypres. Bodies here are meant to elide the divisions of the living. And all of this clearly did something. The Communist *Workers Dreadnought* complained that "millions of bereaved people [were] impressed by the thought that their dead son, their brother, their father, husband or friend they will see no more, has been honored" while unemployment remained high and the government did nothing.

But this tells us less about overt manipulation than it does about deep and complex longings that dwelt in individual and public consciousness. In fact, the British government was completely taken aback by the enormous popularity in 1919 of the Cenotaph—the empty tomb that had been hastily constructed in London as a place to salute the dead for the August 1919 peace celebrations. Lord Curzon thought it would be "foreign to the Spirit of our people . . . too Latin" and Sir Alfred Mond, the Minister of Works, came right out and said it was simply too Catholic. Brig. B. J. Wyatt reported that when he was ordered to produce the body of the Unknown Warrior that would be reburied in the Abbey he thought it a good idea but that only one out of twenty-four people at a luncheon party he attended thought so, the rest thinking that the idea would "never appeal to the British."[13] Both rapidly became shrines with enormous emotional power. Indeed the authorities had planned to remove the temporary Cenotaph but public opinion simply would not allow it. Urging haste in its removal when it was already too late, Sir Lionel Earle lamented that "it is rapidly becoming a war shrine" and that the longer the public was allowed to lay floral tributes at its base the more politically difficult would be its dismantling.[14] My claim however is not that there was no politics of memory but that we need to understand the sensibility that made such a politics possible.

A third and last suggestion that adduces some set of objective conditions would be that the sheer magnitude of the slaughter in the war of 1914–1918 demanded something new. The vast lists and other massings of names as well as fields of individual grave markers might be regarded as an aesthetic of the "arithmetical sublime"—Immanuel Kant's phrase. They make manifest the fact, really the unrepresentability, of stupendous mortality. How does one grasp and remember death on that scale? Edmund Blunden and others try to help by geographic analogues: a column of the dead four abreast would stretch from Durham to Westminster Abbey, from Quebec to Ottawa, and take four days and nights to pass a reviewing spot. But on the ground they look like "this" in all their particularity as one views the thousand or so cemeteries (I speak here only of the British) that mark the western front.

But the question behind this answer is why people would want, for the first time, to make great numbers of dead visible as markers of loss, sacrifice, or even glory. In earlier wars—and we must not forget that some 250,000 British soldiers died in the French revolutionary wars, a number proportionately comparable to the losses of the Great War—the slaughter was best forgotten. Battlefields were allowed to turn to pasture without a murmur of concern. After 1914, however, more was demanded of the landscape. Winston Churchill would propose—the first such suggestion in history I think—that Ypres be kept as a ruin in memory of the place where the empire bled. Australian units fought unsuccessfully after the war to keep Caberet Rouge out of cultivation and as near to its battle state as possible. And, of course, the actual lists and cemeteries I have mentioned do literally mark, if in an obviously sanitized and aestheticized way, the contours of battles. Trenches are still visible on almost every site.

I will now move my focus from what seem to be the seemingly objective conditions for new memorial practices to what might be thought of as two microhistories of subjectivity in relation to which I want to situate naming and anonymity in its various forms. The first might be thought of as the production of antidotes, hopeless, poignant, desperate, but nevertheless antidotes, to what Samuel Beckett called the "poisonous ingenuity of Time."[15]

Modern arts of memory are preoccupied with chronicling this poison. Alain Resnais's camera follows the tracks, now covered in weeds, grass, and wildflowers, to the gate of Auschwitz. Dr. Joseph Mengele's hospital looks in the russet colors of fall more like a slightly dilapidated late-eighteenth-century mill than a house of torture. Claude Lanzman's camera in *Shoah* plays over and over the lovely countryside surrounding, and the grass-covered ruins within, what had been death camps. Even during the slaughter of the Great War, the poison—or perhaps it's the balm—was evident. A young lieutenant, in June 1916, a month before he was to die in the First Battle of the Somme, could write home about the "multitude of lives [that] have been simply wasted," but in the same letter he imagined what would happen when the slaughter ended: the trenches "which in February were grim and featureless tunnels of gloom . . . are already overarched and embowered with green." Children will play there "as in a garden" before summer comes again.[16] Very quickly, the bodies and the scars vanish almost as if they were never there, as if there were nothing to ascribe meaning to. The earth which during the war seemed "diseased, pocked, rancid, stinking of death in the morning sun"[17] would appear to a writer of battlefield guidebooks only a few years later as being "nursed back to health" by Nature: "many of the scars have softened; soon they will be gone altogether, and the old familiar landmarks will be gone forever."[18] "Your death means nothing to these fields," wrote one soldier in the context of musing that all this death meant nothing in any case, no more than if "you had died in your bed, full of years and respectability."[19]

There is evident here a powerful anxiety of erasure, a distinctly modern sensibility of the absolute pastness of the past, of its inexorable loss, accompanied by the most intense desire to somehow recover it, to keep it present, or at least to master it. One thinks here of the end of George Eliot's *Mill on the Floss*, a novel that insists that "the future will never join on the past again," that the "book is quite closed,"[20] while at the same time insisting on the power of history and the necessity for its constant recollection:

> Nature repairs her ravages—repairs them with sunshine, and with human labor. The desolation wrought by the flood [one might read "war" here] had left little visible trace on the face of the earth, five years after. The fifth autumn is rich in golden corn-stacks, rising in thick clusters among the distant hedgerows.

But time has been irreparably rent:

> Nature repairs her ravages—but not all. The uptorn trees are not rooted again; the parted hills are left scarred: if there is new growth, the trees are not the same as the old, and the hills underneath their green vesture bear the marks of the past ending. To the eyes that have dwelt on the past, there is no thorough repair.[21]

Nor did there seem any repair for the gaps between the mute, dead, quick-to-decay, and stolidly material dead body about which war journals, diaries, and letters speak incessantly, on the one side, and the imperative to give it some more permanent meaning, to make something cultural of it, to make it part of national and personal memory, on the other. In a sense, of course, this chasm might be regarded as an aspect of the anxiety of erasure. But it is also more specifically an anxiety about the corporeal integrity and individuality of the dead in an age when the omnipotent God of John Donne's sermons could no longer be relied on to appropriately collect every atom at the day of judgment and more generally about maintaining the dead as part of the world of living.

In fact, one's own dead and the dead of the enemy looked alarmingly alike. The body of the last British soldier of the 119th Infantry killed in the Great War looked very much like the "two blokes" in the neighboring hole—Germans. "He died for his country" reads the penciled note over the former; "I suppose they did too," remarks a subaltern; "yes" says the general, "but unfortunately for them, they were on the wrong side!" But this too is to speak as if they were still persons; the dead do not have fortune, good or ill. "The dead no longer count. War has no use for dead men," as the same general noted on the occasion of surveying some of the once-human carnage near Thiepval.[22] Pell-mell they were mashed together: a garden, "about as big as ours in Hampstead," wrote the poet John Masefield, was filled with ranks of graves: "Foutiane, Marcel, 27 ans . . . sometimes simply 'un Allemand' for in the heavy fighting often the bodies were not found, but heads and parts of bodies, sometimes only rags of flesh."[23] "I remember a pair of hands (nationality unknown) which protruded from the soaked ashen soil . . . and the dead were the dead" writes Siegfried Sassoon in his memoirs.[24]

Indeed, the literature of the Great War is saturated with the disappearance, the disarticulation, of bodies. In some measure this is a response to the objective conditions of this particular mode of warfare: high-explosive shells, constant artillery bombardments, machine guns, and mines employed for four years over a very long but extremely narrow front. It is also, however, a response to the much broader cultural shifts which I will return to in a moment.

To an unprecedented extent in this war vast numbers of bodies and body parts were beaten, not once but repeatedly, into the ground, which soon became a Bosch-like landscape of the Last Days. Few memoirs or diaries fail to dwell on the particulars of this dismemberment, on the smell of decay, and of blood everywhere and always. There are the "[g]rotesque mud bloated dead."[25] There was the head that was like "the fragment of a sculpture" that had been cut in half by a shell so that the "the face lay like a mask, its features unmarred at all, a full foot away from the rest of the head."[26] There were the knocked-in trenches after a bombardment where 200 men were lost without firing a shot—"pieces of flesh, scalp, legs, tunics tattered and parts of soldiers carried away in blankets."[27]

In memoir after memoir we are confronted with such phantasmagoric scenes of persons come apart, bodies never at rest either in their supposedly final resting place or in the realms of meaning. While battlefields—"fields of slaughter" in German—have of course always been places of disordered death and broken bodies, never before the Great War of 1914–1918 had so many fought with such destructive weapons over such a small surface of the earth. Bringing order to this chaos, both in the sense of cleaning it up—a task left by the British to Chinese, Indian, and African laborers hired for the occasion who also lost their lives by the thousands from unexploded mines and shells and other mishaps—and in the sense of fashioning a new cultural order out of it, was a daunting task.

We know how this was attempted in a body-by-body fashion. In 1917, for example, the mother of Pvt. Eric Pinks was told, in a penciled note, on Church Army Recreation Hut stationery, from a corporal in his company, that her son had been killed by sniper fire but that he "has got a good grave" whose precise location he could not reveal. Ten years later she wrote to the War Graves Commission asking for its location, near Langemark in the Ypres Salient, so she thought. By return mail she was told that her son's grave could not be located; "in many areas military operations caused the destruction of crosses and graves registration marks, and completely changed the surface of the ground," the letter said. But in place of a location the Commission comforted her with the fact that "his name has been commemorated on the memorial which has been erected at Menin Gate, Ypres," and included two photographs of the list where it appeared—between W. Pilling and J. H. Pinney, opposite a long, long list of Smiths.[28]

We also know how the universal body—*the* Unknown Warrior—was brought back into the memory of the living; how he was, so to speak, resurrected. The bones in Westminster Abbey were self-consciously bones. They were dug out of the earth where they had moldered for almost six years; they were not transformed to ashes despite suggestions that this might be more appropriate. "There could be no doubt," opined Lord Curzon, "that in the public mind there would be more the idea of identity if bones and not ashes were in the coffin."[29] They proceeded through various stages of honor, a sort of secular beatification, from a mudhole, to a Quonset hut, to a great parade, to the deck of a destroyer, to the greatest funeral in British history. The suggestion that the soldier be buried with a rifle—it was used to mark graves on the front, it was the weapon he fought with, and to bury him with a cross-handled sword would confuse those who might reopen the grave centuries later—was turned down and a handmade crusader's sword that resembled a cross was placed in the grave instead.[30]

The final line on the slab beneath which the Unknown Warrior rests reads, "In Christ Shall All Be Made Alive," and not, as a critic later suggested it should have read, "This is my body broken for you." Had that epitaph been adopted, the sacralization would have been perhaps too literal. But in the bones of a soldier whose universality was to be guaranteed by his eternal anonymity, in the empty tomb—the Cenotaph—that any body might fill, and in the great massings of names, on walls and on gravestones, space is created in which those left behind remake their lives and culture by infusing meaning into earthen, meaningless, interchangeable remains.

Finally, let me suggest that the centrality of names in modern memorial practice must be understood not only, as I have discussed so far, as an antidote to a modern anxiety of erasure or disintegration—to the poisons of time—but also as the result of the modern notion that everyone has a memorable life to live, or in any case the right to a life story. It would be facetious but not altogether false to say that modern commemoration owes its existence to Dickens, Trollope, Balzac, and Eliot.

In considering 1914–1918, we should note again that the meaning of lone uncommemorated graves and of anonymous mass graves had changed dramatically during the course of the nineteenth century. There had been a major remaking of sensibility. The men at the front and those they left behind had perhaps read the end of Balzac's *Père Goriot,* where only Eugène's charity saves the old man from the ignominy of a common, unmarked grave. They almost certainly had read one of the other countless novels, tracts, or newspaper accounts in which the anonymous pauper funeral became during the nineteenth century the cardinal sign of isolation, despair, and social exclusion for both the rich, who contemplated such matters from afar, and the urban poor, who suffered them. Such a reader is drawn, as Walter Benjamin observed, "to a novel in the hope of warming his shivering life with a death he reads about."

Few British workingmen would have enjoyed a marked individual grave in their prewar homeland, but the British State would have to do better by them if it sent them by the hundreds of thousands to die abroad. The Red Cross congratulated itself very soon after it began recording graves of the war dead by reporting that "the remains of soldiers have been saved from the common grave and interred in private plots."[31] (This all too civilian formulation would soon become ludicrous.) In fact, more usual was the report that lamented: "The blackness of their exposed features told me that they had long lain thus: in the bustle of preparing for a push the small services due to the dead were often overlooked. I felt sad; there was no peace here even for the dead."[32]

The cultural norm, if sadly not the practice, was to connect name and body of the dead and to mark their passage with some sort of ritual. Men who met their end at the front, however unreal the landscape and gruesome the circumstances, nevertheless were thought to have died within the cultural and more importantly domestic world of their homeland.

While much has been made about the enormous distance between the two and of the camaraderie of the trenches that isolated soldiers from their families, I am struck by just the opposite. This was a war of unparalleled intimacy. Four thousand postal clerks on the western front saw to it that the war front and the domestic world of Britain were in constant communication. So, a death and a dead body were not some far-off event but a brutal break in family life and narrative, a narrative that is redolent with the sensibility of domesticity and the novel.

Sometimes we have only fragments of this history in an archive, a sheet of brown paper on which is written the contents of the package it once wrapped—foot powder, peppermints, socks, cake—and in capital letters, "RETURNED—RECIPIENT KILLED," along with official notices of death and the burial site. John Bennett had given his little daughter a watch which she promptly overwound; it was repaired, but he told her that he had better keep it until she was old enough to take care of it; it did not come back with his effects because, we learn from a comrade, his left arm had been severed by the shrapnel from which he died. Three days before his death his diary reads: "Bright sunny day. O.P. [our position] had warm time. 200 shells dropped near."[33]

Sometimes we have a much fuller history. Pvt. Eric Pinks' correspondence with his working-class family fills hundreds of pages: a postcard to his sister: "To dear little Eva, with much love and kisses, Eric"; a letter from his Uncle Bill, May 17, 1917: "You are passing through a rough time now my dear boy but keep smiling for I think the good times are coming"; "What a little beggar old Spot is," writes Eric to his mother in response to her report that the dog won't allow itself to be dried after its bath; on August 5 he writes home that he is "glad that Spot is getting on alright," that he "is so glad to hear old chap that you have got over having those teeth drawn alright and that dear old Gran and Harold are better and that all the rest of you dear ones are well and so hope that all the rest of you dear ones will keep well." He asked for one or two razor blades. There is an August 6 standardized postcard on which Eric acknowledged receiving his family's letter of August 2 and crossed out all the alternative messages to the phrase "I am quite well." On August 14 he was killed by a sniper; his body was lost; his name is, as I mentioned earlier, listed on the Menin Gate.

It is in this context that frantic letters go back and forth between parents or wives and the authorities; maps are made and sent, graves are sought and photographed; names are recorded. A narrative of a life is brought to closure; a ghost is laid to rest.

I want to end with an exchange of letters between W. J. Martin, an infantry private and onetime groom, and his fiancée, Emily Chitticks, a farm servant. There are seventy-five manuscript letters from him between August 1916, when he enlisted, and March 27, 1917, a couple of days before he was killed; there are twenty-three from Emily to "her Will" between March 25 and April 5, 1917, including five that were returned unopened and marked "KILLED."

In 1921, she collected into a bundle Will's letters, together with a chronology of their relationship, a penciled verse about how she would not see him on earth again, and a couplet in ink: "sleep darling sleep, on foreign shore / I loved and love you dearly, but Jesus loves You more." There is also a note saying that she wanted the packet buried with her just as her heart was already buried in Flanders' Field. Her life, she said, had ended with his. Emily Chitticks never married and died alone in a Council Estate. She apparently left no heirs. Her papers were found by a neighbor who attended her funeral and were given by him to the Imperial War Museum in spring 1994.

It is a remarkable letter exchange, most importantly for my purposes because it allows each of the correspondents to reveal their inner selves, to think themselves into the lives of the other, and more specifically to imagine death and burial with a quite characteristic nineteenth-century sensibility. A life under these circumstances requires a different sort of narrative closure than in earlier times. "I have dreamt that you were back home with me dear," writes Emily, "and the most strange thing about them, you are always in civilian clothes when I dream of you, & I have never seen you in those dear, so it seems very strange. I hope that will come true. I only wish you were in civilians now." "You must forgive me dear," he writes to her, "if I was reserved on Tuesday night. I wanted to say a lot dear, but I knew that you couldn't stand it. I didn't want to make it worse for you dear. If I do not mistake dear I think you gave vent to your feelings before I was out of hearing." Like Eric Pinks with his family, they share all manner of small news, the sort that produces texture, i.e., the reality effect, in domestic novels. "Two dear little puppies at Suffolk House," Emily re-

ports in one of the letters returned with "KILLED" on the enve-
lope, "two little sheep dogs they are and they are so pretty and
playful one cannot help loving them." He tells her about death at
the front: "I have seen some graves today dear of Officers and men
who were killed in action. They had wooden crosses and wood rail-
ings around the grave. They were really done off very nicely. Well
dear Emily I hope you have received all my letters. . . ."

And when she finally learns of his death she is desperate to fit
it into the sort of story the two of them had been creating. She
wants to know the exact circumstances of his end, and his com-
rades rise to her expectations; "How can I thank you for the information you sent me," Emily writes back to the friend, "regarding
my sweetheart Will Martin. It is a terrible blow to me, no one
knows but myself what it means to me."

Emily's inquiries regarding Will's grave at first elicited a reply
from the War Graves Commission dated October 22, 1917, to the
effect that Pvt. W. J. Martin is buried "at a point just S.W. of
Ecoust St. Mein which is S.E. of Arras." The site, however, was in
the midst of a battlefield and was destroyed in the back and forth of
artillery duels and trench excavation. No trace could later on be
found of Will Martin. After several inquiries the Commmission assured Emily Chittick, however, that Will's "name" would be preserved: "You may rest assured that the dead who have no known
resting place will be honoured equally with the others, and that
each case will be dealt with upon full consideration of its merits as
regarding the site and place of the memorial." Pvt. Will Martin's
name, along with 10,000 others, is on the memorial to the missing
at Faubourg d'Amiens for soldiers lost in the Arras sector of the
Battle of the Somme.

## NOTES

1. Reginald Harold Bryson, clerk, "My War Diary," p. 10. IWM (Imperial War Museum, London), Ms. 72/88/1.
2. Quoted in James Langebach, "'The Fellowship of Men That Perish':
Wallace Stevens and the First World War," *Wallace Stevens Journal*
13, No. 2 (Fall 1989): 96.
3. Imperial (now Commonwealth) War Graves Commission, Maiden-

head, uncatalogued archive, Tyne Cote file no. 2, November 23–July 28, 1924, Blomfield to Col. F. R. Durham, to whom Blomfield is somewhat apologetic for continuing negotiations, but he points out that in a "matter so important … every precaution should be taken to see that we get it right." "Sorry to bother you again," he says, "over the question of the name panels for the Menin Gate. In many ways they will be for the interested public the most important feature of the Memorial." For the responses of the Director of Public Works, see the Commission's Minutes, 68th meeting, Windsor Castle Archives, 7/G24/321/S.

4. Director of Records to General Ware, February 16, 1922, Tyne Cott Boxes, Imperial War Graves Commission Archives, Maidenhead.

5. Chaim Kaplan, *Scroll of Agony: The Warsaw Diary of Chaim Kaplan*, Abraham I. Katsh, trans. and ed. (New York: Macmillan, 1965), March 7, 1942.

6. Interview, *New York Times*, April 23, 1990.

7. *In Search of Lost Time*, Vol. 3: *The Guermantes Way*, C. K. Scott Moncrieff and Terrance Kilmartin, trans., revised by D. J. Enright (New York: Modern Library, 1993), p. 3.

8. William Wordsworth, *Selected Prose*, "Essays on Epitaphs" (Harmondsworth, Middlesex, UK: Penguin Books, 1988), No. 1, 322–323.

9. Paul de Man, "Autobiography as De-Facement," in *The Rhetoric of Romanticism* (New York: Columbia University Press, 1984).

10. Quintilian, *The 'Institutio oration,'* with an English translation by H. E. Butler (London: Heinman, 1953) xi, II. 811, pp. 217–219.

11. Labour Representative Delegation report on the work of the Imperial War Graves Commission, typescript, n.d. JSM/WG/l, Labour Party Archives, National Museum of Labour History, Manchester, UK.

12. Lloyd George Papers, House of Lords Record Office, F/24/3/20, Storr to Davies, October 28, 1920.

13. Brig. L. J. Wyatt file, IWM, 69/84/A.

14. PRO WO (Record Office, Office of Works) 20/1/3, Earle/Mond 24/7/19.

15. Samuel Beckett, *Proust* (New York: Grove Press, 1931), p. 4.

16. Letter from 2nd Lt. Stephen Hewett to Mrs. Robertson, June 2, 1916, in Laurence Housman, ed., *War Letters of Fallen Englishmen* (London: Victor Gollancz, 1930), pp. 137–138.

17. Cecil Lewis, *Sagittarius Rising* (London: Peter Davies, 1936, 1966), p. 113.

18. Lt. Col. T. A. Lowe, *The Western Battlefields: A Guide to the British Line* (London: Gale and Polder, n.d.).

19. Guy Chapman, *A Passionate Prodigality: Fragments of an Autobiography* (London: MacGibbon, 1965), p. 122.
20. George Eliot, *Mill on the Floss,* Carol T. Christ, ed. (New York: Norton, 1994), p. 359.
21. Ibid., p. 422.
22. Brig. Gen. F. P. Crozier, *A Brass Hat in No Man's Land* (New York: Jonathan Cape, 1930), pp. 233, 106.
23. *John Masefield's Letters from the Front, 1915–1917,* Peter Vansittart, ed. (London: Constable, 1980), p. 137.
24. Siegfried Sassoon, *Memoirs of an Infantry Officer* (London: Faber and Faber, 1930), p. 222.
25. Percy Croney, *Soldier's Luck: Memoirs of a Soldier of the Great War* ( Ilfracombe, Devon, UK: Arthur H. Stockwell, 1965), p. 209.
26. Bernard Adams, *Nothing of Importance* (London: Methuen, 1917), p. 264.
27. Housman, *War Letters of Fallen Englishmen,* p. 91. Letter of Pvt. Thomas Dry from Gallipoli, January 15, 1916.
28. IWM, 85/43/1.
29. PRO WO 20/1/3, f. 56.
30. War Museum/Mond PRO WO 20/1/3, f. 133, October 27, 1920; Curator of the Armouries/Earle, WO 20/1/3, f. 155, October 29, 1920.
31. *Red Cross Magazine* (April 1915): 82.
32. Pvt. E. N. Gladston, 1917, in C. B. Purdon, *Everyman at War* (London and Toronto: J. M. Dent, 1930), p. 117.
33. J. Bennett, IWM, 83/14/1.

# PART THREE

# BODIES
# SOCIOPOLITICAL AND
# ECONOMIC

# The Body at Work: Boundaries and Collectivities in the Late Twentieth Century

### Emily Martin

Many attest to the dramatic nature of changes that are now of occurring in the political economy of the globe. As an ethnographer, I am interested in the possible interplay between these changes and alterations in concepts of the person or the body that may be accompanying or even enabling them.

The changes in global political economy include the elements that go to make up what David Harvey terms the condition of postmodernity: the creation of a part-time "home-work" economy at the level of worldwide production; the forging of corporate conglomerates at the level of global management; restructuring within the U.S. economy with increasing cleavages between the top and bottom of the economic ladder, with increasing homelessness, a reduced middle class, and persistent and higher levels of unemployment and underemployment; technological developments with innovations in electronic storage, retrieval, and transmission of information; medical advances in genetic-level research and therapy; and global epidemics (Harvey 1989).

In this chapter I want to explore how these changes at the macro level are being registered more locally, as challenges to units

145

of experience we may easily take for granted, in particular, the individuality and bodily integrity of the person. As boundaries between the person and the world change, we also need to understand changes in how larger social and cultural units are being conceptualized: we need to take account of boundaries and the collectivities they embrace or exclude. I will describe these changes in three domains: the body itself; the global epidemic of HIV (human immunodeficiency virus) infection; and corporate organizations. In all three domains, we will see that a range of possibilities with opposite implications coexists—from tight, bounded, closed units poised in fear and hostility against other units of like kind, on the one end, to harmonious interconnection and unity of all that is, on the other.

The fieldwork on which I am drawing in this discussion was conducted over three years, primarily in Baltimore, Maryland.[1] The major ethnographic sites where a group of five graduate students (Bjorn Claeson, Wendy Richardson, Monica Schoch-Spana, Karen-Sue Taussig, and Ariane van der Straten) and I participated as volunteers, residents, or interviewers included a university immunology laboratory, an AIDS wing in an inner-city nursing home, several AIDS activist service organizations, several socioeconomically diverse urban neighborhoods, and the training activities of a major multinational corporation (Martin, 1994).

## First Domain: The Body

How is the body being imaged in terms of its ability to maintain health? At one end of the spectrum, the body is a tightly bounded unit. Macho heterosexualized T-cells, wielding weapons, graduate from "technical college" (the thymus) and guard the healthy body, like intelligent Rambos, killing invading non-self cells. Flexible, creative, innovative B cells, producers of antibodies, provide additional ever-changing protection, like talented females. Lowly, dumb, primitive macrophages, marked as low-ranked females or racial others, are the infantry/garbage collectors who die in great numbers on the body's battlefield or live to cannibalize the dead bodies or dispose of the garbage. This is the body as nation-state,

146

isolated, precariously defended at its borders, attempting to maintain purity within and to guard from contamination without: "self" is sharply divided from and defended against "non-self." This depiction of the body as defended nation-state allows the medical description of HIV-positive gay men suffering from AIDS to entail a loss of heterosexual potency, in the guise of their progressive loss of virile T cells (Martin, 1992).

But looking ahead in the light of trends that are only now emerging, I sense a shifting of the terms of the argument, the shape of the picture. We are beginning to hear that macrophages, cells once glossed as primitive garbage eaters, are major players in the maintenance of the immune system, and once sabotaged, an able porter for disease organisms. Headline news in June 1991 proclaimed that "AIDS Virus Can Get into Body Through Mucous Membranes" (Garrett, 1991). At the Seventh International Conference on AIDS, researchers reported that HIV can enter the body through dendritic cells (a type of macrophage) and mucosal cells (sticky cells in the mucous membranes that can transport cells much the way macrophages do):

> Neither dendritic nor mucosal cells have CD4 receptors, special proteins long thought to be the doorknobs that HIV uses to gain entry into a cell. For the last 10 years, AIDS researchers have assumed that the primary target for HIV was CD4-bearing cells [T cells] of the immune system. But now . . . it is beginning to look as if the dendritic cells are the first target of the virus and that T cells are secondary. (p. 12A)

This finding will help explain HIV transmission among heterosexuals and people who have no sores or cuts that would allow HIV to enter the bloodstream directly. Everyone has mucous membranes in mouth, anus, or vagina across which HIV can travel via these cells. "Look," Dr. Haseltine said, "let's be candid. AIDS is a venereal disease. . . . it's time people stopped thinking there was something special about somebody else that put them at risk for HIV. Mucosa is mucosa: VD is VD" (p. 12A).

These boundary-blurring images find commonality with imagery that has long been in alternative health discourses and that is coming to seem more relevant to a scientific description of the body. The following quotation from *The Green Lifestyle Handbook*, a guide to New Age deep ecology edited by Jeremy Rifkin, was read by the professor in a class I took on psychoneuroimmunology to illustrate the directions she thought current understandings of immunology were leading us (Dossey, 1990, p. 79):

> Although each of us seems to be bounded by his or her skin, this is a sheer illusion. When we view our physical boundaries with pinpoint accuracy, they are so fuzzy as to be nonexistent. With each bodily movement, we trail such a haze of chemicals, vapors, and gases behind us that we resemble out-of-focus images.
>
> Not only are we constantly blending physically into the world and our environment, we are blending into each other. Quite literally, we are sharing bodies. How? As writer Guy Murchie has shown, each breath of air we inhale contains a quadrillion or 1015 atoms that have been breathed by the rest of mankind within the past few weeks, and more than a million atoms breathed by each and every person on Earth. These atoms don't just shuttle in and out of our lungs, they enter our blood and tissue and make up the actual stuff of our bodies. This means that human bodies are constantly being interchanged with those of any and all things that breathe—not just the bodies of humans but those of cows, crocodiles, serpents, birds, fish, etc. These exhaled "pieces" of our bodies remain after we die to be taken in by other bodies. Yet our roots in the world go even deeper, even to the stars themselves. Many of the elements that comprise our bodies were not born on Earth but were recycled through lifetimes of several stars before becoming localized on our planet. Thus, not only are our roots in each other, they are also in the stars. We are, literally, star stuff.

In our interviews in Baltimore neighborhoods, these boundary-blurring images have clearly made their way into the popular imagination. One example among many is this response to a general question about what it means to be healthy:

> I think your immune system, for me is more that you have a whole network of things that affect you and you order those things to, to work the most efficient way and that you have to make choices in what you do

with yourself and your life, and where you live and what you eat, for that to work. And it's all intertwined, so no one thing is going to save you from illness. (Julia Sarton, forties, African-American, teacher)

## SECOND DOMAIN: REACTION TO THE GLOBAL EPIDEMIC OF HIV, A WAY OF TALKING ABOUT BODIES LINKED TO OTHER BODIES

In the first domain, I described a range of representations, from the body as an isolated and defended nation-state to the body as a "constant blur." A similar range can be found in the domain of HIV transmission. First, here are two examples of the isolated, fearful, defended self. This statement is from a young woman at a center for teen mothers. It illustrates how an absolute shortage of resources for health care forces a kind of social triage:

> I think they should be working on a vaccine for AIDS, because I mean, people say I'm a sinner cause I think this way, but a AIDS patient, is soon, in the long run is going to die anyway. You spending all this money sending him to the hospital, he's in the hospital taking up space, why, some peoples don't even have money to go to the hospital, for just an ordinary disease. Like a person has, well this girl was telling me her mother had cancer, had breast cancer. Her mother was on a fixed income. Now if you're on a fixed income, you only got Medicaid. So she could, if, she ran up a hospital bill of, it was like 45 some thousand dollars. Now, Medicaid didn't pay for it, that whole 40 some thousand dollars. So her mother, after the operation her mother died. So, they have to pay their mother's hospital bill. So, why waste all that money on these AIDS patients? They human beings, I know. I know they're human beings, but you think about this person who got cancer, for no, for no good reason of, they didn't get cancer because they wanted to. . . . Because a baby with AIDS, he didn't get it because he wanted to. It's not his lifestyle because he got AIDS.
>
> [You said that, that they should put money into trying to find cures for people with ordinary diseases?]
> Yes.
> [So what do you mean by an ordinary disease?]
> Cancer, arthritis.
> [And why is that ordinary? What do you mean?]

With arthritis, you don't make yourself get arthritis. You don't make yourself with cancer. You don't make yourself get, like lung disease. But they just, they just, they spend all this money on peoples that has AIDS, that really doesn't really have to have AIDS. That's a disease they inflict upon, on theirself.

[What about, what about behaviors that are found to increase people's chance of getting cancer, like smoking or something like that?]

That still is, that still is not like getting AIDS.

[How is AIDS different?]

AIDS can be passed onto other people, so you going to prolong this person life, so he can stay on and give AIDS to someone else? You can't pass along cancer onto another person. I don't mean to be cynical about it, but that's just the way I feel. I just feel that, I feel that they going to prolong anybody's life, you prolong the babies', cause babies don't ask to come here be born to be a little AIDS patient, so you work on something to help the babies. Forget the others. (Mary Blackstone, forties, African-American, unemployed)

The second example, from a very different position in the socioeconomic structure is from an interview with Peter Black and Frank Wallace, a gay white male couple in their early twenties. In their descriptions of the immune system and AIDS, they draw heavily upon an idiom of boundaries. Their talk of boundaries, safety, and risk in depicting the body and the threat of HIV is consonant with their descriptions of danger of a different scale—the neighborhood and the threat of crime.

Peter laments that AIDS and a preoccupation with protecting oneself, that is, wearing a condom, is at odds with love, which is an act of letting down one's barriers. He explains, "a lot of time, and this happens with straight and gay people . . . the issue of love enters the scenario and sometimes . . . when you love someone they don't feel that . . . you should have to protect yourself, and I think that not using protection is a result of that, because they feel that you love this person, that this person loves them and because you love each other, you shouldn't have to hide or protect anything about yourself from this person." The biology of sex and of HIV mandates a barrier, the condom, between two bodies, while the sociality of lovemaking mandates openness between two people.

In his description of how a fetus might contract HIV from a

infected mother, Peter focuses again upon boundaries, this time describing the function of skin as a barrier to disease: "while the
baby's inside the mother, that baby is part of the mother. . . . all her
body fluids are coming into contact with it. . . . even if its blood
type is different, the blood is still coming into contact with this
baby. . . . it does not have its fully developed skin on it to protect
it." Because of a breach in its skin through which the mother's infected blood can pass, the fetus is vulnerable to HIV. Compromised
boundaries, openings in the skin, constitute vulnerability to HIV.

His partner, Frank, emphasizes that caution toward HIV entails not only vigilance against possible points of entry but also care
toward the fluid medium containing HIV. He draws upon an example from his own life, recounting the time he threw away an X-acto
knife at his office after a coworker cut himself with it. He defends
his act to Peter, who thinks him somewhat paranoid, by arguing
that HIV is highly contagious because of its presence in fluids and
because of fluid's special quality of permeating boundaries. It is the
"bodily fluids" of others, from outside, he suggests, that one must
avoid getting inside oneself: "I mean, you know that this disease is
transmitted through fluid, o.k., simple . . . if I've got an open
wound on me, I'm not going to roll around in bed with someone,
and like, have all this semen or fluid or whatever have a chance to
enter my body, you know." Protesting that he was not paranoid in
throwing out the knife, he argues further that he would act within
reason if he encountered a person with HIV: "if I know someone
has AIDS . . . I will take precautions. I'm not going to be . . . total[ly], well, 'you stay ten feet away from me, and if you sneeze, cov-
er your mouth, don't get any fluid on me.' . . . I'm not going to be
like that, because that would be kind of ridiculous, but on the same
chance, I'm not going to welcome the opportunity by . . . getting
horny and sleeping with the person, [or] . . . shar[ing] a needle."

In order to articulate the value of AZT (azidothymidine) for
someone who has tested positive for HIV, Frank draws upon a
boundary metaphor, describing the medication as at least some
protection, however compromised, against the progression of disease. He explains that while this drug may be of only limited help
to the person, merely delaying the onset of symptoms of AIDS,
that help should not be ignored or criticized: "AZT is good. . . . you

can't fuck with it because it's the only thing we got. . . . You know, it's like you're out in the rain, and you see this awning, and you know, its got a few leaks in it, but you'll be a hell of a lot drier from standing under those few leaks than you will if you stand out in this pouring down rain. There's nothing else there, so you got to go for what's there."

In thinking through issues of health and illness, Frank and Peter employ notions of barriers and their permeation of bodily fluids. Talk of vulnerability shifts easily, however, from the level of the body to that of the neighborhood. Just as skin is seen to circumscribe the body, protecting a vulnerable interior from exterior threats, so are streets seen to delineate the margins of a neighborhood, marking good areas from bad. When describing their area of the central city, Frank and Peter call out street names to outline the "safe" portion of the neighborhood. Frank notes that not only have gentrification efforts on streets south and west of the lines of safety failed but also that "bad" areas are encroaching upon "good" ones: "they tried to build that up, and a lot of yuppies moved in, but for some reason, they just didn't make it. . . . That's really all that's there. . . . I think bad areas are kind of moving in, all the good areas are kind of moving up toward this way."

Peter invokes an image of a safe, enclosed area, outside of which one faces possible dangers: "I mean to me, it's almost as though we're a little box. . . . if you go over past Lake Avenue, you start to get into, you know, an area where you might put yourself at risk, you get down towards Packard Street going north, you're starting to put yourself at risk. . . . if you go toward Central Street, that same thing applies, and it just pretty much . . . it's a nice little square, your safe, little, cozy square right here. If you leave it, you're increasing your chances of crime, not to overly worry about it often, but I walk around all the time, I mean I'm always aware, I always keep my eyes and my ears open." Boundaries mark off or contain an area of safety. In one's neighborhood, one knows what streets to avoid and at what streets "bad" areas appear to begin; second, if one knowingly crosses such borders, one must assume the risk of harm. Cross the street and you may be asking for trouble.

Sentiments on the other end of the separation–constant blur continuum come from many places in our fieldwork. One of the most vivid was Jack Morgan, a retired seaman who, based on his careful reading of many issues of the magazine *Discover*, had devised his own theory of HIV infection. His theory was that all humans carry the human immunodeficiency virus in them; it is only those unfortunate enough to manifest it who have the disease we call AIDS. He stressed the common fate of all humans, equally exposed and at risk. Another position, one that surprised me at first, was that of men and women who are in a long-term study of HIV infection in one of the poorest African-American neighborhoods in Baltimore. Virtually all of the forty men and women we have interviewed in this setting have told us in one way or another that although AIDS is terrible, it has one benefit: since no one is safe, anyone can catch HIV, so the disease is going to bring us together as a society as we face a common danger.[2]

## THIRD DOMAIN: CORPORATE RESTRUCTURING

Again we find a range of ways of perceiving what is going on, from a view of increasingly sharp boundaries, and exclusion from a collectivity, to a view of organic wholeness. On the side of sharp boundaries and cleavages, I would include this eloquent statement from a community leader in an integrated neighborhood affected by poverty and high unemployment, who spoke of their poor health, malformed bodies, and general neglect:

I got bad teeth, o.k.? And one of the things all poor people have is bad teeth, because of being poor, ok? . . . it's one of the first things I noticed when I started moving around, because when I talk to Indian people, they got bad teeth. You know what I mean? And I go down south, and they got bad teeth, so it's one of the things that we all, it's one of the things that poor people share all over the world in common, we all got bad teeth. You know what I mean? [laughs] What I come to realize it's for a number of reasons. One is, I think that government doesn't want us to have, they don't care about our teeth. . . . I never could figure it out, it just pissed me off, you know what I mean, but I figure it's because, you know, it's one of the ways of distinguishing poor people from the rest of the population is we all got bad teeth [laughs]. . . .
And so you won't get rid of the drug abuse or the prostitution or the

crime or stuff, until the people who live here are no longer here. And that to me is the same as the underclass thing, disposable people. . . . As soon as they can't figure out a need for us, they'll get rid of us.

[What's the need for you right now?]

We still make money for somebody or another. They still need us some, like they needed people to come up out of the south to work in the mills, so they attract them all up. Now there's not as much need for the people to work in the mills, they need some people in the service economy, they try to retrain . . . but if not they're no use, they'll put you in jail . . . they'll choke you off so that you can't make a living doing anything else, so they get rid of you, or you know, hopefully you'll go back to Virginia or somewhere else, right? You know, you'll crawl in a crack or you won't have children or something. (John Marcellino, forties, Euro-American, community organizer)

In a similar vein, Sidney Mintz wrote of Taso, the Puerto Rican worker with whom he produced a life history, "the condition of Taso's teeth, for example, can be fairly viewed as the direct consequence of external influences upon local life" (1989, p. 791).

The "external influences" affecting John Marcellino's teeth can only be understood by moving to another context, the corporate sector. Put simply, signs of dramatic change are abroad in the structure, organization, and meaning of work inside corporations. Variously referred to as Total Quality Management, continuous improvement, reengineering, or by the names of its founders, W. Edwards Deming, J. M. Juran, or Philip B. Crosby, certain startling shifts are sweeping the corporate world (Crosby, 1984; Drucker, 1992; Juran, 1988; Kantor, 1989; Peterson, 1992; Walton, 1986).

A capsule description of these changes would go like this: we now assume the worker is a partner with management in a continuously changing process of making quality products that fit customers' continuously changing needs. We assume the worker is good, smart, trustworthy, trying his or her best, and working his or her hardest. We strive not for productivity and efficiency per se but for consistency in the production process. If the system of production is running optimally, products will be produced that are consistently very low in defects. Attention shifts away from the worker per se, and his or her specific actions on an assembly line, to the system as a whole. The" system" includes literally everything: it includes the quality of suppliers' materials (which means vertical linkages hitherto unthinkable are being set up in which suppliers and buyers share confidential information); it includes the entire work environment of all workers, including such diffuse things as the experience of a satisfying and meaningful job. It also includes the entire life environment of workers: happiness in marriage, the availability of child care, adult education, recreation, exercise facilities, and so on.

The reason this penumbra of things comes under the corporation's concern is that the behavior of the individual worker is no longer the starting point of the corporation's concern. What matters is the size of the range of variation, within which, once it is consistently held to appropriate limits, individual performance can vary. This means that once consistent results are held within an acceptable range, by controlling elements of the system at some distance from the worker's behavior on the job, the usual kinds of scrutiny of the individual traditionally found in industry are no longer desirable. Gone are piece rates, quality inspections, first line supervisors. In their place are teams that cross divisions so the whole work process can be understood, workers who take responsibility, managers who become coaches or cheerleaders instead of bosses, and a variety of forms of profit sharing.

The dramatic nature of these changes has called for dramatic ways of instilling them. An increasing number of corporations are using forms of learning that focus on experiential, bodily lessons. One member of the Fortune 500 has just finished sending 22,000 employees (from top management to assembly line workers) through an extensive experiential learning course, involving ropes courses, group workshops, and problem solving. Special facilities were built at rural sites up and down the U.S. east coast where the training took place. Ropes courses involve physical exercises in which participants are protected by sophisticated mountain-climbing helmets and harnesses. In one such, for example, teams of men and women, workers and managers of all ages and physiques, climbed a forty-foot tower and leaped off into space tethered to a steel cable stretched between the top of the tower and a landing platform near the ground; they climbed a forty-foot-high wall and rappelled down again; and they climbed a twenty-five-foot-high telephone pole, stood up on a precarious twelve-inch wide disk at the top, turned around 180 degrees and leaped off into space. In the midst of this leap, each person was caught by a rope attached to his or her harness, which, passing through a mountaineering carabiner, was belayed by a coworker. High obstacles are deliberately used to arouse fear and vulnerability so that new kinds of behaviors and attitudes can be forged.

In the process, linkages are being formed across many former sharp and of course hierarchical boundaries: supplier/buyer; worker/manager; manual worker/mental worker. Even competitors in a single sector of the market are being seen as partners: at a recent conference on work redesign in Florida, I heard a top executive say, "[As] we in our industry all drink from the same well, we have to cooperate to make the well deeper and the water cleaner. Then we can all drink deeper."

But of course there is an underside to these changes: most companies that are now "investing in human resources" have first "restructured," or "delayered," their workforce. The member of the Fortune 500 I referred to reduced its workforce by one-third before beginning to reorganize. Those who are in the layers removed, from line workers to middle managers (the latter group is disproportionately hit), of course in varying degrees, join John Marcellino's "trash heap" (Ehrenreich, 1990; Newman, 1988). In other words, the corporate organic whole, linked globally to its suppliers and counterparts across the earth, includes only a small proportion of the population. For the few there will be a new form of work integrating mind and body and breaking down the old hierarchies of boss and worker.

To return, by way of contrast, to the society seen by John Marcellino, neither the bodies nor the communities he is describing are likely to be able to adapt successfully to serious challenges:

> we think it [AIDS] could kill us. It could just kill a lot of people in our community, that's what I think about. Because, with AIDS, the way they say that you get AIDS, we got a lot of relationships here, because they say that you get AIDS through needles, and a lot of our people shoot up. They say you get AIDS through gay sex, and a lot of our people have, function as prostitutes, and are [a] really sexually active population, so, and then you get it through having relations with one anoth-

er, and you pass it by being close to one another, and our people are very close to one another.

[Close?]

You know what I mean . . . like the way to not get AIDS is to not touch people, you know what I mean? That was the way it first came to us. You know, and then as we learn more and more about it, you know, we learn that it's real specific in terms of how you can catch it. But, the, you know like, you know like being monogamous and only having one partner, you know what I mean, and that kind of stuff, that's not usual in our community, particularly among young people and, you know what I mean. But, it's not usual, and then you have all this interaction between needle users and folks involved in prostitution, and a lot of, and then a lot of interaction in the community, and so it's not like separated, it's not like, well there's a needle community up here and people shoot up, and they don't have nothing to do with our community. They're part of our community, and having relations in our community, and there's people who, you know, are involved in male prostitution, you know what I mean? And they're over here, you know, and there's a gay community over there, you know, it's part, it's integrated in our community. There's, you know, and so our fear was oh my God, you know, when I first heard about it I thought Jesus, we're going to be like death.

[When was this?]

This was maybe 7 years ago, or so, it was before people were even talking much about it. We just heard and I thought, Jesus, if they say that you get it in these two ways, and there's a lot of that in our community, gee, we're going to, you know, this is horrible. And I went to the hospital, you know?

[To get tested?]

No, I went to the hospital to say you got to do something. You know what I mean? I went, this is God's honest truth, I went up to Johns Hopkins Health, Hospital there, it was called Public Health Hospital, and I said we need to know more about this stuff, because this stuff's going to kill us, it's going to wipe us out. You know, and I was sure we were going have an epidemic, because if what they were telling us was true, we would. What I know is when I looked into it, we haven't had nobody dead.

[Really?]

Nobody. And I don't understand why.

. . . then they said, okay, and this is a real glitch, because then they said it can be seven years before you know you have it, and I thought well Jesus Christ then, we're really in trouble. Cause now, all these people got it, but nobody knows they got it, right? And eventually it's going to be like, you know, all of a sudden it's going to be like, you know, like a butterfly, you know? [it's a] little thing and all of a sudden . . . one day, it's all going to be, you know, all through the community (John Marcellino).

John Marcellino fears transformation through death that will lead to loss of the life of an entire community, a butterfly as harbinger of extinction.

## CONCLUSION

I have stressed the range of distinct perceptions in these three domains, from sharply divided isolated boundaries to whole integration, partly in order to make the point that we may be at an open moment in history when there is the potential for events to move in a variety of directions—when no one is totally in charge of the changes that have been unleashed, and therefore when there is the possibility of critical intervention. Let me try to articulate the positive potential and the terrible danger of this combination: the positive potential is an opening away from the rigid, bureaucratic hierarchies of the Fordist mass production era and the body as isolated, defended nation-state. The danger is that the organic, whole vision of "Green Lifestyle" or corporate America will be bought at the expense of a vision of organic unity that is only for some people, high-quality people, more fully evolved people, relegating the rest of us to Marcellino's trash heap.

## NOTES

1. Funding was provided by the Spencer Foundation. All names of individuals who participated in the research are pseudonyms.
2. A more extensive report of this part of our research is in Martin et al. (forthcoming).

## REFERENCES

Crosby, Philip B. 1984. *Quality Without Tears: The Art of Hassle-Free Management*. New York: McGraw-Hill.

Dossey, Larry. 1990. "Personal Health and the Environment." In *The Green Lifestyle Handbook: 1001 Ways You Can Heal the Earth.* Jeremy Rifkin, ed. New York: Holt, pp. 79–85.

Drucker, Peter F. 1992. *Managing for the Future: The 1990s and Beyond.* New York: Penguin.

Ehrenreich, Barbara. 1990. *Fear of Falling: The Inner Life of the Middle Class.* New York: Harper.

Garrett, Laurie. 1991. "AIDS Virus Can Get into Body Through Mucous Membranes, New Studies Show." *The Sun* (June 20): A12.

Harvey, David. 1989. *The Condition of Postmodernity: An Enquiry into the Origins of Social Change.* Oxford, UK: Basil Blackwell.

Juran, J. M. 1988. *Juran on Planning for Quality.* New York: Free Press.

Kantor, Rosabeth Moss. 1989. *When Giants Learn to Dance.* New York: Simon & Schuster.

Martin, Emily. 1992. "The End of the Body?" *American Ethnologist* 19, No. 1: 120–138.

Martin, Emily. 1994. *Flexible Bodies: Tracking Immunity from the Days of Polio to the Age of AIDS.* Boston: Beacon Press.

Martin, Emily, Laury Oaks, Karen-Sue Taussig, and Ariane van der Straten. Forthcoming. "AIDS, Knowledge and Discrimination in the Inner City: An Anthropological Analysis of the Experiences of Injection Drug Users." In *Cyborgs and Citadels: Anthropological Interventions in Emerging Sciences and Technologies,* Gary Downey, Joeseph Dumit, and Sharon Traweek, eds. Santa Fe, NM: School of American Research.

Mintz, Sidney W. 1989. "The Sensation of Moving, While Standing Still." *American Ethnologist,* pp. 786–796.

Newman, Katherine. 1988. *Falling From Grace: The Experience of Downward Mobility in the American Middle Class.* New York: Free Press.

Peterson, Tom. 1992. *Liberation Management.* New York: Knopf.

Walton, Mary. 1986. *The Deming Management Method.* New York: Putnam.

# Feminism and the History of the Face

## Kathy Peiss

The first public action of the women's liberation movement was a demonstration in 1968 against the Miss America Beauty Pageant. One hundred feminists protested women's enslavement to beauty standards, filled a trash can with curlers, hair spray, bras, and other "beauty aids," and crowned a live sheep America's beauty queen. One participant explained that the "purpose was not to put down Miss America but to attack male chauvinism, commercialization of beauty, racism and oppression of women symbolized by the Pageant."[1]

A "central concern of feminism" has been, as Mary Russo argues, "the reintroduction of the body and categories of the body . . . into the realm of what is called the political."[2] The Anglo-American feminist tradition of the eighteenth and nineteenth century condemned women's pursuit of beauty and fashion, and the society that thus taught them to destroy their health and prepare for a life of dependency. "Looks, not books, are the murderers of American women," complained physician Sarah Stevenson in 1881.[3]

Only in the 1960s, however, did a feminist critique emerge whose central focus was the commerce in and objectification of women's appearances. For second-wave feminists, much more so than their foremothers, beauty and its appurtenances have been key sites of women's oppression. The statement from the Miss America protester strikingly specified the "commercialization of beauty" as a form of oppression commensurate with the more generalized categories of sexism and racism.

Feminist writings of the time expanded upon these themes. Betty Friedan's *The Feminine Mystique* argued that the entire apparatus of mass culture—women's magazines, advertising, popular psychology, the fashion and beauty industries—deflected women's aspirations for achievement onto limiting roles as wives and mothers. Although looking for more radical political solutions, younger second-wave feminists shared much of Friedan's analysis of consumerism. Dana Densmore, writing on the "temptation to be a beautiful object," observed that "many of us are scarred by attempts as teenagers to win the promised glamor from cosmetics." The more women achieved beauty and admiration, "the less reality our personality and intellect will have," she wrote. Densmore asked, "How can anyone take a manikin seriously?" Una Stannard similarly sought to demystify women's engagement with beauty culture. Although it appeared to be a woman's greatest desire and glory, it was in fact "the stigma of her inferiority," her beauty practices a consequence of male power and desire. Seeking some explanation to account for women's acquiescence, Stannard turned to a psychological explanation that rested upon women's narcissism and "unconscious" homosexuality, determined by a culture that forced women to look constantly at themselves and other women. This line of thought led her problematically to the statement that femme lesbians "have wholly identified with the beauty ideal" and "are merely more unadulterated narcissists than heterosexual women."[4]

Post-1960s feminism drew upon the theoretical perspective of the Frankfurt School and the New Left in its critique of consumption as social domination, specifying commodity capitalism's effects on women as consumers.[5] The representations, technologies, and economy of beauty, in this view, manipulated female desires and anxieties, and set singular and unattainable standards of appearance. Its effects were at once intensive and narcotic: women were driven into an absorption with beauty, into making themselves the objects of visual pleasure. Beauty practices at once detoured and excluded women from political activity. At the same time, however, the feminist disclaimer about "not [putting] down Miss America" suggests a certain ambiguity or confusion about women's agency and complicity in what was largely an analysis of the psychology of oppression and victimization.

The dominant feminist interpretation of appearance, both in the academy and in popular culture, retains this basic analysis. Naomi Wolf's recent book, *The Beauty Myth*, for example, recapitulates the 1960s critique in a 1990s context. She argues that beauty standards are a means of social control used by a "power elite" to constrain modern women who, as a result of feminism, have begun to make strides in politics and the economy. Wolf claims, in effect, that beauty is compulsory for women, that women are forced to adhere to standards that, if they were "free" in their subjectivity, they would reject. Women who are beautiful or who achieve beauty according to the imposed standards are rewarded; those who cannot or choose not to be beautiful are punished, economically and socially. This analysis targets a profit-maximizing capitalism as the engine of women's subordination through beauty standards. But it also places women's appearance practices on a continuum that erases cultural and historical differences under the rubric of patriarchal oppression. In this view, foot-binding, tight corset lacing, bulimia, and making up the face have more commonalities than differences as cultural rituals.[6]

Since the 1960s, these feminist views have had a profound impact on the way we think about "normative femininity" and the commercialization of appearance. From the perspective of the late twentieth century, it is hard not to view the growth and presence of the beauty industry in any but negative terms. Its promises appear to us as hype, a manipulative tactic to sell products. Decades of advertising and advice have touted the centrality of external beauty in women's successful negotiation of life and the role of cosmetics in enhancing self-esteem. The merchandising of women's faces and bodies in the mass media, the growth of plastic surgery, the pressure to diet: all have been indicted for their role in making external beauty a compulsory aspect of female identity. Strikingly, this view is not only that of self-identified feminists but has reached deeply into American life as a viable interpretation expressed on television talk shows and even in the pages of women's magazines. "Lookism" or "looksism," in which external appearance is the basis for judgments about character, ability, and worth, has been theorized as a civil rights violation; some college campuses and municipalities, including Santa Cruz, California, have issued regulations or ordinances banning such actions as a form of discrimination.

This position rests on several important claims and assumptions. Sociologically it requires a stark opposition between oppressive and powerful institutions (capitalism, consumer society, patriarchy) and women as objects and passive consumers. It supposes that women as consumers have had little ability to resist the confluence of messages about beauty or that they understand those messages only in ways intended by their producers. And it assumes that women have had no part in the *production* of beauty culture or that they have participated solely as "male-identified" women, as ventriloquist's dummies.

The dominant feminist position also insists upon an essential "real" self that is suppressed, distorted, and discriminated against by these institutions and the representations and standards they promote. Freed of these constraints, women would realize their true, multidimensional humanity. This notion of being claims a particular aesthetics, an aesthetics of the natural, that exists outside the "artificial" beauty standards imposed through consumerism and mass culture.

Only recently, since the mid-1980s, has a challenge to this perspective arisen within feminism. The impetus to reexamine this question came about particularly in the wake of the feminist "sex wars" over pornography and sexual practices. Gay and lesbian studies have been at the forefront of this challenge. Dissecting heterosexuality as a category and institution, queer theorists argue that notions of the natural, including a "natural" aesthetics, function to normalize sexual and gender difference. Analyses of camp, drag, and masquerade show the "constructedness," the inevitable artifice, of the relationship between appearance and identity. Judith Butler's work in particular theorizes this new understanding by revealing the performativity of gender, in her words, "an identity tenuously constituted in time [and] instituted through the stylization of the body." "Hence," she says, gender "must be understood as the mundane way in which bodily gestures, movement, and enactments of various kinds constitute the illusion of an abiding gendered self." It is also evident, at the level of cultural practice, that a political and cultural challenge to the earlier feminist aesthetic has occurred for many young lesbians and feminists, who are choosing to play with the conventions of beauty and fashion to destabilize simple expectations about appearance signifying gender and sexual identity. The phenomenon of the "lipstick lesbian," a *bricolage* of conventionally feminine dress and style, offers a direct answer to Una Stannard's claims about the psychology of oppression through beauty standards.[7]

This newer perspective suggests that the possibility of the "natural" has dissolved. It admits no conceptual space apart from consumer culture. Acknowledging that the culture of appearances, display, and "looks" is pervasive and inescapable—and, in important ways, pleasurable—it argues that one can only disrupt beauty standards from within. At the same time, this approach does not fully address the asymmetries in the power to establish the meanings of appearance, given the apparatus of the beauty industry; nor does it come to terms with the psychological and cultural effects of that apparatus on women.

\* \* \*

This feminist debate has taken place with little understanding of the historical context that gave rise to a culture in which beauty ideals and appearance practices are a dominant presence in women's daily lives. A brief look at that history suggests that the opposition between women's "natural" self and a self distorted by the pursuit of beauty long predates the current feminist debate. Scrutiny of the formative moment of modern beauty culture in the twentieth century also suggests that we analyze its production and consumption today with greater nuance and complexity. I will argue that, at the moment of its popular acceptance in the early twentieth century, cosmetics offered women a language with which they could articulate and mediate new demands, concerns, and desires whose terms were bound up in the changing social, economic, and cultural experiences of women. If one effect of the cosmetics industry was to create woman as merchandise or objectified spectacle, another was to destabilize nineteenth-century cultural hierarchies among women, open economic opportunities, and represent, however inadequately, new claims for social legitimacy.

Of all parts of the human body, the face in Western culture has been marked as particularly meaningful, a unique site of expression, beauty, and character. Indeed, nineteenth-century Americans believed in a "physiognomic paradigm," in which external appearance and internal self were commensurate. The "natural," unadorned face transparently revealed beauty and moral goodness. Advice literature and women's magazines advocated "moral cosmetics"—soap, exercise, and temperance—for the development of both character and beauty. This "natural face" was a cultural construction, integrated into a conscious self-presentation in which fashionable dress required such artifice as corsets and crinolines; women who scorned cosmetics nevertheless practiced "complexion management." The face, however, conveyed the fixity and essence of identity against the inconstancy and social nature of dress. Thus the "natural," as an aesthetic and moral category, oriented standards of beauty, respectability, and femininity in middle-class culture. These standards in turn contributed to the marking of bourgeois status. "Natural beauty" represented, and indeed stabilized, middle-class women's new identification with spiritual equality, domestic sovereignty, and sexual purity: the "true woman." [8]

Yet women's faces had long been in doubt—and cosmetics represented profound anxieties about women's identity and authenticity. Paint marked vices that for centuries had been associated with women: corrupt and uncontrolled sexuality, vanity, and deceit. The language of visible cosmetics drew upon older meanings—the painted woman as Jezebel—that tied powder and paint to this archetype. The stereotypical painted woman continued to be the prostitute, who brazenly advertised her immoral profession through the use of rouge, eye color, and lip paint. [9]

At the same time, this older notion of cosmetics was deployed to mark other social identities that were visible and troubling in the nineteenth century. Cosmetics use denoted inappropriate social and economic ambitions, ambitions that women, restricted in the labor force and in politics, might realize by turning beauty into power. Prescriptive literature condemned ultrafashionable, social-climbing women as "a compound frequently of false hair, false teeth, padding of various kinds, paint, powder, and enamel. Her face is touched up, or painted and lined by a professional adorner of women, and she utterly destroys the health of her skin by her foolish use of cosmetics."[10]

Visible cosmetics also marked the debasement of working-class women, who were already discursively linked to prostitution. In the urban North, some working women had developed a cultural style distinct from the aesthetic of the lady. Lowell mill girls, for example, rouged their cheeks as a sign of their independent new status. Yet in the prescriptive literature such practices were considered degrading. "A violently rouged woman is a disgusting sight," observed Lola Montez. "The excessive red on the face gives a coarseness to every feature, and a general fierceness to the countenance, which transform the elegant lady of fashion into a vulgar harridan."[11]

African-American women in slavery also bore the brunt of these prescriptions. While they may have used berries, herbs, and other substances to beautify the skin, those who dared to cross over into the white mistress's "sphere" of beauty and fashion were harshly punished. Delia Garlick, a former slave, recalled her mistress's reaction: "I seed [her] blackin' her eyebrows wid smut [soot] one day, so I thought I'd black mine jes' for fun. I rubbed some smut on my eyebrows an' forgot to rub it off, an' she kotched me. She was powerful mad an' yelled: 'You black devil, I'll show you how to mock your betters.'"[12] Especially disturbing was cosmetics' very instability as signs of identity and status: they could be applied more or less heavily and could be washed off.

By the late nineteenth century, hierarchies of beauty increasingly found expression in the racialist language of social Darwinism and anthropology. For nineteenth-century women of European descent, looking white had long been the height of facial beauty: the natural face was a white face. An advertisement for Hagan's Magnolia Balm captures succinctly the desirable look, in which a stereotyped rural woman, probably African-American, is miraculously transformed into a genteel white "lady" by the use of skin bleach. "Scientific" racial taxonomies reinforced these aesthetic judgments about facial beauty. Cosmetics, according to one commentator, were a "lingering taint of the savage and barbarous." In anthropologist Robert Shufeldt's classification of Indian types of beauty in 1891, the "most beautiful" Native American women were depicted according to the conventions of Victorian portraiture, the body seated, hands in lap, head tilted; the "ugliest" were photographed in the visual idiom of ethnography, their half-naked bodies posed frontally toward the camera, their hair and faces marked with the paint of the "savage."[13]

The nineteenth-century discourse, then, placed cosmetics outside a truthful representation of personal and social identity and identified cosmetics with disrepute, vanity, transgression, and a debased female "other." This was an effort to reinscribe the fixity and naturalness of gender identities. Still, deceit, artfulness, and the desire for beauty threatened to undermine this equation. Even before the extensive commercialization of beauty after 1890, many women used cosmetics—albeit covertly. Handwritten receipt (or recipe) books passed on from mother to daughter included simple moisturizing creams and cleansing lotions, while published household manuals contained formulas not only for skin care products but for paints, powders, and eye makeup.[14]

Moreover, in the post–Civil War decades, cultural tensions over women's "false faces" seem to have deepened substantially, resulting, for example, in warnings about prostitutes disguised as shoppers or saleswomen appearing to be "ladies" and in advice books to bachelors on how to tell authentic beauties from fakes. Some fashionable women embraced the transgressive qualities of cosmetics, part of a skillful performance that mediated respectability and the "fast" life. Ellen Ruggles Strong, the wife of civic leader George Templeton Strong, attended charity balls and receptions "painted like a wanton," according to the diarist Maria Lydig Daly. At an "old New York party" she ran into Ellen, "painted as usual, looking, as [a gentleman friend] said, however, very pretty and very young looking. 'It is well done,' said he. 'I can't see it.'" Daly's sharp reply: "Put on your glasses and thank Providence you are near-sighted, then."[15]

Constituting the self through appearance and gesture became

more visible *as performances* in the late nineteenth and early twentieth centuries, and this altered the way cosmetics were understood. What had been perceived as a falsifying, deceptive practice
began to be seen as self-presentation in a culture increasingly oriented to "looks," display, and spectatorship.[16] It is significant that
the first places where cosmetics use was justified, besides the professional stage, was in the photographer's studio, amateur theatricals, and large-scale balls. In photographer's galleries, women were
urged to understand their physiognomy, choose the appropriate
fashion, and use cosmetics to enhance the face. Sitters, in turn, demanded that the photographs themselves be "made up," a rosy
blush painted onto the cheeks. The changing cultural position of
actresses and professional "beauties" also suggests new measure-
ments of appearance. Performers like Adah Mencken blurred the
lines between the performance of a theatrical role and that of her
"real self"; at the same time, actresses brought theatricality into
everyday life, fostering a contentious debate over the use of blonde
hair dye and visible makeup. By the late nineteenth century, "ordinary" women wore makeup for amateur theatricals and *tableaux vi-
vants*. Cosmetics use was justified for coming-out parties, balls, and
theater-going, all of which involved public or semipublic display.[17]

It is in this context that the modern cosmetics industry arose.
In the late nineteenth century, a growing trade in cosmetics and
beauty products, reinforced by the proliferation of women's magazines, advice literature, and advertising, began to intervene in the
cultural discourse over facial truth and the hierarchy of beauty.
Pharmaceutical houses, beauty salons, drugstores, mail-order cata-
logs, and department stores created the infrastructure for beauty
culture. By the mid-1910s, many beauty products were being advertised in national magazines, and large firms were investing in
full cosmetics lines. Beauty commodities, moreover, were available
at every level of the social scale by this time, to urban immigrants,
African-Americans, and rural women, as well as to middle-class
and elite women—a "democratization" of the aspiration to beauty.

More than in any other area of economic life in the United
States at the time, women were a significant and formative presence in the beauty business, as entrepreneurs, manufacturers, dis-
tributors, and promoters. While men commanded perfumery, phar-

macy, and soap manufacture, women dominated the commercial beauty culture originating in hairdressing and beauty salons. With little capital, women set themselves up in business as beauty culturists, operating out of storefronts or their homes. Many developed their own products: the U.S. patent office registered over 450 trademarks for cosmetics produced by women, many from small towns in the Midwest and the South, from 1880 to 1920. Like Avon or Mary Kay representatives today, women sales agents sold products door-to-door and through home demonstrations. In a period when employment was a pressing problem for many women, beauty culture offered opportunities for steady work, genteel surroundings, and for some the chance to become independent proprietors.[18]

By the 1910s, women owned the leading firms selling to wealthy and upper-middle-class women and those selling to African-American women. The following three brief examples suggest the range of experiences and social origins of beauty entrepreneurs.

Harriet Hubbard Ayer, an early manufacturer of "elite" cosmetics, was born and married into wealth, and as a young woman led the life of a socialite. In 1883, however, when she was thirty-four, her dissipated husband Herbert failed in business and left Harriet to support herself and her two children. After working as a saleswoman and interior decorator in Chicago stores, she moved to New York and gained financial backing to produce and sell face cream. Her Recamier preparations, named after a French beauty of the Napoleonic era, proved to be very successful, at least initially.[19]

Helena Rubenstein, in contrast, came from a poor Jewish family in Austria. Her parents sent Helena to Australia to live with relatives, either because of an inappropriate love affair or to relieve the family of supporting her. In Australia she began to sell informally a cream compounded by an uncle who was a pharmacist; she established a small beauty shop in Melbourne, then successively grander establishments in Paris, London, and finally New York.[20] Other leading figures in the cosmetics industry, both women and men, were immigrants to the United States. Somewhat analogous to the movie industry, the beauty business opened opportunity for the socially and economically marginal, because established business and social elites perceived the trade as vulgar and insignificant.

Finally, there are the African-American entrepreneurs like Madame C. J. Walker. Madame Walker began life as Sarah Breedlove, the daughter of ex-slaves; she was born in Delta, Louisiana, in 1867, orphaned at age seven, married at fourteen, and widowed, with a child, at twenty. She worked in St. Louis as a domestic and laundress for eighteen years. Then, in 1903 or 1904, she developed Wonderful Hair Grower. Sarah moved to Denver in 1905 and married Charles Johnson Walker, a newspaperman and promoter, who helped her advertise and sell her "beauty system" door-to-door and through a mail-order business. She incorporated the business as the Walker Manufacturing Company in 1910; divorced Charles Walker in 1912; and built a large factory in Indianapolis. Walker salons appeared in cities across the country, while agents distributed products in small towns and rural areas. Walker explicitly promoted economic opportunity and independence for African-American women, emphasizing race pride and self-help in a segregated labor market. In speeches and advertising, she connected her efforts to provide as a single mother with the larger "struggle . . . to build up Negro womanhood."[21]

Beyond the cosmetics manufacturers themselves, a network of women as well as men legitimated and reinforced beauty culture. Advertising agencies frequently assigned women to write ad copy for beauty products; women promoted themselves as beauty experts, writing books, newspaper columns, and magazine articles on beauty; and, of course, movie actresses, models, and product demonstrators visually represented the made-up face. Nor were all these women the Tammy Faye Bakkers of their generation: many female ad writers, beauty editors, and public relations specialists identified themselves strongly as feminists and professional women. Helen Lansdowne Resor, for instance, was the brilliant advertising executive who spearheaded the Woodbury's facial soap and Pond's creams campaigns at the J. Walter Thompson Company; she aggressively hired and promoted women within the agency and organized the copywriters to march in the suffrage parades in New York along Fifth Avenue.[22]

What did these women (and men) offer consumers? Even more than the promise of beauty, I would argue that they promoted cosmetics as a means of remaking identity. They offered a system of signification that overturned the association of visible cosmetics with a degraded or false female self by attaching cosmetics to a rhetoric of personal transformation, of self-making—what we know today as the cosmetic "makeover." In American culture, being self-made has meant overcoming historical relationships of dependency through individual effort—the Horatio Alger myth. Self-making for women, however, focused upon self-presentation as the means to self-realization.

How this played out varied in the marketing strategies directed toward different groups of women. Elite cosmetics companies like Elizabeth Arden or Helena Rubinstein invoked status distinctions through fashionable cosmetics. Mass market advertisers, in contrast, suggested that women might use cosmetics to deny or rework traditional nineteenth-century cultural divisions. The Armand complexion powder campaign, for example, advised each woman to "find yourself," through the help of a "famous psychologist and a noted beauty expert." However, individuality was readily submerged into a typology that coded personality in terms of facial appearance and ethnic euphemisms; identities were no longer aligned with immigrant groups, but, rather, conceived as personal styles. Similarly, cosmetics advertisers overturned traditions of Victorian women's culture and the female life cycle. The Pompeian Company advertised its face cream in 1909 using sentimental Victorian images of an elderly mother and adult daughter. Its 1923 advertisements depicted the youthful modern mother, now no older than the 1909 daughter. "You're getting younger every day," observed her child quite accurately.[23]

In many respects, the promotion of cosmetics rested on a deepening emphasis on women as spectacles, as objects of the gaze of husbands, children, employers, and other women. But beauty advertisers and promoters also indicated that women might manage or control their appearances for their own purposes—to achieve success in the workplace, to enhance popularity in social activities, or to gain the right husband. These conflicting meanings and the new legitimacy of cosmetics in the consumer market must be seen in the context of women's relationship to other economies, particularly the labor market and the marriage market. Women's growing presence in the labor force generated anxiety that was frequently represented in bodily and sexual imagery. Indeed, a number of the new jobs open to women required particular attention to appearance. Saleswomen, waitresses, secretaries, entertainers, and others working in the clerical and service sectors transformed themselves into the physical "types" expected in these jobs. Even factory workers found themselves sorted into different kinds of labor based on the appearance of respectability, good grooming, and ethnic identity. The social and economic organization of sexuality and marriage similarly reinforced the importance of appearance in the early twentieth century. Dating and courtship increasingly occurred in a market context, within commercialized leisure and consumption activities where women could trade on their looks. Although the ideology of romantic love masked such exchange, it also promoted notions of personal magnetism and fascination that relied in part on enhanced physical appearance.

Finally, beauty commodities held particular importance for immigrant, working-class, and African-American women. These were the very groups against whom ideals of beauty had been defined in the nineteenth century. For women doubly or triply defined as "other" (as women and as nonwhite and/or lowerclass) beauty could become an arena in which issues not only of appearance but of personal, social, and even political identity were staged and discussed.

Immigrant and second-generation women, for example, frequently composed style and appearance as a language—a "hidden transcript"—for mediating the conditions of American life. Immigrant women's magazines like *Die Deutsche Hausfrau, Froyen Zhurnal,* and the *American Jewess* emphasized that *looking* like a lady aided assimilation. Advertisers certainly appealed to this concern. A 1924 trade advertisement for Zip depilatory, for instance, showed before-and-after photographs of a dark-skinned woman, her appearance suggesting an eastern or southern European immigrant. The images and copy made clear that such women could achieve social acceptance in the United States by ridding themselves of superfluous hair.[24] The egalitarian thrust of this advertisement was counterbalanced by a guilt-inducing and objectifying message.

At the same time, some young working-class women clearly enjoyed the theatricality and outrageous possibilities of cosmetics, incorporating them into a cultural performance that affirmed generational identity and challenged the authority of parents, employers, and school officials. Manufacturers of eye shadow and mascara, products long associated with prostitution, encouraged their association with cultural play and sexual fantasy. Maybelline placed ads in *Photoplay* that used glamorous and eroticized images of film stars to foster young women's identification with the product. Some young women delighted in *showing* the artifice—making up their faces in restaurants or pulling powder puffs out of their stocking tops at dance halls. The most extreme cosmetics users in the early 1920s were working-class truants and delinquents, whose elaborately painted faces involved a self-conscious imitation of their movie idols and explicit rejection of the stigmatizing label others placed on them as "problem girls" or "whores."[25]

African-American beauty culture also suggests the ways in which appearance could be a site for contesting identity and social hierarchy. Significantly, the African-American industry developed in the period of disfranchisement and deepening segregation in the South, worsening economic conditions, and black urban migration. The period is also notable for black women's individual and collective response to decades of abuse, poverty, and discrimination. An important part of this response was the public denunciation of stereotypes of black womanhood and the search for new kinds of self-representation.

This was certainly the view of Madame Walker, Annie Turnbo Malone, and other African-American beauty culturists who promoted a cosmetics-using, modern "New Negro Woman." Controversies over skin bleaches and hair straighteners within the black community heightened discussions over the relationship between aesthetics, racial hierarchies, and economic and social discrimination. The beauty culturists positioned themselves very, carefully, distancing themselves from the blatant racist appeals of white-owned companies to "look 5 or 6 shades lighter." Rather, they focused on the need to overturn stereotypes that reinforced social and sexual debasement. Underlining the centrality of appearance for personal opportunity and racial progress, one Walker ad observed: "Radiate an air of prosperity and who is to know if your purse is lined with gold or not? Personal cleanliness, neatness, whitened teeth, luxurious hair, a flawless complexion and dainty hands—these are the things that impress others and pave the way for your success by building confidence. Look your best. . . . you owe it to your race." Significantly, these ads linked African-American advancement with women's beauty and their economic and social empowerment.[26]

\* \* \*

By recovering what was at stake historically in the creation of beauty culture, my intention here has been to nudge the feminist debate on the politics of appearance in a direction away from simple moral readings of a male-dominated beauty industry and victimized women consumers. What might this history contribute to our thinking about beauty culture? First, we must begin to acknowledge the multiple meanings embedded in the various beautifying practices of women and to examine more closely who has the power to signify what these practices mean at any given time. The expression "to put on one's face" might mean an act of deception, a self-conscious performance, or a naturalizing confirmation of one's identity as a woman; it might also be, quite literally, a "put on," a parody. Few feminist scholars have thought to examine, historically or ethnographically, what it is women are doing with their faces and what it means to them when they put on cosmetics. In the early twentieth century, I argue here, cosmetics figured in, among other things, the representation of women's desire for cultural legitimacy, individuality, self-expression, and social participation. The seemingly magical or enchanted properties of such commodities— as agents of personal transformation—need to be examined not simply as advertisers' hype to putatively irrational or weak women but as part of a larger cultural system in which women participate.

Next, feminists' continuing use of the opposition between "natural" and "artifice" mystifies the ways in which, for women, cosmetics have become part of their embodiment, as other forms of adornment—clothing, hair styling, etc.—are for *both* women *and* men. It also obscures the way a "natural" aesthetic expresses class judgments, its essentialism reinforcing the legitimacy of bourgeois status. Since the early modern period, power and "display" have been inversely related: elite and bourgeois men rejected elaborate and decorative styles in favor of subdued and sober attire, in what is called by costume historians "the great masculine renunciation."[27] It remains the case today that colorful and "heavy" makeup, as well as "big" hair, are semiotic codes for working-class women and reinforce a middle-class perception of their "coarseness" and bad taste, their poor educational and social capital. Mike Nichols' motion picture *Working Girl* exemplifies the class-based reading of these visual codes, as the working-class heroine from Staten Island transforms herself into an arbitrageur by remaking herself in the image of her elite boss, with discreet makeup, short hair, and inconspicuous, well-tailored clothes. White middle-class feminists, from the Miss America protesters to Naomi Wolf, have not avoided this assumption.

Finally, this history suggests that feminist analyses of gender and consumption need to question the conceptual opposition between "industry" and "women." Historically, women were integral to the making of beauty culture. Understanding the dimensions of their agency and motives as producers and consumers, as well as the intended and unintended consequences of their actions, remains a crucial task for the "bodily politics" of feminism.

# NOTES

Some of the historical discussion in this paper appears in my essay "Making Up, Making Over: Cosmetics, Consumer Culture, and Women's Identity," in *The Sex of Things: Gender and Consumption in Historical Perspective*, Victoria de Grazia, ed., with Ellen Furlough (Berkeley: University of California Press, 1996).

1. Alice Echols, *Daring to Be Bad: Radical Feminism in America 1967–1975* (Minneapolis: University of Minnesota Press, 1989), pp. 92–96; Robin Morgan, "No More Miss America," in *Sisterhood Is Powerful: An Anthology of Writings From the Women's Liberation Move-*

*ment* (New York: Random House, 1970), pp. 584–588. See also Blanche Linden-Ward and Carol Hurd Green, *American Women in the 1960s: Changing the Future* (New York: Twayne, 1993), pp. 319–333.

2. Mary Russo, "Female Grotesques: Carnival and Theory," in *Feminist Studies/Critical Studies*, Teresa de Lauretis, ed. (Bloomington: Indiana University Press, 1986), pp. 214.

3. Sarah Stevenson, *The Physiology of Woman* (1881), quoted in Carroll Smith-Rosenberg, "The New Woman as Androgyne," in *Disorderly Conduct: Visions of Gender in Victorian America* (New York: Knopf, 1985), p. 263. On nineteenth-century feminists and fashion, see William R. Leach, *True Love and Perfect Union: The Feminist Reform of Sex and Society* (Middletown, CT: Wesleyan University Press, 1989).

4. Betty Friedan, *The Feminine Mystique* (New York: Norton, 1963); Dana Densmore, "On the Temptation to Be a Beautiful Object" (1968), in *Female Liberation*, Roberta Salter, ed. (New York, Knopf, 1972), pp. 204, 207; Una Stannard, "The Mask of Beauty," in *Woman in Sexist Society*, Vivian Gornick and Barbara K. Moran, eds. (New York: Basic Books, 1971), pp. 187–203 (quotes on pp. 200–201).

5. See the useful overview by Patrick Brantlinger, *Bread and Circuses: Theories of Mass Culture as Social Decay* (Ithaca, NY: Cornell University Press, 1983).

6. Naomi Wolf, *The Beauty Myth: How Images of Beauty Are Used Against Women* (New York: Morrow, 1991). See also Wendy Chapkis, *Beauty Secrets: Women and the Politics of Appearance* (Boston: South End Press, 1986).

7. Judith Butler, "Performative Acts and Gender Constitution: An Essay in Phenomenology and Feminist Theory," *Theatre Journal* 40 (December 1988): 519–531; Butler, *Gender Trouble: Feminism and the Subversion of Identity* (New York: Routledge, 1990). See also Dianna Fuss, ed., *Inside/Out: Lesbian Theories/Gay Theories* (New York: Routledge, 1991). On lesbian style, see Arlene Stein, "All Dressed Up, But No Place to Go? Style Wars and the New Lesbianism," *Out/Look* (Winter 1989): 34–44.

8. Karen Halttunen, *Confidence Men and Painted Women* (New Haven, CT: Yale University Press, 1982), pp. 56–91; Joanne Finkelstein, *The Fashioned Self* (Philadelphia: Temple University Press, 1991), pp. 15–77; Allan Sekula, "The Body and the Archive," *October 39* (Winter 1986): 3–64. See also Jennifer Jones, "The Taste for Fashion and Frivolity," Ph.D. dissertation, Princeton University, 1991. For examples of "complexion management," see Mrs. A. Walker, *Female Beau-*

ty (New York: Scofield and Voorhies, 1840), pp. 286–300, and color plates.

9. Frances E. Dolan, "Taking the Pencil Out of God's Hand: Art, Nature, and the Face-Painting Debate in Early Modern England," *PMLA* 108 (March 1993): 224–239; Annette Drew-Bear, "Cosmetics and Attitudes Toward Women in the Seventeenth Century," *Journal of Popular Culture* 9 (Summer 1975): 31–37. On the image of prostitutes, see Christine Stansell, *City of Women* (New York: Knopf, 1986), 187–188; Mariana Valverde, "The Love of Finery: Fashion and the Fallen Woman in 19th Century Social Discourse," *Victorian Studies* 32 (Winter 1989): 169–188.

10. James D. McCabe, *Lights and Shadows of New York Life* (Philadelphia: National Publishing, 1872), p. 154; George Ellington, *The Women of New York* (1869; reprint, New York: Arno Press, 1972), pp. 42–51, 82–90.

11. Lola Montez, *The Arts of Beauty* (New York: Dick and Fitzgerald, 1853), pp. 48–49.

12. George P. Rawick, ed., *The American Slave: A Composite Autobiography*, Vol. 6 (Westport, CT: Greenwood, 1972), p. 130; Vertamae Smart-Grosvenor, "The Beauty Quest," *Essence* (May 1985): 154–155.

13. Lyon's Manufacturing Company, "The Secret of Health and Beauty," pamphlet, Warshaw Collection, Archives Center, National Museum of American History, Smithsonian Institution, Washington, DC; Harry T. Finck, *Romantic Love and Personal Beauty* (New York: Macmillan, 1887), p. 458; Robert W. Shufeldt, *Indian Types of Beauty*, pamphlet reprinted from *The American Field* (1891), in Department of Rare Books and Manuscripts, Kroch Library, Cornell University.

14. For examples of unpublished receipt books, see those of Mrs. Lowell and Mrs. Charles Smith, Garrison Family Papers, MS Group 60, Sophia Smith Collection, Smith College, Northampton, MA. For examples of published household manuals and beauty guides, see E. G. Storke, ed., *The Family and Householder's Guide* (Auburn, NY: Auburn Publishing, 1859), and *Etiquette for Ladies* (Philadelphia: Lea and Blanchard, 1841); for other works, see Eleanor Lowenstein, *Bibliography of American Cookery Books, 1742–1860* (Worcester, MA: American Antiquarian Society, 1972), and the extensive collection at the American Antiquarian Society, Worcester, MA.

15. Harold Earl Hammond, ed., *Diary of a Union Lady, 1861–1865* (New York: Funk and Wagnalls, 1962), pp. 123, 321–322, 331–332.

16. See Lois Banner, *American Beauty* (Chicago: University of Chicago Press, 1983); Robert C. Allen, *Horrible Prettiness: Burlesque and*

*American Culture* (Chapel Hill: University of North Carolina Press, 1991); John Kasson, *Rudeness and Civility: Manners in Nineteenth Century Urban America* (New York: Hill and Wang, 1990); William Leach, *Land of Desire: Merchants, Power, and the Rise of a New American Culture* (New York: Pantheon, 1993).

17. See, e.g., H. J. Rodgers, *Twenty-Three Years Under a Sky-Light* (Hartford, CT: H. J. Rodgers, 1872); *New-York Times* (November 22, 1868): 3; Olive Logan, *Apropos of Women and Theaters* (New York: Carleton, 1869).

18. Associated Manufacturers of Toilet Articles, *Trade-marks for Perfumes, Toilet Articles, and Soaps* (New York: AMTA, 1925). On women sales agents in beauty culture, see, e.g., George Gaspar, "The California Perfume Company," *Collector's Showcase* 6 (July/August 1987): 62–67; California Perfume Company, *For Beauty's Toilet* (New York: California Perfume Co., 1898), Bella C. Landauer Collection, New-York Historical Society, New York. Bertha Benz to Miss Prim, February 21, 1893, James King Wilkerson Papers, Manuscripts Collection, Perkins Library, Duke University, Durham, NC.

19. "Harriet Hubbard Ayer," *Notable American Women, 1607–1950*, Edward T. James, ed. (Cambridge, MA: Harvard University Press, 1971), Vol. 1, pp. 72–74; Henry E. Hamilton, "Harriet Hubbard Ayer," *Personal Reminiscences of Henry E. Hamilton*, manuscript, c. 1915, Chicago Historical Society; Frances E. Willard and Mary A. Livermore, *A Woman of the Century* (1893; reprint, Detroit: Gale Research, 1967), p. 41.

20. Helena Rubenstein, *My Life for Beauty* (London: Bodley Head, 1965); also her *The Art of Feminine Beauty* (New York: Horace Liveright, 1930). Margaret Allen, *Selling Dreams: Inside the Beauty Business* (New York: Simon and Schuster, 1981); Patrick O'Higgins, *Madame: An Intimate Biography of Helena Rubenstein* (New York: Viking Press, 1971).

21. National Negro Business League, *Report of the Fifteenth Annual Convention*, p. 152. Gwendolyn Robinson, "Class, Race, and Gender: A Transcultural Theoretical and Sociohistorical Analysis of Cosmetic Institutions and Practices to 1920," Ph.D. dissertation, University of Illinois at Chicago, 1984; A'Lelia Perry Bundles, *Madam C. J. Walker* (New York: Chelsea House, 1991); Madame C. J. Walker Papers, Indiana Historical Society, Indianapolis.

22. See "Interview with Margaret King Eddy and Sidney R. Bernstein," Box 1, and Personnel Information, Box 4, Sidney Bernstein Papers, RG3; Applications for Employment, Frances Maule, September 27, 1920, and Therese Olzendam, May 9, 1919, in Personnel Records, all

in the J. Walter Thompson Advertising Archives, Manuscript Collections, Perkins Library, Duke University.

23. Armand Complexion Powder ad proofs, 1929, N. W. Ayer Collection, Archives Center, National Museum of American History. Pompeian Massage Cream advertisements, *Women's Home Companion* (November 1909), and *Pictorial Review* (October 1923). For a fuller discussion, see Kathy Peiss, "Making Faces: The Cosmetics Industry and the Cultural Construction of Gender, 1890–1930," *Genders 7* (Spring 1990): 143–169.

24. Zip advertisement, *Toilet Requisites* (April 1924).

25. Maybelline advertisements, *Photoplay* (1920). Kathy Peiss, *Cheap Amusements: Working Women and Leisure in Turn-of-the-Century New York* (Philadelphia: Temple University Press, 1986); Mary Odem, "Single Mothers, Delinquent Daughters, and the Juvenile Court in Early 20th Century Los Angeles," *Journal of Social History* 25 (September 1991): 33–37.

26. "Amazing Progress of Colored Race," two-page Madam C. J. Walker advertisement, *Oklahoma Eagle* (March 3, 1928), clipping in Box 262, f4, Claude Barnett Collection, Chicago Historical Society.

27. For a brilliant discussion, see David Kuchta, "Inconspicuous Consumption: Masculinity, Political Economy and Fashion in England, 1550–1776," Ph.D. dissertation, University of California at Berkeley, 1991.

# From "Trained Gorilla" to "Humanware": Repoliticizing the Body–Machine Complex Between Fordism and Post-Fordism

Ernest J. Yanarella

Herbert G. Reid

## INTRODUCTION

In his celebrated essay "Americanism and Fordism," Antonio Gramsci (1971) mused over the social and cultural consequences of the transition from craft to mass production introduced in the automobile industry by Henry Ford in the United States and slowly taken shape with considerable resistance in western Europe, including Italy. With a familiarity with the content and import of Frederick Winslow Taylor's scientific management practices and Henry Ford's production and management techniques far surer and more subtle than one might expect from someone rotting in a Fascist prison, Gramsci sought to trace the shift toward Taylorism and

Fordism and their promise of installing a "new way of life," a "new culture," "new methods of work," a "new sexual ethic," even and especially a "new type of worker."

Taking Gramsci's analysis of the dawning of Fordism as a critical but hopeful model of the internal transformation of industrial capitalism in the West, this chapter explores the continuities and ruptures unfolding in the crisis of Fordism in late-twentieth-century capitalism for insights into the changing conceptions of industrial production, labor–management relations, power, work, gender, and sexuality in the mind–body percept of the new worker inhabiting this putative new regime of accumulation and its accompanying mode of production and consumption variously called post-Fordism and lean production. Drawing upon the postmodern writings of John O'Neill, Renate Holub, Hubert L. Dreyfus, Donna Haraway, David Harvey, Martha Banta, and Chantal Mouffe and Ernesto Laclau, among others, this *post*-Marxist/post-*Marxist* reading of the changing structure of hegemony within the automobile industry (historically, the locus of the eruption of Fordism after 1910) raises critical issues about the body of the laboring subject as the multiple site of political struggle to recuperate the democratic core from the largely illusory claims of management theorists and even left academicians about post-Fordism.

Its particular focus will be on the changing boundaries of the animal–human interface, the mind–body percept, and the body–machine complex in the emergence of the Taylorized and then Fordist worker and its incipient successor under post-Fordism under the rubric of the worker as "humanware." Through an examination of the underlying continuities between Fordism and post-Fordism, this chapter will explore the impact and costs of the American body–machine complex to the development of a new politics of democratic politics, culture, and workplace.

### GRAMSCI, TAYLOR, AND FORD: THE EMERGING WORKER AND THE LABORING BODY IN THE FORDIST REGIME

Gramsci's classic text on the making of the Taylorized body and the emergence of Fordism as a hegemonic ideology and a new regime of accumulation simultaneously beckons and repels the late-twen-tieth-century knower-actor confronting the localizing and globaliz-ing, the fragmenting and restructuring, tendencies in political economy and culture reverberating throughout the global village of the dawning information age. Penetrating insight and subtlety of theoretical grasp of an inchoate problematic are combined with es-sentialist residues and optimistic, almost automatic, expectations of a modernist Marxism that his hegemonic theory of power strove to, but could not entirely, surpass. As we will see, these limitations ultimately vitiated its role as both a theory of Fordism and a guide to post-Fordist tendencies in evidence today.

Benefiting from the historically grounded theoretical musings of later students of Fordism and Taylorism, a post-Marxist reading of Gramsci's apprehension of the Fordist worker shows his keen sensitivity to the new borderlines between the animal and the hu-man, the mind and the body, and the human and machine being carved out by the inchoate tendencies of Fordism.

## The Animal–Human and Human–Machine Interface: The Laboring Body and the Problem of Animality in the Taylorist–Fordist Factory

Gramsci and other students of Fordism who have commented on the boundary shifts and transgressions inscribed by the Taylor text demonstrate the many ambivalences of Frederick Winslow Taylor toward the laboring subject in this dawning era. Although his sci-entific management project would heavily shape the contours of the Fordist enterprise, Taylor's effort to redraw the boundaries be-tween animal and human and human and machine would run aground of a simplistic model of human nature. As a result, his rhetorical or narratological strategy for legitimizing these shifting boundaries and representations would ultimately yield an inade-quate ideological strategy of minimalist hegemony.

In two essays, "Americanism and Fordism" and "The Intellec-tuals," Gramsci is moved to quote Taylor's oft-cited characteriza-tion of the worker as "trained gorilla." In the former, he contextu-alizes this reference as a concrete example of the extent to which Fordist and Taylorist work rationalization and Americanist puri-tanical initiatives like the Five-Dollar Day were intended as "the biggest collective effort to date to create, with unprecedented speed, and with a consciousness of purpose unmatched in history, a new type of worker and of man" (Gramsci, 1971, p. 302). While Gramsci notes the irony of juxtaposing the phrase "consciousness of purpose" with the idea of the new worker as trained gorilla, he sees in Taylor's design a cynical drive simultaneously to develop "in the worker to the highest degree automatic and mechanical attitudes, breaking up the old psycho-physical nexus of qualified professional work, which demands a certain active participation of intelligence, fantasy and initiative on the part of the worker, and reducing productive operations exclusively to the mechanical, physical aspect" (p. 302).

At one and the same time, then, the worker is reduced to his physical animality while his bodily operations are pushed to new levels of mechanization. The emphasis that Taylor places on the animal dimension of the new worker in his gorilla metaphor is easy to (dis)miss, since the Taylorization of work tends to foreground the mechanistic facet of work rationalization. For Gramsci, it is a matter of acknowledging the extent to which "the history of industrialism has been a continuing struggle . . . against the element of 'animality' in man" (p. 298). This recognition leads him, unfortunately, to the extreme position of interpreting this process as essentially a historical given, seeing it as "an uninterrupted, often painful and bloody process of subjugating natural (i.e., animal and primitive) instincts to new, more complex and rigid norms and habits of order, exactitude and precision which can make possible the increasingly complex forms of collective life which are the necessary consequence of industrial development" (p. 298). But, in the latter essay, Gramsci himself concedes that Taylor's characterization is better understood as a metaphor pointing to a limit to work rationalization and human degradation—or, in his words, to the fact that "in any physical work, even the most degraded and mechanical, there exists a minimum of technical qualification, that is, a minimum of creative intellectual activity" (p. 8).

In redrawing the lines between the animal and the human and the human and the machine, Taylor was acutely aware and deeply fearful of the animal or instinctual in the worker. Far from subjugating or sublating that natural substratum, Taylor evidences in the many stories populating his manuals on scientific management of the shop floor a concern for, even an obsession with, the instinctual or animal in human beings. Indicative of this fixation, as Banta (1993) and Seltzer (1992) note, is the fact that Taylor's instructional narratives on the new worker under the regime of scientific management continually revert to the telling of beast fables. These beast fables, we would argue, at once symbolically acknowledge and ideologically camouflage the wild, irrational, animal side of human nature as understood and feared by Taylor.

In his continuing stories and references to workers as dray horses, trotting horses, saddle horses, ponies, and birds (Taylor, "Testimony," 1947b, pp. 157, 172–176, 179–180), Taylor insists that he is merely developing such analogies to distinguish between "first-class" and "second-class" laborers without intending to degrade workers (p. 157). Yet Banta's deconstruction of these beast analogies is closer to the truth in highlighting the threatening nature of animalistic or irrational excess in humankind and in seeing Taylor's deployment of these metaphors and stories as a strategy of containment. For Taylor, this savage element and these wild facts continually threaten to introduce onto the shop floor circumstances that would subvert the hope of instituting efficient and ordered management systems into factory production. But instead of revising the orientation, theories, and goals of scientific management in light of the messiness of humankind and its manifold behavior, "'uncouth forms' were expected to do the adjusting: this included all nature of men, but especially women, children, blacks, and immigrants—those social elements designated as the irrational forces requiring careful containment" (Banta, 1993, p. 28). Later human relations specialists, learning from Taylor's mistakes and terrors, would revise his simplistic conceptualization of human nature and introduce more complex assumptions and motivations for the purpose of installing more sophisticated techniques of managerial authority and social control (Noble, 1977, p. 275).

Taylor's problem with coping with the animal dimension of human nature then stemmed in part from his elementary model of human nature. That portrait sees the worker as an animal who thinks and uses language and is primarily motivated by economic (largely monetary) incentives. In entwining a degraded animality with a refined mechanization of the laboring body, Taylor must confront the reality that the worker can reason and communicate through language and therefore cannot be tamed merely through simple coercive instruments of instinctual modification and habit training appropriate to "dumb" animals. The strategy of the discipline of scientific management in taming the animal who thinks and talks is at least twofold. First, Taylorism strives to affect a "mental revolution" in the Fordist worker before the binary division of the corporate body into brain (management) and brawn (labor) by convincing the worker of the superiority of these new scientific techniques in terms of efficiency and productivity and of their greater profitability—not only for corporate management but also for the laborer as well (Taylor, "Shop Management," 1947b, p. 131). Arguing that "nine-tenths of improvements from scientific management have come from cooperative workers" (p. 148), Taylor aims to persuade workers that giving up the secrets of worker shop floor skills and techniques to their appropriation and rationalization by management will lead to happier, more well-paid employees despite the introduction through scientific management of greater regimentation and work discipline into the labor process. In addition, this mental revolution, if successful, will eliminate the natural tendency of workers to engage in individual and collective forms of soldiering (i.e., trimming on the job). Finally, the felt need of a growing number of workers for collective representation of interests through labor unions will be overcome by a recognition of the identity of interests of management and workers.

These rhetorical/narratological devices in the propagation of scientific management in public and in the ideological indoctrination of workers are epitomized in the popular Schmidt anecdote (Taylor, "The Principles of Scientific Management," 1947b, pp. 43–47). Of all the stories fabricated and countlessly retold by Taylor, no other so captured the popular imagination as this story of inspiration and instruction. In reviewing this partly true, partly fictional narrative to identify the essential elements of scientific management, the reader is struck not only by the patronizing tone of Taylor the Teacher's carefully guided pedagogical exercise but also by its authoritarian certitude and manipulative orientation toward this "mentally sluggish" little Pennsylvanian Dutchman (p. 46).

Interestingly, absent from the story is any acknowledgment of the origins of Schmidt's heightened productivity residing in management's appropriation of earlier workers' most valuable possession—worker knowledge of the tacit and explicit skills of production. Also evident is the resort to enhanced financial remuneration as the basic carrot to induce slow-witted Schmidt to worker harder and more efficiently.

Scientific management's "total mental revolution" promoted by the aphorisms, homilies, and anecdotes of Taylorism as an "extended narrative structure and discourse system" (Banta, 1993, p. 4) is complemented and reinforced by the revolution in representing the laboring body on the model of a machine brought about by Taylor. As Banta has cogently argued, the stakes and consequences of this second revolution were high indeed:

> The very presence of people on the factory floor is enough to introduce questions of the troublesome relations among reform, conduct, and control. Yet determined efforts were made to close the gap between theories of efficient production and the effect of those practices upon the bodies involved. It was argued that not only would machine and human muscle be as one but that the machine was the great emancipator of mind and soul as well. (p. 27)

Thus, the progressivist, reformist thrust of Taylor's efficiency and uplift philosophy (Tichi, 1987, p. 81; Haber, 1964) should not be lost sight of, even in the face of its brutalizing impact upon the laboring body.

Here, Taylor's revolution in re-presenting the body must be distinguished from the European science of work movement. Anson Rabinbach has noted both the similarities and differences between the two. One striking affinity was their shared image of work and their single-minded focus on the body rather than the social relations of production in the workplace as "the arena of labor power" (Rabinbach, 1990, p. 11). Likewise, each school began with the breaking down of work into ever more discrete and calculable subtasks and routines that could be measured in terms of quantitative indices (time, motion, work units, fatigue, etc.). Both saw the solution to alleviating social ferment and labor troubles in the factory as modernizing industry and increasing productivity. Above all, Taylorism and the European science of work movement "shared the utopian hope that it was possible to resolve industrial conflict scientifically and rationally in the interests of economic progress" (p. 243).

The scientific management school departed from its European counterpart, however, in a number of crucial respects. First, whereas the science of work school was premised on the assumption that social justice and heightened happiness were the direct result of fostering job satisfaction and increased productivity, Taylorism was less sanguine about the prospects of making industrial work less alienating and more satisfying to the laborer and instead sought to compensate the worker for the negative consequences of work rationalization through monetary dividends—i.e., higher wages—and rewards of leisure and increased consumption of value outside the workplace. Second, because the European school's starting point was the metaphor of the worker's body as a human motor and its focal interest in the physiology of labor lay in reducing fatigue by uncovering the laws of muscles, nerves, and the efficient use of human energy, one of its larger goals was the preservation of the worker's energy in the interest of human well-being and social harmony, whereas Taylorism clearly sided with management objectives of cutting costs and maximizing profits through the increase and intensification of productivity of the individual worker and enterprise (pp. 242–243). No less significant, the hero of the Taylor system was the plant engineer, whereas the European school appealed to scientists studying human physiology and early ergonomists.

The gospel of efficiency preached by Taylor, of course, had its major impetus in the Progressive era's efforts to promote natural resource conservation. Interestingly, Taylor both drew upon this conservationist spirit and attracted exponents and followers of this turn-of-the-century movement. In his introduction to his primer on scientific management, Taylor intones the words of President Theodore Roosevelt on the necessity of conserving America's natural resources and borrows upon Roosevelt's appeal to "the larger question of increasing our national efficiency" (cited in Taylor, 1947a, p. 5) to legitimize his program promoting the principles and axioms of systematic or scientific management. Much could be made of the deeper affinities between the conservationist's objective to protect and preserve scarce natural resources and to eliminate waste and inefficiency in their use and Taylorism's objective to conserve human energy and promote efficiency in the workplace of the dawning "gear-and-girder world" of the twentieth century (e.g., Hays, 1969; Tichi, 1987; Humphrey and Buttel, 1982) . But beneath these parallels between natural resource and industrial efficiencies lies a deeper, more profound cultural association.

Drawing upon a subtle reading and appreciation of the cultural/ideological genesis of the Boy Scouts movement articulated in its founding statements and first handbook, Mark Seltzer has shown how the Woodcraft movement in the United States emerged out of the anxieties over the enervating consequences of the emerging Fordist production and its machine culture. In a system that transforms energetic, self-reliant boys into nervous, chain-smoking shells of manhood with questionable vitality, the only solution to this flight toward bodily exhaustion and moral degeneracy for the Scouting movement founders, Ernest Thompson Seton and Robert Baden-Powell, was the physical regeneration of the male body that involves the spawning of a recreation (re-creation) movement that, taking its inspiration from Teddy Roosevelt and Progressive conservationism, links together male bodybuilding and nation building—processes understood as twins (Seltzer, 1992, pp. 149–150). The regeneration of the male natural body, for Scouting, entailed a double regimen of physical activity and character building, with at least as much emphasis on the latter as the former. Pointing to the evident isomorphism between character and work in industrial America at this time, Seltzer observes that the Boy Scouts itself "is something of a model of uniform, and uniformed mass production" (p. 153) and that "the character factory, like the [Fordist-Taylorist] factory, standardizes the making of men, coordinating the body and the machine within a single system of regulation and production" (p. 154). In so doing, Scouting and Taylorism become housed under a single regime of production such that "these technologies of regeneration, of man in the making, make visible the rewriting of the natural and of the natural body in the idiom of scientific management, systems of measurement and standardization, and the disciplines of the machine process" (p. 154).

In the Taylor text, then, the "American body/machine complex" (Seltzer, 1992) shifted the boundaries of the human–technology interface heavily toward the machine ideal. For Taylor and his successors, the laboring body was extensively analyzed by time and motion studies via the stopwatch and camera that dissected the movement of the body in motion on the shop floor and searched out extraneous motion or expenditure of excess energy, thereby reducing the body into a set of standardized machinelike components capable of discipline and refinement through correct training and constant monitoring. This mechanization of the body was accompanied by the rationalization and degradation of human skills cultivated under the auspices of craft production.

Under the artisanal work regime, the craftsperson's skill was intimately anchored in the human body and formed the basis of the craft laborer's authority in setting the pace and controlling the design of the product. Long apprenticeships with skilled craftspeople were seen as necessary to hone these artisanal skills through tutelage by mentors whose instruction and bodily example communicated them through both explicit and tacit means. Although craft work did not shun explicit measurement, the corporeal basis of craft skills often led to a dependence upon unformalized (but communicable) "rule-of-thumb" methods in the production of craft wares. This, in turn, meant that the products of craftsmanship involved slight human variations in each product—deviations that often enhanced the value of these products because they etched the personal stamp of the individual artisan on the item or made each product in a sense unique. Both rule-of-thumb operations and human variation were common targets of Taylor's scientific management approach.

Abjuring the artisan's deference to corporeal rule-of-thumb methods and the tacit skills underlying them, Taylor strove to formulate an exacting and wholly explicit science of skills. In attacking the artisan's monopoly over craft knowledge and its largely unformalized nature and tacitly communicated means of transfer, the managerial bias of Taylor's science of skills is readily apparent. Less obvious perhaps is the way his project succumbs to the objectivist myth of complete formalization of methods and skills. Believing that rule-of-thumb skills lead to inefficiency, decreased output, and variable products (Taylor, "The Principles of Scientific Management," 1947b, pp. 16, 24–25, 36, 39), scientific management struggled to find the "one best way" through expropriation, objectification, disassembly, formalization, streamlining, and reassembly of work tasks and the means for their performance into the "objectively" single best method. This process, beginning with the analysis and appropriation of workers' traditional knowledge and ending in "classifying, tabulating, and reducing this knowledge to rules, laws, and formulae" (p. 36), is founded upon the objectivist assumption that knowledge can be made totally explicit and formal.

Building on the vital contributions of Martin Heidegger, Maurice Merleau-Ponty, and Michael Polanyi and their interest in how human beings use tools, Dreyfus (1979) has insisted on the role of the body in intelligent behavior, arguing that "man's skillful bodily activity as he works to satisfy his needs generates the human world" (p. 281; see also Chapt. 7 and 8). More recently, Mark Johnson's study *The Body in the Mind* (1987) has explored "the way meaning and rationality are grounded in recurring structures of embodied human understanding" (p. 209). Contrary to the objectivist vision of abstract reason and its dualist view of experience, objectivity is "made possible by the public nature of image-schematic and basic-level structures of understanding, and the metaphoric and metonymic projections based upon them" (p. 212). This alternative perspective illuminating the bodily basis of meaning, imagination, and reason has momentous implications for the corporate state's body–machine complex: it evokes the historic-specific horizons of the technological world-picture and liberal individualism. It also enables more effective concepts of responsibility and justice, as technobureaucratic mystification is replaced by resituating machine intelligence in newly authorized structures of human intelligence. Nevertheless, as Dreyfus indicated a good many years ago, a crisis is upon us:

> People have begun to think of themselves as objects able to fit into the inflexible calculations of disembodied machines: machines for which the human form-of-life must be analyzed into

meaningless facts, rather than a field of concern organized by sensory-motor skills. Our risk is not the advent of superintelligent computers, but of subintelligent human beings. (1979, p. 280)

## The Mind–Body Percept: The Fordist Worker (Some Dis-/Reassembly Required), the Corporate Body, and the Body Politic

The Taylor text, as we have seen, oscillates between the animal and machine in the laboring subject, only reluctantly conceding the rational and other qualities of the worker as human. Gramsci's "Americanism and Fordism" evinced great concern over the impact of brutalizing forces of the newly instituted rationalizing systems impinging upon the worker's psychophysical processes and restricting human drives and instincts—forces and processes generating, in Renate Holub's words, "a pathological crisis" (1992, p. 114). In this dawning age of mass production and work rationalization, Gramsci observes:

> American industrialists are concerned to maintain the continuity of the physical and muscular-nervous efficiency of the worker. It is in their interest to have a stable, skilled labour force, a permanently well-adjusted complex, because the human complex (the collective worker) of an enterprise is also a machine which cannot, without considerable loss, be taken to pieces too often and renewed with single new parts. (1971, p. 303)

The problem, the anomaly, the crisis of Taylorism is, as we have argued, that the worker is an animal who thinks and talks. The minimalist hegemony of the Taylor text is insufficient to address and circumvent this problem. In Gramsci's view, Henry Ford remedied this problem by educating his workers into the doctrine of Americanism (Gramsci, 1971, pp. 303–306, 311–312; see also Holub, 1992, pp. 114–115). In amending the Taylor text, Ford inaugurated a maximalist strategy of hegemony for more fully integrating the new worker into the American body politic and its twentieth-century corporate economy. But the Ford innovations in mass production involved not only recuperating the human domain of the laboring body; it included some horrific insights into the impact of unfolding technology into the slaughter and dressing of animals for human consumption (as discussed below).

It is a commonplace among historians and cultural critics of Henry Ford and Fordist mass production (e.g., Hughes, 1989; Meyer, 1981; Tichi, 1987; Banta, 1993) that Ford's genius lay less in the realm of invention than in the process of systematizing the piecemeal innovations of others into a coherent whole not prefigured by any of the parts. Perhaps surprisingly, other observers of the genealogy of Fordism suggest the cultural ideal of the American body–machine complex and the political ideal of the American(ist) citizen may be found in the animal origins of the Fordist assembly line.

If the essence of mass assembly line production, the product of Ford's contribution to American and eventually world industry, is continuous flow or uninterrupted production within a single, integrated factory or production process, that essential idea must be traced back to its origins prior to the crystallization of industrialization in the United States. Sigfried Giedion (1948) has shed considerable light on the mass assembly line's precursors in the contributions of Oliver Evans' mechanized grain mill in 1783, the British naval arsenal's biscuit production process in Deptford, England, in 1804, and Johann Georg Bodmer's traveling crane invented to convey products in the assemblage process in 1839. But a unified production process was first fully achieved and implemented in the meatpacking industry in Cincinnati and then Chicago after the late 1830s, and it is to the slaughterhouse and to the disassembly of pigs into varieties and cuts of pork that we must look for the genesis and spirit of the Ford auto assembly plant.

As early as the 1850s, observers like Frederick Law Olmsted in his travels through the Midwest were struck by the minute division of labor, mechanization of work, and mechanized processes of Cincinnati's packinghouses even without the benefit of gears and cogwheels. Some years later, Max Weber visited the Chicago stockyards and was stunned and appalled by the pace, intensity, and systematization of the disassembly process:

> From the moment when the unsuspecting bovine enters the slaughtering area, is hit by a hammer and collapses, whereupon

it is immediately gripped by an iron clamp, is hoisted up, and starts its journey, it is in constant motion—past ever-new workers who eviscerate and skin it, etc., but are always (in the rhythm of work) tied to the machine that pulls the animal past them. . . . There one can follow a pig from the sty to the sausage and the can. (Weber, 1975, p. 287)

Viewing Chicago as the "crystallization of the American spirit" (p. 285) and the stockyards as a token of modernity, Weber's wife Marianne quotes her husband as exclaiming, "Look, this is what modern reality is like" (p. 287).

The contributions of the techniques and processes of the slaughterhouse to modern assembly line production were hastened in spite of—or perhaps because of—the fact that the slaughterhouse was inhospitable to full mechanization. That is, given the organic, irregular character of the hog, "all the essential operations in the mass production of pressed meat have to be performed by hand" (Giedion, 1948, p. 94). Ironically, because of the surplus labor extant in the early twentieth century due to waves of mass immigration from Europe to America, Henry Ford and his engineering staff were able to refine and introduce these assembly line techniques transferred from the meatpacking industry so quickly because automobile production was (or could be) so labor-intensive and because the slaughtering and processing of pigs had already been marked by considerable of assembly line experience and scores of incremental innovations.

Giedion chooses to interpret this chapter in an anonymous history of mechanization and modernity in terms of the limits or boundaries of mechanization of death. For him, the slaughterhouse testifies to the fact that death cannot be completely mechanized but instead must remain with the knife guided by the trained hand orchestrated by the organization of human labor on the (dis)assembly line, a process where "death cries and mechanical noises are almost impossible to distinguish" (p. 246). The speedy integration of the assembly line into automobile production from roughly 1902 to 1913 points to the precipitation of the "labor problem" (a codeword for worker alienation and workplace injuries), which in turn spawned the progressivist efforts of Ford and his sociology department to the Lee reforms and then the Five-Dollar Day program.

Gramsci's modernist impulse evidenced in his ultimate reconciliation with Fordism in his classic essay is surely a weak point in his often subtle treatment of this emergent accumulation regime and vitiates his critical analysis. Despite his Marxist mooring, Gramsci unreflectively seems to fuse illicit assumptions from René Descartes's mind–body dualism and Kantian notions of freedom with a dialectical Marxism that can accommodate neither successfully. In two noted passages in "Americanism and Fordism," Gramsci suggests that the new forces of production will issue in a "forced selection" where "a part of the old working class will be pitilessly eliminated from the world of labour" (p. 303); yet, he optimistically continues, while the bloody and mind-numbing rationalization of production brought on by Fordism and Taylorism will exact its toll on the worker's body, "once the process of adaptation has been completed, what really happens is that the brain of the worker, far from being mummified, reaches a state of complete freedom" (p. 309)

Gramsci deploys these arguments, as subsequent passages reveal, to undercut Taylor's image of the worker as "trained gorilla" and to open up the space for the emergence of revolutionary working-class consciousness. Yet this Kantian notion of absolute freedom in the midst of seeming complete bodily subjugation outlined by Gramsci works against his more sophisticated theory of hegemonic struggle in a new politics of civil society and a much broader range of lived relations. (Was he perhaps seeking in this argument some philosophically regressive surcease from his own imprisonment while writing these notes?) The other reason for unfolding this line of argumentation was to set up his discussion of the components of Ford's maximalist hegemonic strategy. Still, one must question Gramsci appeal to historical inevitability and his relatively sanguine attitude in regard to Fordism and its human costs, especially given the butcher's knife wielded by Ford in bisecting and disassembling so many realms of lived existence in the new factory system he was in the process of installing.

In his autobiographical and mythmaking book, My Life and Work, Henry Ford (1922) opens up Chapter 7, "The Terror of the

Machine," by taking note of the frightening character of repetitive, monotonous work on the assembly line and the dissatisfaction of all but the dull-witted to accept a job involving so much routinized physical exertion. He dismisses the role of charity toward the physically handicapped in his philosophy of life and work but then quickly sketches a chilling and nightmarish image of the requisites of a Ford auto factory based on a dispassionate analysis of its labor or human resource needs. Acknowledging that nearly 50 percent of the 7882 jobs required able-bodied men, just over one-half—or 4034—called for less than full capacity. Using this impersonal accounting method, his production managers discovered that "670 could be filled by legless men, 2,637 by one-legged men, 2 by armless men, 715 by one-armed men, and 10 by blind men" (Ford, 1922, p. 108). Extending the rationalizing impulse to its logical conclusion, Ford's horrific fantasy of the completely rationalized factory (pp. 110–111) went on to speculate on the superior merits of these partially disassembled human beings ("the blind man was able to do not only his own work but also the work that had formerly been done by the sound men") and to experiment with employing the bedridden in some phase of production ("they slept and ate better and recovered more rapidly"). Despite its professed humanitarianism, this fantastic image of the fully realized Fordist factory clearly lapses into a totalitarian dream of human resource deployment and management. It also demonstrates the processes of disassembly carried over from the packinghouse origins of the mass assembly line.

When not speculatively placing the laboring body on a corporate Procrustean bed, Ford's carving knife was also dissecting the factory organism into brain (management) and brawn or muscle (worker) and excising the skilled tradesman from the production process. Through the high-wage policy of the Five-Dollar Day program, the Ford Motor Company divided the worker into a producer, whose work habits were guided by careful monitoring and rigid discipline, and a consumer, whose personal, hygienic, and social habits and behavior were subject to the closest scrutiny. These educational or puritanical initiatives had the intent, as Gramsci so rightly surmised, "of preserving, outside of work, a certain psychophysical equilibrium which prevents the physiological collapse of the worker, exhausted by the new method of production" (Gramsci, 1971, p. 303). Work rationalization and rational consumption, for Ford, must go hand in hand. Overall, the systematic disassembly of the laboring body into mechanical operations and simplified skills is paralleled by the reassembly of these component parts into the corporate factory body-system.

Today, after "deindustrialization," a political focus on the "body–machine complex" is in some says more difficult. The stakes, however, may not be much different. Taylor's extreme rationalization of the division of labor was aimed at fitting human labor to the machine. Taylor's reduction of human to beast divided or abstracted the worker from bodily presence to a "hermeneutical space for praxis" (cf. Schrag, 1986). The Taylorite subjectivization of the worker included a program of cultural evisceration aimed especially at stripping remnants of the republican producer ideology obstructing smoother operations of industrial capitalism. It is a mechanized body (a Cartesian body as machine) that Taylor attempted to fit to the machine as the center of rationalized production. Taylor wanted to be done with the time-forming, decentering practices of the worker as body-subject, replacing them with the spatialized time produced by the machine and controlled by its managers. Today, what O'Neill (1985, pp. 100–107) has termed "the fetishization of the productive body," including the self-reproducing "fantasy work" of the consumer, reflects not only new levels of capitalist engineering but also new types of contradictions. The latter bear at least potential uncertainties and disturbances that might open up new fields of action; indeed, that is the ground new social movements sometimes cultivate. However, from Taylor and Marie Bernays to our own era of pervasive image management and image "politics," corporate state hegemony has depended on endless variations of the subjectivization of political and economic life. In the body–machine complex of our corporate state, the recycling of consumers and the reshaping of "needs" for new styles of consumption amount to a massive containment policy in the cool war between capitalism and democracy. Nevertheless, the eruption of labor unrest and the upsurge of the union movement after World War II demonstrated that corporate hegemony had its limits and that the boundaries of instinct, reason, and mechanism could not be completely redrawn in a manner that permitted reification to triumph in the corporate body of the new Fordist factory, whatever Ford's fantasies.

We American theorists should take the opportunity to contextualize Gramsci's text on "Americanism" in ways that enable us to recover his insights without concealing his blindspots. While his grasp occasionally faltered, it is remarkable not only that he saw "Americanism" as an organic extension of the earliest phases of liberal-capitalist ideology but also that he put into focus major elements of the emergent phase of corporate liberalism and anticipated the shift toward technocratic modes of legitimation. In the case of the United States, a comparative historical analysis of politics, policies, and ideologies reveals the relative absence of many "passive" or "parasitic" sedimentations—a lack facilitating the construction of a capitalist economy and the comprehensive rationalization of social existence. The pervasive instrumentalism that Alexis de Tocqueville detected amid a dynamic civil society should be appreciated not only in relation to the growing mystique of the free market as a mechanistic model of natural order but also in relation to the institutionalization of the technological world-picture which Henry David Thoreau, for one, opposed with an alternative philosophy of nature, reason, and work.

The nineteenth-century process of institutionalizing of the technological world-picture became a key component of the twentieth century's corporate state by advancing a major cultural horizon for most of our social policies. Activities undertaken within the horizon of the technological worldview are ultimately aimed at domination, "mastery," or "control" inasmuch as the "outside world" is pictured as a field of resource objects to be exploited by calculative/manipulative approaches. In other words, the institutional anchoring of this horizon, which entails the bureaucratization of various modes of instrumental rationality, has facilitated the industrialization of cultural life as surely as it has the economy. "Mainstream politics," its mediating structures institutionally linked to the corporate capitalist economy and allegedly grounded in a "pragmatic-realist" tradition, has evoked for decades "progress," "growth," and now "environmental management." To put it another way, the hegemony of the monopoly sector of the capitalist economy is exercised not only through its profit-oriented hierarchical control of the mode of production but also through the increasing control and distribution of "legitimate" modes of experience, what Grossberg (1992, Chap. 12) terms the "disciplined mobilization of everyday life."

## THE POST-FORDIST WORKER AND THE POST-FORDIST BODY: HUMANWARE, DISCIPLINARY INDIVIDUALISM, AND THE AMERICAN BODY–MACHINE COMPLEX

Much has changed and much has remained the same since Gramsci penned his thoughts about the hegemonic processes taking shape in the early stages of Fordist mass production in America and beginning to diffuse with considerable resistance in western Europe. The playing out of Fordism as a regime of accumulation in various capitalist societies has, it has been argued, given way to the dawning of a new post-Fordist accumulation regime. This new paradigm of industrial production and regulatory system has stood at the center of theoretical debate and political controversy. For the French regulationists and other radical political economists, Fordism as a new phase in capitalism took more than four decades to crystallize into a mature, full-fledged regime of accumulation; and the new post-Fordist phase being born will similarly have a lengthy gestation period. Recent proponents of this putative internal transformation in capitalism have extolled the virtues of an incipient post-Fordist regime synthesizing mass and craft production into lean management and innovation-mediated production taking form once again in the automobile industry (Womack et al., 1990; Kenney and Florida, 1988, 1989, 1993). Others, while acknowledging new tendencies manifested in Japanese production techniques, have developed a theory of neo-Fordism that highlights the deeper continuities between Fordist and so-called post-Fordist production paradigms (Dohse et al., 1985; Jürgens, et al., 1993; Meyer, 1989; Foster and Woolfson, 1989). Still others have pointed to more synthetic modes of production and consumption that incorporate the best of Fordist and post-Fordist elements into a new regime that acknowledges the shortcomings of Fordist mass production but preserves a critical role for organized labor in shaping such hybrid regimes (Mahon, 1987, 1991; Streeck, 1985).

Against the background of industrial restructuring of the global political economy and the crisis of Fordism permeating mass production industries, labor–management relations, labor and consumer markets, government policies, and international trade, fundamental changes in the boundaries between animal, human, and machine seem once more to be taking place in the ideological and cultural realms and to be reconstructing dominant notions about work, workers, and the laboring and gendered body, as well as the relationship between new forms of technology and new skill requirements of workers in the Age of the Smart Machine (Zuboff, 1988).

Within the broad literature on post-Fordism, two schools of thought have emerged which have opened up reconsideration of grounding images of workers, bodies, and skills in the new post-Fordist workplace and have sought to transgress old boundaries and lines of division shaping these cultural tokens. Despite internal quarrels, the MIT International Motor Vehicle Project (IMVP) team headed by James Womack and the Florida and Kenney team have both stressed the unfolding of an increasingly integrated production system and model of the new worker known as "humanware." The appearance of the term can be traced at least to the early 1980s (to an *Independent School* article, "Hardware, Software, Humanware," 1984) and has had an elastic meaning depending upon where it has been employed. Indeed, given its extensive diffusion across academic disciplines and throughout management and marketing circles, "humanware" has come to inhabit the cultural zeitgeist informing the post-Fordist turn in globalizing capitalism.

For some educators, it carves out a technological space between hardware and software and seems to connote the effort on the part of human beings to adapt to the incipient era of microcomputer technology ("Hardware, . . ." 1984). For corporate designers like Arnold Wasserman, it refers to the integration of product designers into corporate strategic planning in order to make product design—whether an automobile, a photocopy machine, or a software interface—more user-friendly (de Forest, 1990). Within the rapidly changing global economic environment increasingly geared to highly differentiated consumer tastes and markets, product development planners have increasingly turned to "humanware" solutions to integrate product innovations and manufacturing or process innovations to keep so-called fast-track corporations on top of fast-paced changes in the global marketplace (Gehani, 1992, p. 45). In addition, in the construction industry, where post-Fordist trends in the organization and management of housing and other building construction have been in evidence (Florida and Feldman, 1988), occupational safety concerns among professional and consultants have prompted a growing focus on the role of humanware failures (as opposed to software and hardware deficiencies) in these production systems as the main source of injuries on the construction sites (Nishigaki et al., 1994).

The increasingly porous nature of the boundary between human beings and technology implied by the term "humanware" is well captured in most of the renderings above. But it is in the automobile industry, the historic innovator of industrial manufacturing in the twentieth century, where humanware has achieved its most detailed and systematic articulation and where the dividing line between human beings and technology has all but disappeared. For the IMVP school and its students, the humanware dimension of the Japanese production system, rather than any particular aspect of its hardware or social organization, is the defining and most innovative feature of this approach to automobile production. This theory of Japanese production methods (JPM), or "lean production" or post-Fordist management, as Shimada and MacDuffie (1987) argue, begins with a definition of humanware as the technology–human resources interface, or the "linkage between hardware and human resources" into a larger system of industrial production (p. 2). In contrast to the approach to automobile production innovation in the United States, where high-technology improvements have been seen as the driving force of increased productivity, Shimada and MacDuffie claim that Japanese automakers spearheaded by Toyota Motor Company have worked to coordinate and integrate hard technology and human beings in more tightly coupled relationships. Whereas the Lordstown, Hamtramck, and Saturn plants have symbolized the high-technology bent of America's General Motors, NUMMI (New United Motor Manufacturing, Inc., in Fremont, California), TMM (Toyota Motor Manufacturing, in Georgetown, Kentucky), and Honda (in Marysville, Ohio) have been emblems of the Japanese commitment to humanware development. This is not to say that Japanese auto manufacturing does not introduce technological advancement into the production process. Rather, for the IMVP school, it is the dynamic interweaving of changes in technology and changes in human resources that is singular to the Japanese production system.

Acknowledging that Americans generally think "of particular hardware technologies [as] *requiring* certain capabilities, but don't tend to consider how the use of hardware technology . . . can create and reinforce the qualities which make human resources effective," the Japanese humanware approach offers a more dynamic view of the interaction between hardware and humanware, which "sees the production process creating the opportunity for continuous, ongoing learning (as opposed to a one-time 'learning curve' effect)" (p. 6). As a result, "the greater the interdependence [between hardware and human resources], the greater the dependence of the overall production system on human resources, and the greater the vulnerability of the system to human variability" (p. 5).

For proponents of the post-Fordist or lean production model, this humanware perspective radiates outward and affects virtually every facet of the Japanese production system, revolutionizing the traditional automobile manufacturing plant and turning the post-Fordist factory into a "learning bureaucracy" (Adler, 1993; Adler and Cole, 1993). Among the components of the human resource strategy underlying the new organization of humanware and innovation-mediated production are new forms of human control, including self-generating innovative capacity ("giving wisdom to the machine"), continuous improvement (*kaizen*), lifelong worker training, and (in the case of transplanted or hybrid renditions of post-Fordism in the United States) the new Americanism.

In important respects, the key to understanding the deeper cultural and ideological impact of post-Fordist tendencies unfolding in the crisis of Fordism is to examine the interplay between the larger hegemonic processes being developed within this alternative accumulation regime and mode of production and consumption and the microprocesses between instituted at the level of the shop floor relating to worker self-image, skills development, and the human–technology interface. The popularity of the term "humanware" itself testifies to the further blurring beyond Taylorism and Fordism of the line of demarcation between human being and technology. Indeed, despite the pseudoegalitarianism evident in lean production factories and the absence of symbols of organization hierarchy between management and labor, the language of the post-Fordist text marginalizes the human dimension to the point of obliteration, absorbing the laboring subject as humanware completely into the corporate circuitry of the post-Fordist organization and production system.

In "Americanism and Fordism, " Antonio Gramsci speculated on the hegemonic struggle being fought out in the transition from craft production to Fordist mass production, pointing out how the effort to achieve a psychophysical equilibrium within the worker and in the workplace could "become internalised if it is proposed by the worker himself, and not imposed from the outside, if it is proposed by a new form of society, with appropriate and original methods" (1971, p. 303). This passage is, in striking ways, even more applicable to the hegemonic control strategy emanating from post-Fordism. The emergent post-Fordist management and production system is grounded in a series of organizational, social, and educational components dedicated to persuading the new laboring subject to become his or her own agency of hegemonic discipline and control. Through careful recruitment, screening, and selection of flexible, problem-solving workers, post-Fordist enterprises cultivate a process of worker training, combining company-specific technical (or "hard") skills and more generalized social (or "soft") skills, seeking to indoctrinate the worker into the corporate worldview and shape his or her self-image as a self-disciplined component that is expected to be fully integrated into the artificial corporate body (Yanarella, 1996). Contrary to the team organization and team spirit championed in the post-Fordist text, the deeper reality of the post-Fordist factory in the United States and elsewhere is the emergence of a form of "disciplinary power" (Sakolsky, 1992) operating under an increasingly complex and ideologically camouflaged social "regime of subordination" (Garrahan and Stewart, 1992).

This assessment is confirmed by constructing some the terms and concepts residing on the margins of post-Fordist discourse. For example, an integral feature of the self-generating innovative capability of the Japanese production system is the practice of *kaizen*, or continuous improvement. Combining rigid enforcement of the work production process (approximating Taylor's "one best way") with work flexibility and production innovation, the JPM in its variants in the auto industry holds forth an expectation that workers will regularly offer a certain number of suggestions for improving the production process within their work area. Recognizing that the performance of machine technology can be dramatically improved by small or subtle refinements, the Japanese production system integrated "this process of incremental improvements of hardware emerging from the experience of production workers," calling it "giving wisdom to the machines" (Shimada and Mac-Duffie, 1987, p. 12). While this transfer of worker intelligence and skills to technology is in some ways continuous with Taylorism, the appropriation of worker capital under this new factory regime departs significantly from the old Taylor system. As Kenney and Florida (1993, p. 16) argue, the uniqueness of post-Fordist production lies in the "organizational forms of the new shop floor [which] mobilize and harness the collective intelligence of workers as a source of continuous improvement in products and processes, of increased productivity, and of value creation." Yet, adopting an almost Gramscian optimism in the face of grim realities, they candidly admit that "far from being romantic or naive, this view recognizes quite explicitly that the new industrial revolution exploits the worker more completely and totally than before" (p. 17).

The character of this exploitation and its underlying purposes are not, however, part of the post-Fordist text. The new American body–machine complex called humanware receives typically 90 hours of orientation and training before being inserted into the corporate circuitry of the post-Fordist factory and then from 40–90 hours of retraining off the assembly line to upgrade company-specific knowledge and skills in the manner of the latest microcomputer chip. The honing of the corporeal and social dimensions of humanware and its meshing with the technological circuitry of the post-Fordist corporate body is also advanced in the integration into the initial orientation and training program of an outdoor training regimen (Wagner et al., 1991; Yanarella, 1996). In the spirit of the philosophy of the Scouting movement, outdoor training of all salaried employers (managers) and nonsalaried employees (workers) has been incorporated into post-Fordist training programs for bodybuilding and character-building purposes. The nature trail runs, rope and mountain climbs, and other physical training courses are better seen as constituting a kind of team-building bootcamp for inculcating values of team spirit, mutual trust, risk taking, leadership and followership, problem solving, and sense of corporate ownership.

Corporate hegemony within the workplace is complemented by broader community and even national hegemony in the post-Fordist system. At transplanted automobile manufacturing plants in the United States, Japanese corporations have to varying degrees sought to extend hegemonic processes and patterns into the surrounding communities and states wherein they are located. Community hegemony has been an integral part of corporate life in the Japanese auto industry (e.g., Toyota City). The geographic and economic restructuring that took place in America's industrial heartland has seen the pervasive attempt by the auto transplants to incorporate hegemonic design into the community life of small towns like Georgetown, Kentucky, Smyrna, Tennessee, and Marysville, Ohio, through the replication of some of the elements of their hegemonic integration of corporate–community, economic–social, and business–cultural spheres of Japanese company towns.

Through a steady stream of corporate giving, a complex web of company–community institutions (including political, industrial, education, and cultural ties), and a vigilant staff of public relations employees working to polish or defend the corporate image, management-driven mobilization campaigns have sought to reshape the local community into a supportive environment for corporate programs and plans and to turn the community into a showcase for a mass-mediated national audience in the United States. One form taken by this hegemonic mobilization strategy has been extensive efforts through product advertising to manipulate symbols of local culture (e.g., the Bluegrass in central Kentucky) and meld company products and corporate symbols into that cultural landscape. In addition, in building on American shores a somewhat nativized *keiretsu* (vertical industrial group) structure integrating secondary and tertiary suppliers into its production complex, post-Fordist corporations have used their training centers as means for schooling and disciplining wider elements of the production network into integrating into their production processes their particular model of the Japanese production system. Finally, as part of their voluntary activities, factory workers are actively encouraged to participate in local civic organizations to further the company's community image—thus serving as a vital link between processes of company and community hegemony. Like other levels of its hegemonic processes, these too have been subject to criticism and challenge, necessitating corporate adaptation in a continuing effort to rebalance and augment the ongoing and dynamic hegemonic equilibrium.

Exemplary of the hegemonic efforts to forge a new Americanism among post-Fordist enterprises is the mobilization strategy of GM's Saturn Corporation. Unlike various Japanese transplants, Saturn has launched its hegemonic initiatives onto a national arena in the form of molding the mass consumer image of the car and the corporation through mass advertising (Serafin, 1992) while employing its training program as a model for innovative public education (Bennett and King, 1991) and as an instrument for instructing its retail force in its market philosophy and its mechanics in the principles of its training and production system. In the process, it has elaborated a new species of Americanism—albeit a much weaker and shallower version of patriotism and good citizenship than the one Gramsci saw linked to Fordism. In addition to trying to sell American citizens through the mass advertising of an image of Saturn as a different kind of car and a different kind of company, this new Americanism has tried to convince the mass citizenry of the need for a different kind of unionized workforce guided by a more cooperative approach to union–management relations that transcends the traditional adversarial model (Yanarella and Green, 1993). Not least of all, in the face of economic challenge and the experience of a falling standard of living for many

Americans, Saturn's new Americanism presents the company and its philosophy as a catalyst for reversing America's declining economic fortunes and making the twenty-first century the new American century.

## POST-FORDISM AND THE IRONIC MYTH OF THE CYBORG

In carrying the hegemonic processes of corporate power onto a new plane and to new heights and by more fully and completely integrating the collective intelligence of the workforce into a more exploitative regime of subordination, post-Fordism raises the question of how radical and dissident forces should respond to more subtle forms of disciplinary power being manifested in this inchoate accumulation regime and to its changing images of work, laboring subject, and skills development and redrawn boundaries between animal, human, and machine. One response to the tightening of hegemony under the regime of post-Fordism, which is simultaneously a socialist feminist countercorrelate to post-Fordism's reconfiguration of the body-machine complex (i.e., "humanware"), is Donna Haraway's promulgation of the ironic myth of the cyborg.

Written in the mid-1980s as a double reaction to latent technofascist possibilities surfacing in Reaganite corporate America and to the ecological and spiritualist turn in the multivalent feminist movement, Haraway's "Manifesto for Cyborgs" (1985, 1991a) seized new cultural ground and opened up a liberatory space for cultural and political intervention for socialist feminists and other radicals not on the margins but in the belly of the patriarchal, technocapitalist, heterosexist beast (Penley and Ross, 1991, p. 6; Csicsery-Ronay, 1991, p. 397). While consciously framing her cyborg manifesto in a postmodern language written at the furthest reaches of posthistoric times, she conceived her blasphemous image of the cyborg in terms of "an ironic political myth faithful to feminism, socialism, and materialism" (Haraway, 1991a, p. 149).

Within science fiction and cultural studies, the cyborg has been understood as a hybrid fusing organism and machine. Rorvik (1971) has pointed to the origins of the cyborg in the coupling of injured bodies and prosthetic limbs in the medical field and McLuhan and Fiore have more generally seen its genesis in the conception of all technological innovation as "a literal amputation of ourselves in order that it may be amplified and manipulated for social power and action" (1968, p. 73). Haraway herself, noting affinities between the cyborg and emergent trends in late-twentieth-century society, acknowledges how "modern production seems like a dream of cyborg colonization of work, a dream that makes the nightmare of Taylorism seem idyllic" (1991a, p. 150). Convergent with Martin (1992), Csicsery-Ronay has interpreted the fictional cyborg as deriving from "the radical anxiety of human consciousness about its own embodiment at the moment that embodiment appears almost fully contingent" (1991, p. 395).

The audacious radicalism of Haraway's thesis, however, cannot be captured solely by projecting unfolding realities or working through and deconstructing nightmarish dreams. In her manifesto and subsequent elaborations, Haraway critically appropriates and radicalizes the cyborg, and in the process transgresses those traditional animal–human–machine boundaries that have hitherto been shifted and made increasingly porous but have never been regarded as totally breached and overcome. Csicsery-Ronay has superbly summarized this critical point:

> Cyborgs represent for Haraway beings that combine mechanical and organic qualities, of animal and human qualities, within the limits of their physical bodies. But for Haraway these are localizations of a set of systematic relations in postmodern, high-tech cultures. . . . The cyborg is the site of a categorical breakdown, a system of transgressions, and an irrecoverable one, [and] since the condition of cyborg existence cannot be reversed, essential differences cannot be restored with the laser-scalpel of classical rationalities. (1991, p. 396)

In other words, the boundaries between animal and human and between human and machine, in Haraway's new political mythology, have been erased by developments in modern biology and evolutionary theory and by communications and cybernetics (Haraway, 1991a, pp. 152, 153).

Ironically, Haraway's postmodern discourse on post-Fordism

and the (feminist) cyborg manifests certain striking—and troubling—affinities with Gramsci's modernist discourse on Fordism
and female liberation. While the latter sees the new worker and
the former sees the cyborg as sites of cultural and political contestation, each seems to reach an accommodation with processes of instrumental rationality too quickly and without enough sensitivity
to the theoretical and political costs of the ontological losses.
Granting that Gramsci avows the fundamental importance of
women's liberation for any Marxist project of human emancipation
and sexuality as the site of domination and oppression (1971, p.
296), his narrative seems at critical junctures in his argument for
women's liberation to misplace the foundations of liberation in the
rationalization processes of Fordist production. Departing from his
complex theory of hegemony, which sees power residing not only
in the realm of state or class power but also at the interstices of
everyday life and in the institutions of civil society, Gramsci curiously links the "woman's inalienable rights of control over her sexuality and her body to processes of rationalization of production,
[believing] that new and liberated forms of sexuality for women,
and ways of validating these new forms of sexuality, a new ethics,
are contingent on the demands of the sphere of production atten-
tive to restraining the passions of the body" (Holub, 1992, pp.
197–198). This regressive and productivist form of Marxist analysis
and liberal, deterministic view of progress, in contrast to Foucault's
discourse on human sexuality (1979b), vitiate Gramsci's subtle
grasp of hegemonic processes combining coercion and consent, the
state and civil institutions, in the production and reproduction of
structures of inequality and domination, just as it sanctions as the
cost of liberation in women (and men) the institutionalization of
more intensified forms of discipline over the human body and sexual desires as a requirement of the latest phase in the industrialization process.

As a cultural critic and radical social theorist, Haraway un-
equivocally works to uncover moments in the process of cultural
production and reproduction where critical interventions are both
possible and desirable (Penley and Ross, 1991, p. xv). Moreover,
she clearly sees the cyborg as a site of struggle where the stakes in
this border war are nothing less than the issues of production, re-

production, and imagination (Haraway, 1991a, p. 150). Yet in her haste to advance the agenda of women's (and, by implication, male and animal) liberation, her delight in the confusion and erasure of boundaries provoking the construction of the female as cyborg raises a number of difficult and troubling issues, some of which parallel Gramsci's. Leaving aside the repressive egalitarianism residing in her utopian hope of a world without gender and the underlying Christian (indeed, Catholic) impulses of her manifesto, Haraway's claim that "the cyborg has no origin story in the Western sense" is contradicted by her own admission that the main trouble with cyborgs . . . is that they are the illegitimate offspring of militarism and patriarchal capitalism, not to mention state socialism" (p. 151).

Still, Haraway's equanimity with the militaristic and cybernetic origins of the cyborg and her erasure of all boundaries lead to a number of difficulties. For one thing, the former weakens the grounding for political and cultural contestation among feminists of emergent high-tech sources of the continuing domination of women's bodies by, e.g., modern medical science's ongoing intervention into the female body, in contrast to Elshtain's critique of technological and pharmacological intervention into the male body imagined in Marge Piercy's *Women on the Edge of Time* (Elshtain, 1981, p. 212). It must also contend with the fact that, despite her attempt to develop a positive hermeneutic of popular culture, Haraway's feminist cyborg ideal of smooth, fluid, "semi-permeable constructions, hybrid, almost makeshift attempts at counterrationality," as opposed to the technofascist, masculinist ideal of the invincible armored cyborg, has found precious little cultural expression in mass culture. Instead, as contemporary cyborg films testify, "violent, forceful cyborg imagery participates in contemporary discourses that cling to nineteenth-century notions about technology, sexual difference, and gender roles" (Springer, 1993, p. 89), leaving the hoped-for new cultural constructions without foundation or prefigurations. In the face of the muscular circuitry of these Arnold Schwarzenegger look-alikes, the "essentialism" of gendered resistance of women's peace organizations and ecofeminist groups seems much less anachronistic and to be preferred!

While it is incontestable that boundaries between animal, human, and machine are indeed undergoing radical reconfiguration, advanced in part by the mediation of technology, the radicality of Haraway's thesis, which celebrates the complete collapse of boundaries, is too extreme and cannot be sustained as a strategy for cultural and political intervention. In the post-Fordist realms of work and reproduction, Haraway's "informatics of domination" at least marks the general way microelectronics mediate "the translations of labor into robotics and wordprocessing, sex into genetic engineering and reproductive technologies, and mind into artificial intelligence and decision procedures" (1991a, p. 165). In this new work environment, if the workforce is not to become reconciled to the construct of the worker as humanware, where else will workers go to organize for collective representation if not to their physical and emotional distress brought on by the rapidly proliferating post-Fordist induced illnesses and injuries to the laboring body such as carpal tunnel syndrome, CRT eye stress, and other repetitive stress injuries and to their rights as persons to full voice and participation in the true democratization of the new workplace (no doubt in places mediated by communications technology)?

Going beyond the immediately mobilizable issues of the shop floor, our argument refuses the terms of discourse set by the professional advocates of the body–machine complex. We contend, with Carol Bigwood, that we "need to remain true to our embodied experience that shows us the world is, as Maurice Merleau-Ponty (1962) explains in detail, not what I think but what I live through. We are not separate from the world-earth-home but are *of* it to the very depths of our sentient being" (1993, p. 285). As Bigwood shows, we need "alternative models of subjectivity based on an openness to the other and the body." Haraway's "taboo fusions" (1991a, p. 173) have these auspices for exposing, as Bigwood says, discourses of domination such as patriarchy "to contradiction and difference" (1993, p. 7). Haraway's cyborg suffers from its own version of Western homelessness. We would bring it back to earth to reclaim its territory, its living space that has been commodified by transnational predators and their global shopping malls (never in reach for millions anyway).

As Bigwood puts it, the trouble with the "poststructuralist's culturally inscribed body is [that it is] disembodied and lacks terrestrial weight and locatedness because, like both empiricist and idealist accounts of the body, it has left out . . . the anonymous noncognitive cleaving of our bodies to others and things, to the general incarnate structure of the world" (pp. 52, 55). Haraway claims in her postscript to the cyborg manifesto that we "have no choice but to move through a harrowed and harrowing artifactualism to elsewhere" (1991b, pp. 24–25). If we adhered to the liberal myth/ideal of self-enclosed subjectivity, we might agree. The acceptance of a dichotomy between life and thought, the reification of space, and the ontological demise of nature might then leave us with little more than "the promises of monsters" (ibid.). This monster talk may be another way of saying we are among the "endangered species." But "endangered species are not simply accidents of our way of living," as Charles Bergman has observed. "They are the necessary consequences of our way of knowing animals" (see Evernden, 1992, p. 105ff.). If we are condemned to the vocabulary and the style of rationality of technological experts, then we are not likely to reimagine these "things." The question is whether we are going to regard ourselves as trapped in our "conceptual domestication of nature" or whether we can rediscover the things themselves through what Merleau-Ponty once termed "the secret order of embodied subjects" (Evernden, 1992, pp. 107–124; Reid, 1977, esp. pp. 117–126; Merleau-Ponty, 1968). As Evernden indicates, the totalizing tendency of the technocratic mind is to leave the "genuinely ultrahuman being of nature . . . invisible . . . no place" (1992, p. 121; emphasis his).

Drew Leder's important, cognate study, The Absent Body (1990), has identified the "ecstatic and recessive nature of the lived body" as one of the invariants shaping human experience. His analysis helps us understand how the notion of abstract or immaterial reason is made possible by the body's tacit and self-concealing structure. Much of modern Western thought has "lost," or rather misplaced, the sense of corporeality as a generative principle. The taken-for-granted body and its tacit structures (unthematized) permit or contribute to the fetishization of our tools and to the denial of responsible forms of interpretation—in academe as well as political economy.

At one point in the cyborg manifesto we read that indeed "myth and tool mutually constitute each other" (Haraway, 1991a,

p. 164). These are insufficient auspices for a cyborg or any other politics struggling "against perfect communication" (p. 176). (On this, cf. Dreyfus' [1979] prolonged debate with proponents of artificial intelligence.) To use Haraway's terms, we need more thematics of embodiment to deal with the "informatics of domination" (1991a, pp. 163, 180). This might also enable us to avoid confusing (collapsing) the Western myth of the Autonomous Self with the Western self. The former is implicated in the cyborg as the telos of an "ultimate self untied at last from all dependency" (p. 151). Later, we learn that cyborg writing (Haraway provides several examples) "is about the power to survive, not on the basis of original innocence, but on the basis of seizing the tools to mark the world that marked them ['all colonized groups'] as other" (p. 175). Is this a new version of the old instrumentalism of "seizing state power"?

Seizing the tools would seem to offer us another episode in which the ideal of absolute self-determination is linked to instrumental rationality, another project for recolonization of the lifeworld. "Global vengeance" indeed (p. 181)! Must we acquiesce in the world system in allowing nothing but desperate struggle based on Universal Otherhood (see Reid, 1995)? Recalling Haraway's cyborg postscript (1991b), we grant that history is monstrous—but is it not more than that? Surely the Western self has generated more than a global system for world-historical domination. What sort of investment leads Haraway to advise us to refuse "an anti-science metaphysics, a demonology of technology" (1991a, p. 181)? To put it another way, does her commitment to biotechnology include a bioregional matrix for what Leder calls the "general corporeal field" (1990, pp. 24–25)? The point we are getting at is concisely put by Castells' *Informational City* when he refers to reinventing democracy by matching "the space of flows with the power of places" (1989, p. 347).

It is the American body–machine complex underlying the new communications technologies at the core of our corporate state's consumer culture that blocks a new pluralistic politics of place and a new global politics of democratic will-formation (*pace* Haraway, 1991a, p. 168). Simultaneously, it prolongs the crisis of Fordism, proliferating concepts of the laboring subject, work, and skill formation between Fordism and post-Fordism that at once

camouflage their bodily auspices and impede the evolution of a truly democratic culture, politics, and workplace even as post-Fordism
celebrates their dawning.

## REFERENCES

Adler, Paul S. 1993. "The 'Learning Bureaucracy': New United Motor
Manufacturing, Inc." *Research in Organizational Behavior* 15:
111–194.
Adler, Paul S., and Robert Cole. 1993. "Designed for Learning: A Tale of
Two Auto Plants." *Sloan Management Review 34* (Spring): 85–94.
Alaimo, Stacy. "Cyborg and Ecofeminist Interventions: Challenges for an
Environmental Feminism." *Feminist Studies 20* (Spring): 133–152.
Banta, Martha. 1993. *Taylored Lives: Narrative Productions in the Age of
Taylor, Veblen, and Ford.* Chicago: University of Chicago Press.
Barns, Ian. 1991. "Post-Fordist People? Cultural Meanings of New Tech-
noeconomic Systems." *Futures 23* (November): 895–914.
Bennett, David A., and Thomas D. King. 1991. "The Saturn School of
Tomorrow." *Educational Leadership 48* (May): 41–44.
Bigwood, Carol. 1993. *Earth Muse: Feminism, Nature, and Art.* Philadel-
phia: Temple University Press.
Braun, Rudolf. 1991. "The 'Docile' Body as an Economic-Industrial
Growth Factor." In *Favorites of Fortune: Technology, Growth, and
Economic Development Since the Industrial Revolution,* Patrice
Higonnet, David S. Landes, and Henry Rosousley, eds. Cambridge,
MA: Harvard University Press.
Castells, Manuel. 1989. *The Informational City: Information Technology,
Economic Restructuring and the Urban–Regional Process.* New York:
Blackwell.
Child, Mary. 1990. "Does Humanware Need Unions?" *Journal of Com-
merce and Commercial 385* (August 23): 8A.
Csicsery-Ronay, Istvan. 1991. "The SF of Theory: Baudrillard and Har-
away." *Science-Fiction Studies 18* (November): 387–404.
Clarke, Simon. 1990. "New Utopias for Old: Fordist Dream and Post-
Fordist Fantasies." *Capital and Class 5* (Winter): 131–155.
de Forest, Ann. 1990. "Wasserman." *ID: A Journal of International Design
37* (March/April): 69–71.
Dohse, Knuth, Ulrich Jürgens, and Thomas Malsch. 1985. "From
'Fordism' to 'Toyotism'? The Social Organization of the Labor
Process in the Japanese Automobile Industry." *Politics & Society 14*
(March): 115–146.

Dreyfus, Hubert L. 1979. *What Computers Can't Do: The Limits of Artificial Intelligence*. New York: Harper & Row.

Dunford, Mick, and Georges Benko. 1991. "Neo-Fordism or Post-Fordism? Some Conclusions and Further Remarks." In *Industrial Change and Regional Development: The Transformation of New Industrial Spaces*. New York: Belhaven Press, pp. 286–305.

Edwards, Richard C. 1979. *Contested Terrain*. New York: Basic Books.

Elshtain, Jean Bethke. 1981. *Public Man, Private Woman: Women in Social and Political Thought*. Princeton, NJ: Princeton University Press.

Evernden, Neil. 1992. *The Social Creation of Nature*. Baltimore: Johns Hopkins University Press.

Fitting, Peter. "The Lessons of Cyberpunk." In *Technoculture*, Constance Penley and Andrew Ross, eds. Minneapolis: University of Minnesota Press, pp. 295–315.

Florida, Richard, and Marshall Feldman. 1988. "Housing in U.S. Fordism: The Class Accord and Postwar Spatial Organization." *International Journal of Urban and Regional Research* 12 (April): 187–210.

Ford, Henry (in collaboration with Samuel Crowther). 1922. *My Life and Work*. New York: Doubleday, Page.

Foster, Bellamy, and Charles Woolfson. 1989. "Corporate Restructuring and Business Unionism: The Lessons of Caterpillar and Ford." *New Left Review 147* (March/April): 51–66.

Foster, Thomas. 1993. "Meat Puppets or Robopaths?: Cyberpunk and the Question of Embodiment." *Genders 18* (Winter): 11–31.

Foucault, Michel. 1979a. *Discipline and Punish: The Birth of the Prison*. New York: Vintage Books.

Foucault, Michel. 1979b. *The History of Sexuality*. London: Allen Lane.

Garrahan, Philip, and Paul Stewart. 1992. *The Nissan Enigma: Flexibility at Work in a Local Economy*. New York: Mansell.

Gehani, R. Ray. 1992. "Concurrent Product Development for Fast-Track Corporations." *Long Range Planning* 25(6): 40–47.

Giedion, Sigfried. 1948. *Mechanization Takes Command: A Contribution to an Anonymous History*. New York: Oxford University Press.

Gramsci, Antonio. 1971. "Americanism and Fordism," 277–318, and "The Intellectuals," 5–23. In *Selections from the Prison Notebooks*, Quintin Hoare and Geoffrey Nowell Smith, eds. and trans. New York: International Publishers.

Grossberg, Lawrence. 1992. *We Gotta Get Out of This Place: Popular Conservatism and Postmodern Culture*. New York: Routledge.

Haber, Samuel. 1964. *Efficiency and Uplift: Scientific Management in the Progressive Era, 1890–1920*. Chicago: University of Chicago Press.

Haraway, Donna. 1985. "A Manifesto for Cyborgs: Science, Technology, and Socialist Feminism in the 1980s." *Socialist Review 80*: 65–108.

Haraway, Donna. 1991a. "A Cyborg Manifesto: Science, Technology, and Socialist Feminism in the Late Twentieth Century." *Simians, Cyborgs, and Women: The Reinvention of Nature*. New York: Routledge.

Haraway, Donna. 1991b. "The Actors Are Cyborg, Nature Is Coyote, and the Geography Is Elsewhere: Postscript to 'Cyborgs at Large'." In *Technoculture*, Constance Penley and Andrew Ross, eds. Minneapolis: University of Minnesota Press, pp. 21–26.

"Hardware, Software, Humanware." 1984. *Independent School 43* (May): 39–42.

Harvey, David. 1989. *The Condition of Postmodernity: An Enquiry into the Origins of Cultural Change*. New York: Oxford University Press.

Hays, Samuel P. 1969. *Conservation and the Gospel of Efficiency: The Progressive Conservation Movement, 1890–1920*. New York: Athenaeum.

Herman, Andrew. 1982. "Conceptualizing Control: Domination and Hegemony in the Capitalist Labor Process." *Insurgent Sociologist 11* (Fall): 7–22.

Holub, Renate. 1992. *Antonio Gramsci: Beyond Marxism and Postmodernism*. New York: Routledge.

Hughes, Thomas. 1989. *American Genesis: A Century of Invention and Technological Enthusiasm, 1870–1979*. New York: Penguin.

Humphrey, Craig, and Frederick Buttel. 1982. *Environment, Energy & Society*. Belmont, MA: Wadsworth.

Johnson, Mark. 1987. *The Body in the Mind*. Chicago: University of Chicago Press.

Jones, J. P., Wolfgang Natter, and Theodore Schatzki, eds. Forthcoming. *Democratic Theory and Democracy*. New York: Guilford Press.

Jürgens, Ulrich, Thomas Malsch, and Knuth Dohse. 1993. *Breaking from Taylorism: Changing Forms of Work in the Automobile Industry*. New York: Cambridge University Press.

Kakar, Sudhir. 1970. *Frederick Taylor: A Study of Personality and Innovation*. Cambridge, MA: The MIT Press.

Kenney, Martin, and Richard Florida. 1988. "Beyond Mass Production: Production and the Labor Process in Japan." *Politics and Society 16* (March): 121–158.

Kenney, Martin, and Richard Florida. 1989. "Japan's Role in a Post-Fordist Age." *Futures 21* (April): 136–151.

Kenney, Martin, and Richard Florida. 1993. *Beyond Mass Production: The Japanese System and Its Transfer to the U.S.* New York: Oxford University Press.

Knouse, Stephen B., Paul Phillips Carson, and Kerry D. Carson. 1993.

"W. Edwards Deming and Frederick Winslow Taylor: A Comparison of Two Leaders Who Shaped the World's View of Management." *International Journal of Public Administration* 16 (October): 1621–1658.

Leder, Drew. 1990. *The Absent Body*. Chicago: University of Chicago Press.

Mahon, Rianne. 1987. "From Fordism to ?: New Technology, Labour Markets and Unions." *Economic and Industrial Democracy* 8: 5–60.

Mahon, Rianne. 1991. "Post-Fordism: Some Issues for Labour." In *The New Era of Global Competition*, Daniel Drache and Meric S. Gertler, eds. Montreal: McGill–Queen's University Press, pp. 316–332.

Martin, Emily. 1992. "The End of the Body?" *American Ethnologist* 19 (February): 121–140.

McLuhan, Marshall, and Quentin Fiore. 1968. *War and Peace in the Global Village*. New York: Bantam Books.

Merleau-Ponty, Maurice. 1962. *Phenomenology of Perception*. Trans. Colin Smith. London: Routledge and Kegan Paul.

Merleau-Ponty, Maurice. 1968. *The Visible and the Invisible*. Evanston, IL: Northwestern University Press.

Meyer, Stephen, III. 1981. *The Five-Dollar Day: Labor, Management, and Social Control in the Ford Motor Company, 1908–1921*. Albany: State University of New York Press.

Nichols, Peter, ed. 1979. "Cyborgs." In *The Science Fiction Encyclopedia*. Garden City, NY: Doubleday, p. 151.

Nishigsaki, Shigeomi, Jeannette Vavrin, Noriaki Kano, Toshiro Haga, John C. Kunz, and Kincho Law. 1994. "Humanware, Human Error, and Kiyari-Hat: A Template of Unsafe Symptoms." *Journal of Construction Engineering and Management* 120 (June): 421–441.

Noble, David F. 1997. *America by Design: Science, Technology, and the Rise of Corporate Capitalism*. New York: Oxford University Press.

O'Neill, John. 1985. *Five Bodies*. Ithaca, NY: Cornell University Press.

Penley, Constance, and Andrew Ross. 1991. "Cyborgs at Large: Interview with Donna Haraway." In *Technoculture*, Constance Penley and Andrew Ross, eds. Minneapolis: University of Minnesota Press.

Rabinbach, Anson. 1990. *The Human Motor: Energy, Fatigue and the Origins of Modernity*. New York: Basic Books.

Radhakrishnan, R. 1990. "Toward an Effective Intellectual: Foucault or Gramsci?" In *Intellectuals: Aesthetics, Politics, and Academics*, Bruce Robbins, ed. Minneapolis: University of Minnesota Press.

Reid, Herbert G. 1977. "Critical Phenomenology and the Dialectical Foundations of Social Change." *Dialectical Anthropology* 2: 107–130.

Reid, Herbert G. 1995. "Democratic Theory and the Public Sphere Project: Rethinking Knowledge, Authority, and Identity." Forthcoming.

Rorvik, David. 1971. *Man Becomes a Machine*. Garden City, NY: Doubleday.

Rowand, Roger. 1989. "Humanware: Interaction Between Man and Machine Will Rise in the '90s." *Automotive News* (November 29): 28.

Sakolsky, Ron. 1992. "'Disciplinary Power,' the Labor Process, and the Constitution of the Laboring Subject." *Rethinking Marxism* 5 (Winter): 114–126.

Schrag, Calvin O. 1986. *Communicative Praxis and the Space of Subjectivity*. Indianapolis: Indiana University Press.

Seltzer, Mark. 1992. *Bodies and Machines*. New York: Routledge, Chapman & Hall.

Serafin, Raymond. 1992. "The Saturn Story: How Saturn Became One of the Most Successful New Brands in Marketing History." *Advertising Age* 63 (November 16): 1–3.

Sheehan, James J., and Morton Sosna, eds. 1991. *The Boundaries of Humanity: Humans, Animals, Machines*. Berkeley: University of California Press.

Shimada, Haruo. 1989. "New Economic and Human Resource Strategies: A Challenge for the Japanese Automobile Industry." International Motor Vehicles Program (IMVP) Policy Forum Paper, MIT, Cambridge, MA.

Shimada, Haruo, and John Paul MacDuffie. 1987. "Industrial Relations and 'Humanware': Japanese Investments in Automobile Manufacturing in the United States." International Motor Vehicles Program (IMVP) Briefing Paper, MIT, Cambridge, MA.

Springer, Claudia. 1993. "Muscular Circuitry: The Invincible Armored Cyborg in Cinema." *Genders* 18 (Winter): 87–101.

Stone, Allucquere Rosanne. 1991. "Will the Real Body Please Stand Up?: Boundary Stories About Virtual Cultures." In *Cyberspace: First Steps*, Michael Benedikt, ed. Cambridge, MA: MIT Press.

Streeck, Wolfgang. 1985. "Introduction: Industrial Relations, Technological Change and Economic Restructuring." In *Industrial Relations and Technological Change in the British, Italian and German Automobile Industry*, Wolfgang Streeck, ed. Berlin: Wissenschaftszentrum.

Taylor, Frederick Winslow. 1947a. *The Principles of Management in Science Management*. New York: Harper.

Taylor, Frederick Winslow. 1947b. *Scientific Management* [comprising "Shop Management"; "The Principles of Scientific Management"; and "Testimony Before the Special House Committee"]. New York: Harper.

Tichi, Cecelia. 1987. *Shifting Gears: Technology, Literature, Culture in Modernist America*. Chapel Hill: University of North Carolina Press.

Wagner, Richard J., Timothy T. Baldwin, and Christopher C. Roland. 1991. "Outdoor Training: Revolutions or Fad?" *Training & Development Journal* 45 (March): 51–57.

Weber, Marianne. 1975. *Max Weber: A Biography.* New York: Wiley.

Womack, James, Daniel Jones, and Daniel Roos, 1990. *The Machine That Changed the World.* New York: Rawson Associates.

Yanarella, Ernest J. 1996. "Worker Training at Toyota and Saturn: Hegemony Begins in the Training Center Classroom." In *North American Auto Unions in Crisis: Lean Production as Contested Terrain,* William C. Green and Ernest J. Yanarella, eds. Albany: State University of New York Press, 125–157.

Yanarella, Ernest J., and William C. Green. 1994. "The UAW and CAW Confront Lean Production at Saturn, CAMI, and the Japanese Automobile Transplants." *Labor Studies Journal* 18 (Winter): 52–75.

Zuboff, Shoshana. 1988. *In the Age of the Smart Machine: The Future of Work and Power.* New York: Basic Books.

# Index

INDEX

## G

Gardener, Helen, 103, 104–112
Gellert, George, 115
Gender
  as being, 58
  brain research related to concep-
    tions of, 104–113, 116–117
  discursive constitution, 58, 61–62
  as doing, 59–60, 61, 164–165
  performance conception, 58–59
  properties of atomistic self, 11–12
  social constitution, 63
  social normatization, 60–61
  substance conception, 58
  women's cosmetics use as social
    transgression, 166–168
Giddens, Anthony, 8
Giedion, Sigfried, 193, 194
Gorski, Roger, 112, 114
Gramsci, Antonio, 20–21, 181,
    182–183, 192
  on Americanism, 198
  feminist thought, 209
  on outcomes of Fordism, 195
  on Taylorism, 183–184

## H

Habitus, 4, 15–16
  in acquisition of social rules, 32
  formative nature of, 32–34
  in generation of dispositions,
    33–34
  generative dimensions, 31
  ideal of adaptation, 34
  linguistic, 37–39
  objective–subjective dimensions,
    32–36
  and practices, 30
  significance of, 30
  via unofficial performativity, 43
Hamer, Dean, 118
Hammond, William, 104–105, 107
Haraway, Donna, 182, 207–214
Harvey, David, 13–14, 19, 145

Health and illness, 6
  body as nation-state, 146–147
  body boundary imagery, 147–149
  protective barrier imagery,
    150–151
  and thoughts of death, 94
Hobbes, Thomas, 3
Homosexuality, 56
  brain research, 112–119
  implications of biological basis,
    117–119
Human bodies
  boundary imagery in HIV,
    146–153
  expression of mentality by, 66,
    67–69
  individuality and, 57–58, 63
  as site of resistance to power, 52
  social constitution of, 2–3
  social-historical constitution,
    51–52
  techniques of social constitution,
    51–52
Humanware, 200–205

## I

Incitement, 52–54
Individuals
  characteristics of, 50–51
  concept of, and concept of death,
    79
  constituting modalities, 7–8
  constitution via social practices,
    16–17, 73–74
  contextualized bodily constitu-
    tion, 5–8
  personhood, 51
  relation to bodies, 57–58, 63
  social shaping, 2–3
  socioeconomic context, 12–14
  subjecthood, 51
Institutions
  appropriateness of performative
    acts, 42–43
  as behaviors, 56, 57

224

## DATE DUE